AF395684

# Making the Revolution Global

# Making the Revolution Global

## Black Radicalism and the British Socialist Movement before Decolonisation

Theo Williams

VERSO

London • New York

First published by Verso 2022
© Theo Williams 2022



1 3 5 7 9 10 8 6 4 2

**Verso**
UK: 6 Meard Street, London W1F 0EG
US: 388 Atlantic Avenue, Brooklyn, NY 11217
versobooks.com

Verso is the imprint of New Left Books

ISBN-13:  978-1-83976-198-0
ISBN-13:  978-1-83976-201-7 (US EBK)
ISBN-13:  978-1-83976-200-0 (UK EBK)

**British Library Cataloguing in Publication Data**
A catalogue record for this book is available from the British Library

**Library of Congress Cataloging-in-Publication Data**
A catalog record for this book is available from the Library of Congress

Typeset in Minion by Biblichor Ltd, Scotland
Printed and bound by CPI Group (UK) Ltd, Croydon, CR0 4YY

# Contents

*For Bakari*

# Acknowledgements

I must begin by thanking Richard Drayton and Dan Matlin, who mentored me through this research project. The germ of this book was formed in Richard's undergraduate special subject course, Caribbean Intellectual History. In that dingy basement on the Strand, I was introduced to activist-intellectuals such as C. L. R. James and George Padmore, alongside other Black Marxists like Aimé Césaire, Claudia Jones and Walter Rodney. As a White Marxist attempting to wrestle with questions of how race and gender intersected with class exploitation, I found their works to be a revelation. I have also known Dan since my undergraduate days, when he supervised my free-standing long essay about the regulation of Black sexuality in the United States. Dan's wisdom and conscientiousness know no bounds, and his patient guidance has helped me immeasurably to refine my ideas. Before I began spending my life in universities, Adam Tomes and John Westmoreland sparked my interest in radical histories while I was an A Level student at York College.

During the time I spent working on this book, I had the good fortune to be involved in several vibrant reading groups. They counted among their members Prerna Agarwal, Kate Ambler, Agnes Arnold-Forster, Uta Balbier, Chris Birkett, Oliver Carter-Wakefield, Vincent Chabany-Douarre, Jen Chochinov, Francesco Cioffo, Molly Corlett, Pete Docking, Saffron East, George Evans, James Fisher, Laura Forster, Lenny Hodges, Michael Humphries, Sandip Kana, Tom Kelsey, Ajmal Khattak, Anna Maguire, Hélène Maloigne, Christian Melby, Naomi Oppenheim, Kelly Power, Paul Readman, Grace Redhead, Norris Saakwa-Mante,

Dongkyung Shin, Martin Spychal, Ian Stewart, Viswanathan Venkataraman, Brian Wallace, Kat Webb-Bourne and Matthew White. Many of these people are now friends as well as colleagues. The Institute of Historical Research, especially the Imperial and World History seminar, also provided a lively intellectual space.

Beyond those already mentioned, I was supported and intellectually nourished during the preparation of this book by scholars including Hakim Adi, Matheus Cardoso da Silva, Michael Collins, Amy Downes, David Edgerton, Gaiwin Eley, Bérénice Guyot-Réchard, Alana Harris, Vincent Hiribarren, Christian Høgsbjerg, Erika Huckestein, Leslie James, Laura Newman, Kennetta Perry, Kate Quinn, Simon Sleight, Gil Shohat, Richard Vinen and Bart Zielinski. Special mention must go to Marika Sherwood, who generously invited me into her home to view her collection of historical documents, and has so often turned a friendly and critical gaze to my work.

Perhaps the most testing experience during this book's gestation was a month-long research trip to Moscow in 2016. Nick Morgan offered invaluable advice and assistance before my visit. In Moscow, Masha Fedorova-Warden and Vijay Singh helped me find my feet and negotiate the archives. Masha and Vijay, alongside the Foreign Historians Conference in Moscow (especially Aleksandra Brokman, Aaron Hale-Dorrell, Thornton Miller and Oscar Sanchez-Sibony), infinitely improved my experience in Russia through our time spent eating, drinking and being tourists together.

Many friends and colleagues offered generous and helpful advice as I sought to publish the book. Advice and assistance offered by James Bowen and Tom Dark was especially valuable. The team at Verso has provided me with much support, and Sebastian Budgen in particular has helped to guide me through the process. I am also indebted to the two anonymous reviewers, whose insightful comments on the first version of the manuscript helped to make this book a better piece of scholarship.

Finally, I want to thank my friends and family. My friends have consistently provided a welcome distraction from the often solitary world of historical research. Mum and Dad have always given me love and encouragement, but never pressure. I have been able to stretch my wings knowing that they provided a safety net beneath me. Grandma June, who died before this book was completed, did the same. She is dearly missed. My brother, grandparents, aunts, uncles and cousins have all shaped and supported me. My partner Jaynaide has filled my life with love, compassion and humour for almost a decade. I would not have dared to start this project without her, let alone have been able to finish it.

Elements of this book were originally published in Theo Williams, 'George Padmore and the Soviet Model of the British Commonwealth', *Modern Intellectual History* 16 (2019); and Theo Williams, 'Collective Security or Colonial Revolution? The 1938 Conference on Peace and Empire, Anticolonialism, and the Popular Front', *Twentieth Century British History* 32 (2021). I thank Cambridge University Press and Oxford University Press, respectively, for permission to reproduce parts of these articles.

# List of abbreviations

| | |
|---|---|
| ABB | African Blood Brotherhood |
| BCAI | British Centre Against Imperialism |
| CIB | Colonial Information Bureau |
| Comintern | Communist International (or Third International) |
| CP | Communist Party |
| CPGB | Communist Party of Great Britain |
| CPUSA | Communist Party of the USA |
| FCB | Fabian Colonial Bureau |
| IAFA/IAFE | International African Friends of Abyssinia/Ethiopia |
| IASB | International African Service Bureau |
| IBRSU | International Bureau for Revolutionary Socialist Unity |
| ILP | Independent Labour Party |
| ITUCNW | International Trade Union Committee of Negro Workers |
| KCA | Kikuyu Central Association |
| LAI | League Against Imperialism and for National Independence |
| LCP | League of Coloured Peoples |
| LDRN | Ligue de Défense de la Race Nègre |
| LSI | Labour and Socialist International (or Second International) |
| NAACP | National Association for the Advancement of Colored People |
| NAC | National Administrative Council (of the ILP) |
| NCCL | National Council for Civil Liberties |
| NMM | National Minority Movement |
| NWA | Negro Welfare Association |

| | |
|---|---|
| PAF | Pan-African Federation |
| PCF | Parti Communiste Français |
| POUM | Partido Obrero de Unificación Marxista |
| RILU | Red International of Labour Unions (or Profintern) |
| RPC | Revolutionary Policy Committee |
| RSL | Revolutionary Socialist League |
| SL | Socialist League |
| SMM | Seamen's Minority Movement |
| TUC | Trades Union Congress |
| UNIA | Universal Negro Improvement Association |
| USSE | United Socialist States of Europe |
| WANS | West African National Secretariat |
| WASU | West African Students' Union |

# Introduction

Readers of the *Chicago Defender*, picking up a copy of the African American newspaper on Saturday 27 October 1945, were greeted with a notice reminding them to set their clocks back one hour on retiring to bed that evening. Their attention, however, was more likely to be drawn to the banner headline below: 'Colonials Demand Freedom'. The article, written by the newspaper's London correspondent, the Trinidadian socialist George Padmore, reported the deliberations and decisions of the Fifth Pan-African Congress, held the previous week in Manchester. The first speech reported by Padmore, however, was not by one of the many leading radicals of Africa and its diaspora present at the congress (who included Amy Ashwood Garvey, W. E. B. Du Bois, Jomo Kenyatta, Kwame Nkrumah and Padmore himself), but rather was by the White general secretary of the British Independent Labour Party (ILP), John McNair.[1] Born in 1887, McNair was a lifelong socialist activist who had travelled to Barcelona as the ILP's representative during the Spanish Civil War of 1936–39.[2] He told the Pan-African congress delegates that they must 'battle for complete political independence'. This would be achieved not through 'trusting the hypocrisy of the British Imperialist class', who would never voluntarily leave Africa. Instead, the congress

---

1 George Padmore, 'Colonials Demand Freedom', *Chicago Defender*, 27 October 1945, p. 1.

2 ILP, *Annual Report of the NAC, 1937* (London, 1937), pp. 3–4.

John McNair addresses the Fifth Pan-African Congress
Getty Images

delegates must return to their homelands and take their independence through struggle.[3]

The pride of place given to McNair's speech may seem strange, especially to those familiar with much of the historiography of Black
radicalism. This moment therefore invites us to consider the histories of
Black radicalisms, and the role played by White socialists in constituting
global movements against imperialism and racism. This example of
collaboration between the ILP and British-based pan-Africanists was in
fact a continuation of a deep political comradeship that had developed
over the previous decade. Moreover, it was a strand in a larger web of
relationships forged between 'the Black' (the antiracist and anticolonial

---

3  Padmore, 'Colonials Demand Freedom', p. 1.

movements of Africa and its diaspora) and 'the Red' (the international socialist and Communist movements).[4] From Ireland to India, colonial subjects pressed their desire for liberation with greater force and frequency during the First World War and its aftermath. This compelled metropolitan socialists to consider more fully the ways in which colonialism shaped both their own domestic politics and the global capitalist system. Furthermore, the Bolsheviks, following their 1917 revolution in Russia, vigorously advanced an anticolonialist programme, agitating for an alliance of the metropolitan proletariat and colonial liberation movements to overthrow imperialism. Lines of connection formed between previously disparate activists, who were gradually bringing together, however unevenly, a world-revolutionary movement.

McNair's speech also invites us to reconsider familiar perspectives on modern British history. Too often, race and empire are deemed niche subjects on the margins of British life. In fact, race and empire have often been central to British political discourse. Britain has been a great power throughout its modern history, and, despite declining influence, remains a major global player. Its citizens have regularly engaged – often critically – with their nation's role as imperial centre and global power, from the anti-slavery movement of the eighteenth and nineteenth centuries to the huge demonstrations against the 2003 invasion of Iraq.[5] The history of Britain cannot be disaggregated from the history of empire, or of the rest of the world. It is impossible to tell the story of Britain's Empire without also telling the story of Empire's Britain. The confluence between Black radicalism and British socialism allows us to examine one significant way in which race and empire have shaped modern Britain.

Nine years before the Manchester congress, Padmore published *How Britain Rules Africa* (1936). This was the first book he published while living in Britain, and came two years after his acrimonious split from the Third International, or Comintern, in 1934, as it began to prioritise antifascism over anti-imperialism. C. L. R. James – Padmore's childhood friend, fellow pan-African socialist, and ILP member – reviewed the book in the ILP's weekly newspaper, the *New Leader*. He told his readers:

<hr>

4 David Featherstone and Christian Høgsbjerg, eds, *The Red and the Black: The Russian Revolution and the Black Atlantic* (Manchester, 2021).

5 For an account of British dissent that is both scholarly and cinematic, see Priyamvada Gopal, *Insurgent Empire: Anticolonial Resistance and British Dissent* (London, 2019).

Africans must win their own freedom. Nobody will win it for them. They need co-operation, but that co-operation must be with the revolutionary movement in Europe and Asia. There is no other way out. Each movement will neglect the other at its peril, and there is not much time left.[6]

This book explores the engagement of socialists and Black radicals in Britain with James's idea that 'each movement will neglect the other at its peril'. It focuses in particular on the group of activists that coalesced in London around Padmore's International African Service Bureau (IASB), formed in 1937, as well as its predecessor, the International African Friends of Ethiopia (IAFE), formed in 1935, and its successor, and the Pan-African Federation (PAF), formed in 1944. It also discusses the Comintern's International Trade Union Committee of Negro Workers (ITUCNW), in which several Black radicals cut their political teeth. These organisations are central to the history of twentieth-century Black radicalism. Alumni include activists who became post-independence presidents (Jomo Kenyatta and Kwame Nkrumah), mentors to African heads of state (Padmore), and one of the century's most important thinkers (James). These organisations, committed to the idea that the metropolitan and colonial revolutions would necessarily be interdependent, each acting as a catalyst and prop to the other, regarded interventions within the British socialist movement as central to their activism. While these organisations were consciously led exclusively by people of African descent, they considered interracial socialist collaboration – collaboration in which Black radicals defended their right to set the terms – to be essential to African liberation.

No previous study has satisfactorily identified the place of Black radicalism within the interwar British socialist movement. Historians of British and European socialism have rarely engaged with histories of Black radicalism and pan-Africanism. They have examined, for instance, the formation of the Communist Party of Great Britain (CPGB) in the early 1920s, the disaffiliation of the Independent Labour Party from the Labour Party in 1932, and the reasons for the ascendancy of the Labour Party in 1945, while directing little attention to the politics of empire.[7]

---

6 C. L. R. James, ' "Civilising" the "Blacks": Why Britain Needs to Maintain Her African Possessions', *New Leader*, 29 May 1936, p. 5.

7 There is little or no discussion of the British Black radicalism of the 1930s and 1940s in Ian Bullock, *Under Siege: The Independent Labour Party in Interwar Britain* (Edmonton, AB, 2017); John Callaghan, *Socialism in Britain Since 1884* (Oxford, 1990);

The focus on political parties has often obscured the history of people of colour who formed socialist organisations at the periphery of party politics. This omission has important implications for how the history of European socialist ideas and movements are framed. As David Featherstone argues, 'To acknowledge the contributions of anti-colonial movements to European left politics is not just to add an excluded dimension that develops a fuller or more complete history. Rather, it is to challenge the very terms on which left politics is understood and articulated.'[8] Historians of Black radicalism, while more sensitive to the engagements between Black radicalism and European socialism, have yet to account for the extent of Black radicals' enmeshment in and influence on the wider British socialist movement.

Black radicals were nonetheless at the heart of many of the debates within the British socialist movement. They worked with the CPGB before tensions developed over the Popular Front strategy (through which socialists would make antifascist alliances with 'progressive' capitalists, leading to a blunting of the Comintern's anti-imperialism). They intervened in debates about how to combat Italian aggression towards Ethiopia. They became immersed within the networks of the ILP, whose journal Padmore edited. Even though, among this group, only James was ever a member of the ILP, Black radicals helped to influence that party's shift away from a paternalistic anticolonialism and towards one that recognised the agency of African peoples. By the late 1930s, Black radical thought had become a vital component of the ILP's political philosophy.

This book demonstrates that the international movements of socialism and Black radicalism, rather than forming separate strands of radicalism, were imbricated in Britain. This book therefore argues that we must de-provincialise the history of the British socialist movement

Gidon Cohen, *The Failure of a Dream: The Independent Labour Party from Disaffiliation to World War II* (London, 2007); Paul Corthorn, *In the Shadow of the Dictators: The British Left in the 1930s* (New York, 2006); James Jupp, *The Radical Left in Britain, 1931–1941* (London, 1982); Keith Laybourn, *The Independent Labour Party, 1914–1939: The Political and Cultural History of a Socialist Party* (Abingdon, 2020). Considering the historiography of European socialism more broadly, not a single IASB member is mentioned in Geoff Eley, *Forging Democracy: The History of the Left in Europe, 1850–2000* (New York, 2002); Donald Sassoon, *One Hundred Years of Socialism: The West European Left in the Twentieth Century* (London, 2010 [1996]).

8  David Featherstone, *Solidarity: Hidden Histories and Geographies of Internationalism* (London, 2012), p. 11.

of the 1930s and 1940s, recognising its multiracial character, and its global as well as domestic preoccupations. It achieves this through an examination of Black radical organisations, and locates these organisations not only within Black internationalist networks, but also within the British socialist movement. It explores the reasons for both conflict and cooperation between Black radicals and other elements of the British socialist movement, and examines how the politics of class intersected with those of race and anticolonialism. This serves as a counterweight to histories of Black radicalism that have failed adequately to explain the interactions of leading Black radical figures with European socialists, and a corrective to histories of British socialism that have marginalised the significance of anti-imperialism and the influence of Black activists on the wider movement. Black radicalism, and more generally the politics of anticolonialism, should occupy a more significant space in the historiography of British socialism. There was no 'White left' during the interwar period, insulated from the activism of socialists of colour.

Black radicals – especially those from the Caribbean – can be understood as 'British', having been imbued with a British identity from childhood. I therefore invoke the idea of 'British Black radicalism', meaning not just 'Black radicalism in Britain', but also a Black radicalism moulded by the British imperial system through language, education and geography. Furthermore, while pan-African solidarity crossed national and imperial boundaries, it was this British imperial system that figured most prominently in British Black radicals' writings and activism.[9] This was, no doubt, further influenced by their predominantly Anglophone transnational network, the British Empire's status as the world's largest colonial empire, and the fact that they were resident in Britain. This Britishness is key to understanding Black radical activism. This book therefore articulates its aim as locating Black radicals within the *wider* British socialist movement, rather than treating them as *distinct* from British socialism.

One of this book's interventions is to explain why, when both the Black radicals and the other British socialists addressed in this study nominally

---

9 However, it is important to remember that opposition to US imperialism in Haiti and Liberia was perhaps the most dominant theme of Padmore's writings during the early 1930s. See Raphael Dalleo, *American Imperialism's Undead: The Occupation of Haiti and the Rise of Caribbean Anticolonialism* (Charlottesville, 2016), Chapter 6.

shared the twin goals of anticapitalism and anti-imperialism, there were regular conflicts between and within these groups about colonial matters. James's position during the Italo-Ethiopian War of 1935–36 is illustrative here. He was a member of the Independent Labour Party – a party that, although central to the Labour Party's formation, essentially became a left-wing faction within the party after the First World War, and disaffiliated in 1932. From the outbreak of war in October 1935, James, like the majority of ILP members, positioned himself against the Labour and Communist policy of endorsing League of Nations sanctions against Italy. This position placed James at odds even with the majority of the International African Friends of Ethiopia. Indeed, he resigned from the IAFE due to its support for League of Nations sanctions. Nevertheless, James advocated the alternative of 'workers' sanctions' against Italy. When the ILP leadership opposed any form of sanctions on the grounds that they would lead to an inter-imperialist war, James was a key figure in the internal opposition. The opposition successfully pursued a motion in support of workers' sanctions at the 1936 annual conference. However, this was later overturned when James Maxton, the party's chair and most prominent MP, threatened to resign from his leadership roles if workers' sanctions were adopted as ILP policy.[10]

Tom Buchanan posits that, for many activists, antifascism superseded anti-imperialism in the 1930s.[11] Buchanan's argument is convincing when applied to the CPGB and many elements of the Labour Party, but does not fit the ILP's Ethiopia debate. If anything, opposition to both war and British (if not Italian) imperialism was a priority for the ILP leadership. Nonetheless, Buchanan usefully observes that a simple opposition to capitalist-imperialism was not enough to sustain left-wing unity, as complex tensions tended to emerge. Conflicting analyses of the relationships between capitalism, imperialism, fascism and war are a recurring theme of this book. As we will see, by the end of the 1930s, after James clashed with the ILP leadership in 1935–36, the International African Service Bureau and ILP had reached a confluence in their analyses of these phenomena.

10  This episode is discussed in Chapter 2, below.
11  Tom Buchanan, '"The Dark Millions in the Colonies are Unavenged": Anti-Fascism and Anti-Imperialism in the 1930s', *Contemporary European History* 25 (2016), pp. 645–65.

The complex analyses of race, class and imperialism pursued by Black radicals, and particularly by James and Padmore, created a form of pan-Africanist Marxism. Hakim Adi has described pan-Africanism as a phenomenon that

> is concerned with the social, economic, cultural and political emancipation of African peoples, including those of the African diaspora. What underlies the manifold visions and approaches of Pan-Africanism and Pan-Africanists is a belief in the unity, common history and common purpose of the peoples of Africa and the African diaspora and the notion that their destinies are interconnected.[12]

James and Padmore considered the Black emancipatory politics of pan-Africanism and the proletarian emancipatory politics of Marxism to be part of the same programme for world socialism. But there is a school of thought that counterposes pan-Africanism to Marxism and Communism. This tendency has been most pronounced in the historiography of Padmore's political thought. His first biographer, James Hooker, argued that Padmore's career can be neatly divided into a pre-1935 Communist phase and a post-1935 pan-Africanist phase.[13] This bifurcation, however, fails to recognise Padmore's continued commitment to Marxism after he left the Comintern. In recent years, this bifurcation has been subjected to robust critique by historians, most notably Leslie James, who observes that Padmore's anticolonial activism was informed not just by his principles, but also by political strategies that responded to a rapidly changing world.[14]

---

12 Hakim Adi, *Pan-Africanism: A History* (London, 2018), p. 2. For more on the history and conceptualisation of pan-Africanism, see P. Olisanwuche Esedebe, *Pan-Africanism: The Idea and Movement, 1776–1991* (Washington, DC, 1994); Imanuel Geiss, *The Pan-African Movement: A History of Pan-Africanism in America, Europe, and Africa*, transl. Ann Keep (London, 1974); Sidney J. Lemelle and Robin D. G. Kelley, eds, *Imagining Home: Class, Culture and Nationalism in the African Diaspora* (London, 1994); George Shepperson, 'Pan-Africanism and "Pan-Africanism": Some Historical Notes', *Phylon* 23 (1962).

13 James R. Hooker, *Black Revolutionary: George Padmore's Path from Communism to Pan-Africanism* (London, 1967). For recent examples, see Vincent B. Thompson, 'George Padmore: Reconciling Two Phases of Contradictions', in Fitzroy Baptiste and Rupert Lewis, eds, *George Padmore: Pan-African Revolutionary* (Kingston, 2009); Anthony P. Maingot, *Race, Ideology, and the Decline of Caribbean Marxism* (Gainesville, FL, 2015), pp. 174–5.

14 Leslie James, *George Padmore and Decolonization from Below: Pan-Africanism, the Cold War, and the End of Empire* (Basingstoke, 2015).

While few scholars now indulge Hooker's simple binary, there remains a vexed but more nuanced debate about the relationship between Black radicalism and Marxism. Perhaps the most influential voice in this conversation has been that of Cedric Robinson, who, after 'map[ping] the historical and intellectual contours of the encounter of Marxism and Black radicalism, two programs for revolutionary change', has posited the existence of a 'Black radical tradition'.[15] Robinson has pursued an archaeology of Black resistance to racial capitalism, beginning with the rebellions of enslaved people. He reminds us: 'Resistances were formed through the meanings that Africans brought to the New World as their cultural possession'.[16] For Robinson, these enslaved Africans stood for the complete rejection of European culture and racial hierarchies. After emancipation, a Black petit-bourgeois intelligentsia emerged, 'no longer as impervious to the penetrations of Western cultures as they had been in their "native" circumstance'.[17] During the interwar period, members of this intelligentsia, including Du Bois, James and Padmore, were drawn to Marxism. However, 'the events that did most to shape their era – the crises of world capitalism, the destructive dialectic of imperialism, and the historical and ideological revelations of the naivety of Western socialism – drove them into a deeper consciousness'.[18] Each of these activists subsequently 'turned his face to the historical tradition of Black liberation and became Black radicals'.[19]

For Robinson, Marxism and Black radicalism are distinct, and occasionally antithetical, revolutionary traditions. While they may have interacted with each other, and each 'tradition' contains a plurality of political philosophies, they hold different origins and epistemologies.[20] Taking a similar, though not identical, approach, Anthony Bogues argues that:

---

15 Cedric J. Robinson, *Black Marxism: The Making of the Black Radical Tradition* (Chapel Hill, NC, 2000 [1983]), p. 1.

16 Ibid., p. 5.

17 Ibid., p. 178.

18 Ibid., pp. 183–4.

19 Ibid., p. 184.

20 David Scott, in theorising the plurality of Black radicalisms, argues that different articulations of Black radicalism are 'rival positions within a black radical *tradition*, that they are engaged in contending interpretations of what is equally perceived to be a common possession, namely, the present of an African past, and that an authoritative reading of that common possession has implications for how we think about the aftermaths of colonial slavery and the place of African culture in the moral shaping of contemporary black identity'. David Scott, 'On the Very Idea of a Black Radical Tradition', *Small Axe* 17 (2013), pp. 5–6. Emphasis in original.

> Black radical intellectual production oftentimes began with an engagement and dialogue with Western radical political ideas, and then moved on to a critique of these ideas as their incompleteness was revealed . . . In other words, black radical intellectual production engages in a double operation – an engagement with Western radical theory and then a critique of this theory.[21]

For Bogues, Marxism was one of several 'tributaries' (along with Black Power, pan-Africanism and West Indian nationalism) in James's political thought.[22]

Both Bogues and Robinson are attuned to the insufficiencies of classical Marxism (by which I mean the writings of Karl Marx and Friedrich Engels) in dealing with the question of Black oppression and liberation. Writing about the origin of the 'Black radical tradition' in the Atlantic slave trade, Robinson notes: 'Marx had not realized fully that the cargoes of laborers also contained African cultures, critical mixes and admixtures of language and thought, of cosmology and metaphysics, of habits, beliefs, and morality.'[23] However, both Bogues's and Robinson's treatment of 'Western' radicalism, socialism and Marxism are not without problems of their own. Both, for example, locate the Russian revolutionary leader Vladimir Lenin within a 'classical' or 'orthodox' Marxist tradition.[24] While they acknowledge Lenin's original contributions to Marxist thought (particularly his theories of imperialism and the role of the peasantry in socialist revolution), they do not consider these to be a critique of or departure from classical Marxism in the same way as, for example, James's claims about the world-historical significance of the Haitian Revolution. But if we turn to Padmore's own *Pan-Africanism or Communism?* (1956), we find Lenin's ideas about imperialism described as 'a heretical departure from orthodox Marxism' – the same language, incidentally, that Bogues uses to describe Black radical 'critiques' of Marxism.[25]

---

21 Anthony Bogues, *Black Heretics, Black Prophets: Radical Political Intellectuals* (New York, 2003), p. 13.

22 Anthony Bogues, *Caliban's Freedom: The Early Political Thought of C. L. R. James* (London, 1997), p. 16.

23 Robinson, *Black Marxism*, pp. 121–2.

24 Ibid., p. 1; Bogues, *Caliban's Freedom*, p. 4.

25 Padmore, *Pan-Africanism or Communism? The Coming Struggle for Africa* (London, 1956), p. 293.

My contention is not that Black socialists did not draw on lineages of African forms of resistance, or that they failed to move beyond established Marxist thought, but rather that it limits our understanding to treat the latter as an essentialised 'Western Marxism'. The most influential exponent of Marxism during the interwar period was Lenin – a Russian revolutionary who was only 'Western' in a relatively loose sense. Leon Trotsky, perhaps the second most important Bolshevik theorist, was, like Marx himself, Jewish (Robinson, for example, fails to engage with this Jewishness and how it placed Marx or Trotsky in relation to 'Western' civilisation and racial formations). At the Second Congress of the Comintern, in 1920, Lenin formulated the theses on the national and colonial questions in comradely debate with M. N. Roy, an Indian Communist who three years earlier had founded the Mexican Communist Party.[26] Drawing on Brent Edwards's idea of 'Black Globality', Tiffany Ruby Patterson and Robin Kelley point to, among other phenomena, the global revolutionary ferment of the 1910s, of which Lenin and Roy were a part, to ask us to think more deeply about the 'international connections' of Black radicalism, which 'sometimes . . . lives through or is integrally tied to other kinds of international movements – socialism, communism, feminism, surrealism, religions such as Islam, and so on'.[27] Their emphasis on dialogue and hybridity in shaping Black radicalisms is also useful in deconstructing the formation of European radicalisms, which, as this book demonstrates, were shaped by Black radical ideas.

It was with the Leninist form of Marxism that James and Padmore engaged most thoroughly, developing ideas and opening new vistas through the use of an explicitly Marxist methodology. As Minkah Makalani argues in his nuanced critique of Bogues and Robinson, 'Marxism's currency is the ability of activist-intellectuals to theorize it in a given time beyond its initial elaborations and points of analysis, its refusal to remain static and unchanged and thus easily identified in sacred texts by Marx

---

26  Kevin McDermott and Jeremy Agnew, *The Comintern: A History of International Communism from Lenin to Stalin* (Basingstoke, 1996). pp. 160–1; George M. Fredrickson, *Black Liberation: A Comparative History of Black Ideologies in the United States and South Africa* (Oxford, 1995), p. 187.

27  Brent Edwards, 'Black Globality: The International Shape of Black Intellectual Culture', doctoral thesis, Columbia University, 1998; Tiffany Ruby Patterson and Robin D. G. Kelley, 'Unfinished Migrations: Reflections on the African Diaspora and the Making of the Modern World', *African Studies Review* 43 (2000), pp. 26-8.

and Lenin'.[28] Makalani, like me, remains 'somewhat hesitant about the disjuncture Bogues suggests between the black radical intellectual and Western radical thought', and finds Robinson's 'central claim that black radicalism and Marxism are incongruent . . . difficult to follow'.[29]

Moreover, James and Padmore were both products of a British colonial education, were both immersed in the British and European socialist movement, and were both concerned with transforming European imperial systems, including their metropoles. They should, in that sense, be understood as constituents of 'Western Marxism' just as much as Marx or Lenin, developing a living intellectual movement from within, and making that movement all the richer for it. Their thought belongs within both Western *and* Black diasporic frameworks. Barbara Bush, while observing that neither Marxism nor 'black discourses of liberation' were 'monolithic', concludes that 'ultimately, neither Marxism nor liberalism provided black activists with an adequate ideological framework for political action'.[30] The problem with this formulation is that it places Black radicals outside Marxism, rather than recognising their ideas as elaborations and iterations of Marxism. In fact, Black radicals were not involved simply in the *consumption* of Marxism, but also its *production*.

Bogues has legitimate concerns about the discipline of intellectual history, decrying the 'great chain of thought constructed around a hierarchical order wherein Africana thinkers are located on the margins. In this chain, radical Africana thinkers piggyback on Marx or Sartre, their intellectual validation passing through the ideas of the accepted "giants." '[31] My approach, in response, is to examine the co-development of radicalisms in order to acknowledge the influence of Marx and Lenin on Black radical thought, while simultaneously showing that Black thinkers were themselves intellectual producers and should not be placed at the bottom of any Marxist intellectual hierarchy. In this respect, I elaborate on Stephen Howe's characterisation of the history of British anticolonialism as a 'story of contact and of the exchange of ideas between British

---

28  Minkah Makalani, *In the Cause of Freedom: Radical Black Internationalism from Harlem to London, 1917–1939* (Chapel Hill, NC, 2011), p. 12.

29  Ibid., p. 13.

30  Barbara Bush, *Imperialism, Race and Resistance: Africa and Britain, 1919–1945* (London, 1999), pp. 244–5.

31  Bogues, *Black Heretics*, p. 2.

socialists and colonial radicals'.[32] It is only by examining the imbrication of Black and White socialists' ideas and activism that the centrality of Marxism to certain forms of Black radicalism may be acknowledged.

Indeed, it is crucial to locate British Black radicals within the legacies of the 1917 Bolshevik Revolution. Their activism is just one example of the impact of the revolution on Black diasporic intellectual life.[33] During the short twentieth century, the Soviet Union emerged as a beacon for many, shining against the racial capitalism of the West. Communism was a strong current in African American intellectual life, beginning during the early interwar years with Cyril Briggs's African Blood Brotherhood (ABB). Jacob Zumoff has examined how the ABB did not consist simply of passive recruits to the Communist Party of the USA (CPUSA), but rather agitated within the party to make it address the 'Negro Question'.[34] It was from this African American milieu that Padmore, who spent much of the 1920s studying in the United States, was drawn into the Communist movement. As Peter Abrahams, the South African writer who joined the IASB in 1940, recalled, the Soviet Union's promises of 'freedom and opportunity' were 'intoxicating'.[35]

Writing shortly before the revolution, Lenin argued that 'imperialism', characterised by monopolisation and colonialism, was 'the highest stage of capitalism'. The great powers divided the world between themselves as an outlet for finance capital and to extract super-profits from the labour of colonial peoples. Moreover, he argued that the First World War had

---

32  Stephen Howe, *Anticolonialism in British Politics: The Left and the End of Empire, 1918–1964* (Oxford, 1993), p. 25.

33  For works that have explored the impact of the Bolshevik Revolution on Black radicalism, see Hakim Adi, *Pan-Africanism and Communism: The Communist International, Africa and the Diaspora, 1919–1939* (Trenton, NJ, 2013); Kate A. Baldwin, *Beyond the Color Line and the Iron Curtain: Reading Encounters between Black and Red, 1922–1963* (Durham, NC, 2002); Earl Ofari Hutchinson, *Blacks and Reds: Race and Class in Conflict, 1919–1990* (East Lansing, MI, 1995); Makalani, *In the Cause of Freedom*; Meredith Roman, *Opposing Jim Crow: African Americans and the Soviet Indictment of US Racism, 1928–1937* (Lincoln, NE, 2012); Mark Solomon, *The Cry Was Unity: Communists and African Americans, 1917–36* (Jackson, MS, 1998); Holger Weiss, *Framing a Radical African Atlantic: African American Agency, West African Intellectuals and the International Trade Union Committee of Negro Workers* (Leiden, 2014); Jacob A. Zumoff, *The Communist International and US Communism, 1919–1929* (Leiden, 2014).

34  Zumoff, *Communist International*, Chapter 14.

35  Peter Abrahams, *The Coyaba Chronicles: Reflections on the Black Experience in the Twentieth Century* (Kingston, 2000), p. 131.

been caused by imperialist rivalry.[36] The Comintern's theses on the national and colonial questions, adopted at the Second Congress in 1920, proclaimed the need for a conjoining of anticolonial forces with the European proletariat in order to overthrow global capitalist-imperialism. The formation in 1928 of the International Trade Union Committee of Negro Workers was a response to this recognition of the need for revolutionary unity. At the Second Comintern Congress, Tom Quelch of the British Socialist Party (which later merged into the CPGB) argued that 'the rank-and-file British worker would consider it treasonable to help the enslaved nations in their uprisings against British rule', drawing Lenin's rebuke in the final report.[37] Crucially, this prompted Black Leninists to decry White socialists who did not appreciate the importance of the colonial revolution in building world socialism. Black radicals used Lenin's theses to denounce those not committed to anticolonialism as 'so-called' socialists.

The Comintern's commitment to anticolonialism was mirrored by a commonly held belief that the Soviet Union had eliminated racism within its own borders – both the antisemitism and other forms of racism that had structured life in the old Russian Empire, and a wider racial mode of thought that positioned Europeans as biologically or culturally superior to the rest of the world. Meredith Roman has argued that, while the Soviet Union was of course not free from racism, there was 'a sincere commitment among many Soviet authorities and citizens to creating a new society', and that African Americans contributed significantly to this discourse of antiracism.[38] One popular story was that of Robert Robinson, an African American man working in a tractor factory in Stalingrad in 1930. When White American workers, who like Robinson had been recruited from the Ford Motor Company in Detroit, attempted to attack him during a lunch break, Russian workers leapt to his defence. The White Americans were found guilty of 'racial chauvinism' and deported from the Soviet Union.[39] Such stories were immensely powerful at a time

36 Vladimir Lenin, *Imperialism: The Highest Stage of Capitalism* (London, 1996 [1917]).

37 Vladimir Lenin, 'Report of the Commission on the National and the Colonial Questions' (1920), at marxists.org.

38 Roman, *Opposing Jim Crow*, p. 24.

39 Ibid., Chapter 1; Negro Delegation of the 5th Congress RILU, 'Down with Racial and National Chauvinism', *Negro Worker*, February 1931, p. 16.

when the vast majority of African and Caribbean peoples were under the heel of European colonialism, and lynchings were common occurrences in the United States. Shortly afterwards, during the campaign to free the Scottsboro Nine (a group of African American teenagers and young men falsely accused of rape in 1931), the Communist International Labor Defense's militant campaign attracted significant support from sections of the Black working class who were frustrated with the more moderate campaign of the National Association for the Advancement of Colored People (NAACP).[40]

The putative antiracism and anti-imperialism of the Soviet Union and the Comintern had profound effects on Black radicalism. Many of the activists who would later form the International African Friends of Ethiopia and the International African Service Bureau (including Padmore, Kenyatta and I. T. A. Wallace-Johnson) were in the late 1920s and early 1930s drawn into the Communist movement, and the ITUCNW in particular. After working for the Comintern's Negro Bureau in Moscow, Padmore moved to Hamburg to lead the ITUCNW.[41] He became particularly attached to the Soviet project, remaining so even after his break from the Comintern – an oft-misunderstood aspect of his political thought.

But there was a plurality of Black radicalisms, even within the IAFE and IASB, and there were clearly forms of Black radicalism that developed independently of, or in opposition to, Marxism. Undoubtedly the most potent Black radical force during the early interwar years was the Universal Negro Improvement Association (UNIA), led by the Jamaican-born Marcus Garvey, which animated millions of Black people across the world. Robinson, locating the UNIA within the 'Black radical tradition', argues that the organisation had an 'eclectic' ideology, 'incorporating elements of Christianity, socialism, revolutionary nationalism, and race solidarity'.[42] Robbie Shilliam observes that Garveyism invoked a 'Black biblical hermeneutic' that made the slave 'the subject of the Bible'.[43] This hermeneutic can

---

40  For an account of the Scottsboro campaign in Britain, see Susan D. Pennybacker, *From Scottsboro to Munich: Race and Political Culture in 1930s Britain* (Princeton, 2009), Chapter 1.

41  The ITUCNW is discussed thoroughly in Chapter 1. See also Adi, *Pan-Africanism and Communism*; Weiss, *Framing a Radical African Atlantic*.

42  Robinson, *Black Marxism*, p. 213.

43  Robbie Shilliam, ' "Ethiopia Shall Stretch Forth Her Hands unto God": Garveyism, Rastafari, and Antiquity', in Daniel Orrells, Gurminder K. Bhambra and Tessa Roynon, eds, *African Athena: New Agendas* (Oxford, 2011), p. 108.

be termed 'Ethiopianism', and, following Psalm 68:31 ('Princes shall come out of Egypt. Ethiopia shall stretch forth her hands unto God'), it 'allowed a vision of Pan-African liberation and healing adequate to challenge the global colonial order of slavery and differential racial rule'.[44] Adam Ewing sees Garveyism 'not as an ideology but as a method of organic mass politics' that, in different local contexts, could take the form of religious millenarianism, labour activism or the formation of welfare associations.[45]

Importantly, even non- or anti-Marxist Black radicalisms influenced Marxist and Communist racial politics. As Robinson suggests, the Comintern's emphasis on Black 'self-determination' after 1928 was a response to the 'Black nationalism' of the UNIA.[46] Of course, Black socialists such as James and Padmore remained critical of the class politics of Garvey and more moderate Black British organisations like the West African Students' Union (WASU) and League of Coloured Peoples (LCP). Yet the political philosophies, terminologies and forms of organisation advanced by these contemporaries and near contemporaries profoundly influenced the IAFE and IASB in how they positioned themselves within the constellation of Black politics. Furthermore, the IASB, LCP and WASU often cooperated with each other, and the organisations' memberships to a certain extent overlapped.

The IASB's language of 'pan-Africanism' was indebted to the 1900 Pan-African Conference organised by Henry Sylvester-Williams and, following that, the four Pan-African Congresses organised by Du Bois between 1919 and 1927.[47] Indeed, Padmore and his comrades would invoke the lineage of the congresses when organising the Fifth Pan-African Congress in 1945. James remembered Padmore, his childhood friend, reading both Du Bois and Garvey as a youth in Trinidad.[48] The IASB member Ras Makonnen, having grown up in British Guiana, remembered Garveyism as a 'racist doctrine' that stoked tensions between Black people and Guiana's large Indian population, but reflected

---

44 Robbie Shilliam, 'Intervention and Colonial-Modernity: Decolonising the Italy/Ethiopia Conflict through Psalms 68:31', *Review of International Studies* 39 (2013), p. 1,143.

45 Adam Ewing, *The Age of Garvey: How a Jamaican Activist Created a Mass Movement and Changed Global Black Politics* (Princeton, 2014), p. 6.

46 Robinson, *Black Marxism*, p. 218.

47 For a recent history of pan-Africanism, see Adi, *Pan-Africanism: A History*.

48 C. L. R. James, 'George Padmore: Black Marxist Revolutionary – A Memoir' (1976), in C. L. R. James, *At the Rendezvous of Victory* (London, 1984), p. 253.

that 'there was something in Garvey's opinion and philosophy to make most of us stop and reflect why the black man was making no headway'.[49] Ewing observes that Garveyism also had an influence on Kikuyu nationalist politics, the milieu from which Kenyatta would arrive in Britain in the late 1920s.[50] Nkrumah, who became a leading figure in British Black radical circles at the end of the Second World War, wrote that he was 'particularly impressed' by the ideas of Marx and Lenin, but that Garvey's writings fired his enthusiasm in a way that other works could not.[51] The UNIA was an important model of Black self-organisation and racial self-assertion. Subsequently, Black British organisations like the LCP and WASU, while lacking the radical class politics of the IASB, provided examples for how Black-led organisations seeking racial equality could operate in interwar Britain. WASU was founded in 1925 by a group of law students resident in Britain, including J. B. Danquah and Ladipo Solanke, who were influenced by the Sierra Leonean politician Herbert Bankole-Bright. The organisation followed in the footsteps of similar organisations, such as the Nigerian Progress Union and the Union of Students of African Descent, and was composed of students from Britain's West African colonies – Gambia, the Gold Coast, Nigeria and Sierra Leone. WASU opposed the colour bar in Britain and aimed to nurture West African nationhood. The LCP was founded by Harold Moody, a Jamaican physician, in 1931. Informed by Christian faith and notions of respectability, it was a multiracial organisation that lobbied against racial discrimination in Britain. Its journal, *The Keys*, invoked the symbolism of Black and White piano keys in order to promote racial harmony.[52]

Something of the plurality of Black radicalisms was reflected within the IASB itself. Pan-Africanism was crucial to the political identity of the IASB, and was the glue that bound its members together. Moreover, all of its major figures were, at least in some sense, socialist. However, while

---

49 T. Ras Makonnen, *Pan-Africanism from Within*, ed. Kenneth King (London, 1973), pp. 32–4.

50 Ewing, *Age of Garvey*, Chapter 8.

51 Kwame Nkrumah, *The Autobiography of Kwame Nkrumah* (Edinburgh, 1957), p. 45.

52 For more on the LCP and WASU, see Hakim Adi, *West Africans in Britain, 1900–1960: Nationalism, Pan-Africanism and Communism* (London, 1998); David Killingray, '"To Do Something for the Race": Harold Moody and the League of Coloured Peoples', in Bill Schwarz, ed., *West Indian Intellectuals in Britain* (Manchester, 2003); Anne Spry Rush, 'Imperial Identity in Colonial Minds: Harold Moody and the League of Coloured Peoples, 1931–50', *Twentieth Century British History* 13 (2002).

Makonnen was an avowed socialist, unlike James and Padmore he rejected both Marxism and any significant role for the European proletariat in achieving colonial liberation; Kenyatta developed a form of revolutionary Kikuyu nationalism with religious-spiritual dimensions; and Ashwood Garvey – Marcus's first wife and herself a former UNIA leader – undoubtedly remained shaped by the politics of Garveyism. As Adom Getachew has demonstrated, Black radicals could simultaneously be both nationalists and internationalists, and these political tendencies could be complementary.[53] Nevertheless, many activists placed greater emphasis on either nationalism or internationalism. While this book most thoroughly examines the political thought of Padmore, and to a lesser extent James, as they were the intellectual and political leaders of the group, it also explores this plurality of political philosophy at some length. It illustrates that Black forms of resistance to capitalism and imperialism in Britain have sometimes been non- or even anti-Marxist. I therefore use the term 'Black radicalism' to capture several tendencies of political thought – Marxist, pan-Africanist, nationalist – while acknowledging the overlap between these ideas, which often developed into synthesis.

As well as addressing the histories of Black radicalism and socialism, this book also contributes to our understanding of what can loosely be termed the 'new imperial history'. During the late twentieth century, historians, anthropologists and literary critics such as Catherine Hall, Bill Schwarz and Wendy Webster challenged the dichotomy between 'metropole' and 'colony', instead treating the history of Britain as indivisible from that of its empire. These scholars also moved beyond the traditional historiographical concern with high politics, and instead offered a deeper reading of culture, race, gender and sexuality in the history of Britain and the empire.[54]

In fact, many Black radicals can themselves be seen as pioneers of this approach. James demonstrated the entanglement of the French and Haitian revolutions in *The Black Jacobins* (1938), examining how each revolution reacted to and catalysed the other.[55] He was also an intellectual

---

53 Adom Getachew, *Worldmaking after Empire: The Rise and Fall of Self-Determination* (Princeton, 2019).

54 For an anthology of some of the most influential essays within this movement, see Stephen Howe, ed., *The New Imperial Histories Reader* (Abingdon, 2010).

55 C. L. R. James, *The Black Jacobins: Toussaint L'Ouverture and the San Domingo Revolution* (London, 1938).

ally of the Trinidadian economic historian Eric Williams, whose *Capitalism and Slavery* (1944) showed how the Atlantic slave system had transformed British capitalism.[56] It has therefore been asserted for some time, albeit not without resistance, that distinctions between colony and metropole are artificial, and that the empire transformed Britain culturally, economically and politically.[57] This book contributes to our understanding of the entanglements between colony and metropole by illustrating important ways in which migration from African and Caribbean colonies transformed the political thought and forms of activism of the metropolitan British left during the 1930s and 1940s. Moreover, the activists discussed in this book were themselves aware of the ways in which the regions of the British imperial system interacted with each other through culture, trade and exploitation, as well as networks of resistance. Through their own scholarship they examined many of the phenomena that later animated the 'new imperial history'.

Of course, previous work on Black radicalism in Britain has also contributed to our understandings of the ways in which race, empire and migration shaped the metropole. Howe, despite an overreliance on published sources, is one of a handful of historians to locate Black activists within British political culture. He notes that, from the mid 1930s onward, the ILP's colonial debates had 'an important additional dimension' due to the presence of James and Padmore in the party's orbit.[58] Priyamvada Gopal, taking this argument further, demonstrates that Asian and Black anticolonialists in the metropole 'not only internationalized British opposition to empire, but also pushed it in more radical directions'.[59] Crucially, Gopal problematises the ' "Caliban" model' of anticolonial resistance by moving beyond 'the ways in which colonial subjects took up British ideas and turned them against empire', instead focusing on the 'reverse influence' from the colonies to the metropole.[60] Historians such as Barbara Bush and Susan Pennybacker have also

---

56  Eric Williams, *Capitalism and Slavery* (Chapel Hill, NC, 1945 [1944]).

57  For a summary and rebuttal of the criticisms levelled against *Capitalism and Slavery*, see Robinson, 'Capitalism, Slavery and Bourgeois Historiography', *History Workshop Journal* 23 (1987). For an influential argument that imperialism had little impact on metropolitan British culture, see Bernard Porter, *The Absent-Minded Imperialists: Empire, Society and Culture in Britain* (Oxford, 2004).

58  Howe, *Anticolonialism in British Politics*, p. 71.

59  Gopal, *Insurgent Empire*, pp. 212–13.

60  Ibid., p. 5.

examined race and imperialism in British political culture of the 1930s and 1940s.[61] Work by Christian Høgsbjerg (on C. L. R. James), Leslie James (on Padmore), W. O. Maloba (on Kenyatta), and Minkah Makalani, Marc Matera, Carol Polsgrove and Daniel Whittall (each addressing, among other things, the IAFE and IASB more broadly) has greatly added to our understanding of British Black radicalism.[62] This scholarship demonstrates that British political life was not an exclusively White domain. The place of Black radicals within the British socialist movement receives varying degrees of attention within these studies. Leslie James, for instance, does far more to illuminate Padmore's transnational pan-Africanist networks than the British political context of his activism, while Matera and Whittall are more concerned with mapping Black networks in London than with interracial socialist collaboration. Nevertheless, all of these works have made profound contributions to our understanding of aspects of British Black radicalism.

This book, unlike those discussed above, centres the relationship between Black radicalism and the wider British socialist movement, and demonstrates the importance of understanding the former in understanding the latter. An exploration of the IASB's place within British socialism allows us to see with new depth and clarity how the relationship between Black radicalism and European socialism involved far more than a simple Black importation of European ideas. Furthermore, a more thorough understanding of the IASB's political thought, which this book explores more fully than any previous study, allows us to grasp the importance it attached to working within the British socialist movement. Polsgrove has implied that Padmore's journalistic work for the ILP was

---

61 Bush, *Imperialism, Race and Resistance*; Pennybacker, *From Scottsboro to Munich*.

62 Christian Høgsbjerg, *C. L. R. James in Imperial Britain* (Durham, NC, 2014); James, *George Padmore*; W. O. Maloba, *Kenyatta and Britain: An Account of Political Transformation, 1929–1963* (Cham, Switzerland, 2018); Makalani, *In the Cause of Freedom*, Chapter 7; Marc Matera, *Black London: The Imperial Metropolis and Decolonization in the Twentieth Century* (Oakland, CA, 2015); Carol Polsgrove, *Ending British Rule in Africa: Writers in a Common Cause* (Manchester, 2009); Daniel Whittall, 'Creolising London: Black West Indian Activism and the Politics of Race and Empire in Britain, 1931–1948', doctoral thesis, Royal Holloway, University of London, 2012. For the history of postwar Black Britain, including Black radicalism, see Kennetta Hammond Perry, *London Is the Place for Me: Black Britons, Citizenship, and the Politics of Race* (New York, 2015); Rob Waters, *Thinking Black: Britain, 1964–1985* (Oakland, CA, 2019).

motivated largely by his wish to address a larger audience.[63] However, the IASB's idea of interdependent metropolitan and colonial revolutions impressed on him the necessity to embrace and enter into the European socialist movement in a more fundamental way. Padmore deemed his work with the ILP (and, more broadly, his enmeshment in the British socialist movement) to be strategically vital.

As well as reshaping our understandings of Black radicalism and socialism, this book aims to make another major historiographical intervention. The most prevalent historiographical trope concerning the ILP is the futility of its disaffiliation from the Labour Party in 1932 and its subsequent decline into obscurity and ineffectiveness. Robert Dowse charts the history of the ILP from its foundation in 1893 until almost a decade after its disaffiliation. The latter part of Dowse's book suffers from his determination to expose the idiocy of disaffiliation. James Jupp contributed to this trend when he heavily criticised the group's disaffiliation from the Labour Party, accusing the ILP of 'busily isolating themselves from the labour movement'.[64] Dowse is highly sympathetic to the earlier ILP, but concludes: 'By 1939 a party with a great and noble past clearly had no prospects at all of a future'.[65]

In these analyses, the ILP's anticolonial politics of the 1930s and 1940s are almost completely ignored. This failure to engage with anticolonial activism contributes to the notion that the post-disaffiliation ILP was a political failure. While the party's role in the downfall of European colonialism was modest, the ILP was a constituent part of a transnational anticolonial network that was ultimately successful. It was, after all, the ILP's McNair, rather than any other figure on the British left, who was invited to deliver fraternal greetings to the 1945 Pan-African Congress.

David James, Tony Jowitt and Keith Laybourn's 1992 edited collection on the history of the ILP adheres to the 'rise-and-fall' narrative of Dowse and Jupp, though this time failing to document the 'fall'. Commenting on the temporally skewed nature of the contributions, the editors remark:

---

63 Carol Polsgrove, 'George Padmore's Use of Periodicals to Build a Movement', in Baptiste and Lewis, *George Padmore*, p. 99.

64 Jupp, *Radical Left in Britain*, p. 23.

65 Robert E. Dowse, *Left in the Centre: The Independent Labour Party, 1893–1940* (London, 1966), p. 202.

It could be argued that we have devoted too much space to the years of growth and development before 1914 and give much less space and attention to the years after 1918 which culminated with disaffiliation from the Labour Party in 1932 and the ILP's consignment to the margins of the British political Labour movement.[66]

Interestingly, the volume concludes with a short contribution from Barry Winter, the political secretary of the renamed Independent Labour Publications. In a book devoid of discussions of the ILP's anticolonialism, Winter reminds his audience: 'When ILPers supported the independence movements in India and other British colonies, the supporters of the empire were incensed. Yet independence came.'[67]

Gidon Cohen attempts to move past the dominant historiographical narrative, which he describes as a 'caricature'.[68] He agrees that disaffiliation ultimately led to a decline in the ILP's influence, but rejects arguments that the ILP left the Labour Party simply to retain its political purity. Instead, the split occurred largely because the ILP's radicalism was restricted by the Labour Party's standing orders in parliament. He argues that the 'larger party pushed the smaller towards its death, and must bear some responsibility for its fate'.[69] He also highlights ways in which the diminishing membership of the ILP after 1932 could be a strength as well as a weakness, citing its greatly improved political coherence by the late 1930s.[70] More recently, Ian Bullock and Keith Laybourn have also produced work that discusses the interwar and post-disaffiliation ILP in more balanced and nuanced ways.[71] However, domestic and European affairs still dominate these analyses. Cohen's argument against the narrative of unmitigated decline could have been strengthened further through greater analysis of the ILP's anticolonialism. By more fully exploring the relationship between the ILP and Black radicals, and focusing on the transnational politics of anti-imperialism

---

66  'Introduction', in David James, Tony Jowitt and Keith Laybourn, eds, *The Centennial History of the Independent Labour Party* (Halifax, 1992), p. 14.

67  Barry Winter, 'The ILP: A Century for Socialism', in James, Jowitt and Laybourn, *Centennial History*, p. 365.

68  Cohen, *Failure of a Dream*, p. 1.

69  Ibid., p. 15.

70  Ibid., p. 211.

71  Bullock, *Under Siege*; Laybourn, *Independent Labour Party*.

rather than domestic matters or electoral success, this book seeks to rehabilitate the post-disaffiliation ILP.

The insertion of White socialists into the story of transnational anti-imperialism also reveals the extent of Britain's (and especially London's) role as, in Ian Duffield's formulation, a 'junction-box' for colonial activists.[72] Although much of Britain's Black population was in other port cities, like Cardiff and Liverpool, most colonial activists, students and intellectuals made London their home. Abrahams later remembered that 'London was the critical point of contact where Pan-African, socialist and anti-colonial ideas were shared and enlarged.'[73] As Duffield argues, 'Until the 1950s, it was easier for blacks to make contact with others and develop common viewpoints and strategies in Britain than in their diverse homelands.'[74] Howe explicitly endorses this idea, and it has found echoes elsewhere.[75] It is central to Matera's work on 'Black London', which observes that 'the conversations, alliances, and boundary crossings that [the metropole] made possible, as well as the tensions and conflicts such encounters produced, influenced the changing political commitments and personal identifications of Africans and Afro-Caribbeans.'[76] Michael Goebel has demonstrated that interwar Paris likewise facilitated intellectual exchanges between Africans, Asians, and Latin Americans that became crucial to Third World anti-imperialism.[77]

The geography of this book, however, is not simply that of 'Black London'. Certainly, there were hubs of Black radical congregation, such as Padmore's flat in Camden and Ashwood Garvey's restaurant on New Oxford Street, but the geography of Black radicalism was also more diffuse and fluid. Black radicals inserted themselves into the spaces of

---

72  Ian Duffield, 'Black People in Britain: History and the Historians', *History Today* 31: 9 (1981).

73  Abrahams, *Coyaba Chronicles*, p. 36.

74  Duffield, 'Black People in Britain', p. 35.

75  Howe, *Anticolonialism in British Politics*, p. 25. Pennybacker observes that 'London served as an unofficial center of colonial and antifascist exile'. Pennybacker, *From Scottsboro to Munich*, p. 1.

76  Matera, *Black London*, p. 2.

77  Michael Goebel, *Anti-Imperial Metropolis: Interwar Paris and the Seeds of Third World Nationalism* (Cambridge, 2015). For a review of several recent books about internationalist anti-imperialist activists in Europe, see Daniel Brückenhaus, 'Challenging Imperialism across Borders: Recent Studies of Twentieth-Century Internationalist Networks against Empire', *Contemporary European History* 29 (2020).

London's broader left. They travelled to Friends House on Euston Road and the ILP offices in the City, and even occasionally ventured south of the river to visit Ethel Mannin and Reginald Reynolds in Wimbledon. This book, then, while not rejecting the existence of a 'Black London', also shows an alternative way of mapping Black radical political activity by demonstrating its imbrication with a broader socialist London (and socialist Britain more widely). Britain's 'junction-box' not only housed connections between colonial radicals, but also connections between radicals of metropolitan and colonial origin.

Partly an intellectual history, this book grounds Black radical intellectual activities in the material world. This involves observing how events like the Italo-Ethiopian War or the Caribbean labour rebellions shaped and reshaped ideas about imperialism. It also entails examining, on the one hand, Black radical and socialist theories about the relationship between colonial liberation movements and metropolitan socialism, and, on the other hand, the practical, quotidian relationships between Black radicals and the various parties, individuals and institutions of the British left. Through this method, it will be seen how ideas and practices influenced one another, as the materialist philosophy of the IAFE and IASB necessitated that political thought reflect concrete conditions. Yet it also involves a deeper understanding of the personal circumstances of political theorists and writers. Most Black radicals lived in perpetual poverty, which inflicted stresses and strains that, in turn, had consequences for their work.

As Polsgrove has demonstrated, the need for income, agents and publishers can be a roadblock for radical writers.[78] Take, for instance, *A History of Negro Revolt* (1938), which James wrote at the request of British socialist publisher Raymond Postgate. James later recalled that he and Padmore had written 'a number of provocative statements which we knew Postgate would object to. But by putting in those and then agreeing to take them out, much really good stuff was sure to get in.'[79] This illustrates a tension in the relationship between the IASB and its publishers, as Black radicals pre-empted editorial interference in an attempt to retain as much of their voice as possible. The alternative of self-publication was

---

78  Polsgrove, *Ending British Rule in Africa*, p. xiii.

79  Rare Book and Manuscript Library, Columbia University, New York, C. L. R. James papers, box 5 folder 21, C. L. R. James, 'Notes on the Life of George Padmore', p. 38.

expensive and time-consuming. It took Padmore two years to self-publish his report on the 1945 Pan-African Congress. His comrade and partner, Dorothy Pizer, wrote that he 'had 2,000 printed at a cost of just under £100, and has only been able to send out small lots to the Colonies'. The copies therefore sold out extremely quickly, and, due to discounts applied in the colonies to encourage a wide readership, the return from sales barely covered the cost of production.[80] A great deal of labour was involved in Black radical writing, and these constraints must be considered when discussing intellectual production.

Another important factor in Black radical intellectual production was the role played by women. Ashwood Garvey was the only Black woman at the core of these groups, having co-founded the IAFE.[81] As Makalani has demonstrated, Ashwood Garvey was a 'tireless organizer' who created 'centers of activism' at her club and restaurant that were invaluable in creating and maintaining the dynamism of Black radical politics in London.[82] Additionally, several White women, such as Pizer and Dinah Stock (notably from Jewish and Irish backgrounds, respectively), were central to the IASB's activism. On a practical level, they collected material, and edited and typed their male companions' work. They have remained relatively unacknowledged – a process in which male Black radicals have been complicit. Moreover, there is a broader sense in which intellectual production is always a collective effort, informed by conversations, experiences and environment. The attribution of a work to a single 'author' expunges this collective production in ways that are particularly prone to efface women's intellectual labour. This book therefore aims, as far as possible, to reconstruct the process of intellectual production, highlighting, for instance, the influence of Pizer on Padmore's writings.

A further significant aspect of the IAFE and IASB was the preponderance of Caribbean activists (Ashwood Garvey, James, Chris Jones,

---

80  Beinecke Rare Book and Manuscript Library, New Haven, CT, Richard Wright papers, box 103 folder 1521, Dorothy Pizer to Richard Wright, 29 May 1948.

81  For important studies of Black female internationalist activists, see Keisha N. Blain, *Set the World on Fire: Black Nationalist Women and the Global Struggle for Freedom* (Philadelphia, 2018); Imaobong D. Umoren, *Race Women Internationalists: Activist-Intellectuals and Global Freedom Struggles* (Oakland, CA, 2018).

82  Minkah Makalani, 'An International African Opinion: Amy Ashwood Garvey and C. L. R. James in Black Radical London', in Davarian L. Baldwin and Minkah Makalani, eds, *Escape from New York: The New Negro Renaissance Beyond Harlem* (Minneapolis, 2013), pp. 86–9.

Makonnen and Padmore), although there were also African activists (Kenyatta and Wallace-Johnson, and, during the 1940s, Abrahams and Nkrumah).[83] In his study of Caribbean radicalism in the United States, Winston James has suggested several reasons for the prominence of Caribbean radicals, including 'their majority consciousness; their prior political and organizational experience; their extensive prior experience of travel and migration'.[84] This is a compelling model to explain the radicalism of the IASB. The vast majority of Black radicals in Britain had come from either Africa or the Caribbean, and therefore not all of Winston James's distinctions between African Caribbeans and African Americans are applicable. Yet it is notable that the IASB, as the most radical Black British organisation of the day, was predominantly Caribbean.

Bill Schwarz has highlighted 'the unusually deep penetration of the institutions of Victorian civic life into the cultural organisation of the colonial Caribbean'.[85] James and Padmore, both well-educated and middle class, were particularly shaped by these institutions. James himself contended decades later (in a striking erasure of Caribbean transculturation): 'Having no native culture, no native language, no native religion and being raised entirely in the British tradition, [West Indians] mixed easily in English intellectual and left-wing political circles'.[86] The IASB's pamphlet *The West Indies To-day* (1938) described Caribbean people as 'almost entirely European in outlook'.[87] These denials of Black diasporic culture were incorrect. However, claims to Britishness and Europeanness made by the likes of James and Padmore were usually part of appeals for Caribbean self-determination. This aspect of Black radical thinking was therefore a contradictory one, which demanded colonial liberation while effacing colonial cultures.

---

83  This preponderance may in part be explained by Britain having a larger Caribbean than African population during this period. Winston James estimates that, between 1911 and 1931, Britain's Black population was around 14,000, of which the Caribbean and Africa accounted for 9,000 and 5,000, respectively. Winston James, 'Harlem's Difference', in Andrew M. Fearnley and Daniel Matlin, eds, *Race Capital? Harlem as Setting and Symbol* (New York, 2018), p. 127.

84  Winston James, *Holding Aloft the Banner of Ethiopia: Caribbean Radicalism in Early Twentieth-Century America* (London, 1998), p. 50.

85  Bill Schwarz, 'Introduction: Crossing the Seas', in Schwarz, *West Indian Intellectuals*, p. 12.

86  C. L. R. James, *Nkrumah and the Ghana Revolution* (London, 1977), p. 76. For 'transculturation', see Fernando Ortiz, *Cuban Counterpoint: Tobacco and Sugar*, transl. Harriet de Onís (Durham, NC, 1995 [1940]).

87  International African Service Bureau, *The West Indies To-day* (London, 1938), p. 5.

James's ideas about Britishness shaped divisions within the IAFE and IASB over the place of Marxism within the movement. Makalani argues that James's 'diasporic moment' in London reoriented him away from a concern with Caribbean self-government and towards African liberation struggles.[88] This is correct, but Makalani overreaches when he declares that James came to see Caribbean modernity 'as a mark of [the Caribbean's] limited revolutionary potential'.[89] Later in life, James commented that when he had met Nkrumah in the United States, Nkrumah was 'quite ignorant about Marxism'; it was in Britain that Padmore 'educated him'.[90] James also lamented the supposed insularity of many Africans in London. He opined that they 'were Marxists in general and so forth, but when you pressed them hard on this or that, it turned out they were primarily concerned with the national question'.[91] He acknowledged that there were prominent Africans in the IASB, but insisted that 'the main burden of the organisation in theoretical and practical matters was carried by the West Indians'.[92]

Contrary to Makalani's claims, Black radicals in fact located Caribbean people within modernity so as to weaponise their anti-imperialist appeals. The IASB's memorandum to the West India Royal Commission noted that the oilfield workers' form of industrial action and their demand for a forty-hour week were in line with 'the most advanced bodies of workers in France and America'.[93] James's and Padmore's Marxist understanding of the progression of history emerging from class conflict meant that, for them, the level of development of colonial countries, and particularly of their labour movements, could be measured against those in Europe, which represented the vanguard of modernity. Appealing to the British labour movement in 1945, Padmore stated: 'coloured workers . . . are to-day passing through their Tolpuddle period'.[94] Importantly, though, this did not lead Black radicals to accept notions that cultural or economic 'advancement' should be a condition of colonial independence, and Makalani is correct that the IASB generally focused its activism on Africa rather than the Caribbean.

---

88  Makalani, 'International African Opinion', p. 88.
89  Ibid., p. 78.
90  C. L. R. James papers, box 2 folder 15, James to Robert Hill, 31 October 1982.
91  C. L. R. James papers, box 4 folder 7, C. L. R. James, 'Autobiography, 1932–38', p. 48.
92  James, 'Notes on the Life of George Padmore', p. 37.
93  *Africa and the World*, 2 September 1937, p. 11.
94  George Padmore, *The Voice of Coloured Labour* (Manchester, 1945), p. 7.

Some clarifications are necessary regarding the parameters of this book. The IASB – alongside related organisations such as the ITUCNW, IAFE and PAF – is my main focus, because this book is primarily an intervention in the historiography of the British socialist movement. This is not to say that other Black activists, such as Una Marson, Harold Moody and Ladipo Solanke did not interact with British socialism, but rather that the IASB, as the most left-wing Black organisation in Britain, is the best vessel through which to explore the ways in which Black radicalism shaped British socialism during the 1930s and 1940s. While most of the book is dedicated to locating these Black radicals within the British socialist movement, it should be remembered that they were also part of transnational pan-Africanist networks. The relative absence of discussions of these networks should not be understood as dismissing their importance, but rather as an acknowledgement that much of this work has been performed by other scholars.

I do not offer a prescriptive definition of 'socialism', but most of the actors in this book shared a belief that capitalism should be totally abolished (albeit at varying speeds and by diverse means) and replaced by an economic system in which the means of production would be commonly owned. This includes the Independent Labour Party and the Communist Party of Great Britain, the two most significant organisations to the left of the Labour Party, but also those on the left wing of the Labour Party, and unaffiliated activists such as Nancy Cunard. As one recent history of the Labour left puts it, paraphrasing Tony Benn, the Labour Party should not be thought of as a socialist party, but rather as 'a party with socialists in it'.[95] Similarly, Paul Rich, contrasting 'liberal' with 'socialist' critics of empire, places Labour members Norman Leys and William McGregor Ross in the liberal camp.[96] Nevertheless, this book discusses Black radical analyses of the nature of the Labour Party, and considers the interactions of Black radicals with several figures on the centre-left of British political life (if not in the same depth as those figures who can be understood as unambiguously socialist).

Temporally, the book covers the period from the late 1920s until the immediate postwar years. It was in the late 1920s and early 1930s that

---

95  Simon Hannah, *A Party with Socialists in It: A History of the Labour Left* (London, 2018).

96  Paul B. Rich, *Race and Empire in British Politics* (Cambridge, 1986), Chapter 4.

many of the people who would form the IAFE and IASB became full-time activists, and it was in this period that several of them first came to Britain. Correspondingly, in the postwar period there was a reorientation away from metropolitan activism and towards Africa itself as the site of struggle. As part of this reorientation, Kenyatta returned to Kenya in 1946, and Nkrumah to the Gold Coast in 1947. Several Black radicals had earlier left London, if not Britain, because of the Second World War. By the summer of 1948, the only core IASB activists remaining in Britain were Makonnen and Padmore – albeit in different cities (Manchester and London, respectively).

Chapter 1 charts the 'prehistory' of the IAFE and IASB in the late 1920s and early 1930s. Of course, in the broadest sense this prehistory lies within the pan-Africanist movements and the entanglements between 'Black' and 'Red' highlighted above. But the purpose of this chapter is to show more specifically how the book's principal actors' experiences of migration and political engagement led them to reformulate aspects of this intellectual and political inheritance. The most detailed discussions are of Padmore's work for the ITUCNW in Hamburg, Kenyatta's agitation on behalf of the Kikuyu Central Association (KCA) in London, and James's immersion in the working-class town of Nelson. Chapter 2 focuses on the Italo-Ethiopian War of 1935–36, and the formation in July 1935 of the IAFE. It was in this period that the activists who would form the IASB began working closely with each other in London. The chapter tracks the false starts of Black radicals' relationships with each other and with the organisations of the British left, as the debate about the correct form of action to take against fascist Italy divided the socialist movement. Chapter 3 discusses the formation of the IASB in 1937 and the crystallisation by the end of 1938 of its coalition with the ILP against the Popular Front strategy advocated by the CPGB. The IASB argued that it was necessary to oppose imperialism in order to oppose fascism, and their winning of the ILP to this position represents an important milestone in the dissemination of Black radical ideas throughout the wider British left. Chapter 4 follows the IASB through much of the Second World War, from 1939 to 1943. The group dispersed as a result of the war, leaving only Chris Jones and Padmore – later joined by Peter Abrahams – to continue organising in London under the IASB banner. The group became even more enmeshed with the ILP in this period. Chapter 5 discusses the postwar manifestos developed by the British socialist and pan-Africanist movements from 1944 to 1947. In particular, it explores the affinities and differences between Padmore's proposal for a socialist 'British' commonwealth, the ILP's agitation for a United Socialist States of Europe, and the pan-Africanism of the 1945 congress. It argues that all had at their heart a desire for world socialist federation, and should generally be understood as complementary. The Epilogue briefly considers the post-1947 period, as the maturation of African nationalist movements, the onset of the Cold War and the failure to achieve socialist revolution in Europe led Black radicals to place less emphasis on the role to be played by the European proletariat in the defeat of imperialism.

This book demonstrates the cross-pollination between Black radicalism and British socialism. This observation challenges the dominant historiographies of British socialism by revealing the ways in which Black radicalism impacted the movement. The role played by Black activists and the importance of anti-imperialist thought need to be given greater consideration in histories of British socialism. This book seeks to enrich our understanding of Black radicalism as a movement which, while also situated in transnational pan-African networks, helped constitute socialist networks in Britain. Yet it is important to remember that Black radicals did not participate in British socialist networks as uncritical foot-soldiers, but rather as influential activists and theorists in their own right. They often criticised the British left not because they *rejected* it, but because they wished to *change* it – to reshape and redefine it from within. Finally, this book counters familiar narratives of ILP decline. When we shift our focus away from domestic concerns and electoral politics, the ILP's position in a transnational network of anti-imperialists (many of whom would lead countries to independence in the postwar period) becomes apparent. This points to the ways in which a confluence of White metropolitan socialists and colonial activists helped to shape decolonisation. This is a story that needs telling, and one wonders how many Black Chicagoans, distracted by the exciting display of pan-African solidarity and White socialist support on the other side of the Atlantic, forgot to set their clocks back on 27 October 1945.

# 1

# Hamburg, London, Nelson, 1929–1934

The International African Friends of Ethiopia was not formed until 1935, and the International African Service Bureau not until 1937, but these organisations have a prehistory without which it is impossible to understand their position within the British socialist movement during the later 1930s and 1940s. Most of their future members, operating in different corners of the Black world, became politically active during the 1920s. Through this activism, they encountered the socialist and trade union movements of Europe and North America. For many of these activists (especially George Padmore, Johnstone Kenyatta, Arnold Ward and I. T. A. Wallace-Johnson), this meant primarily a relationship with the Communist International and its national parties.

This chapter traces this prehistory from the late 1920s until the formation of the International African Friends of Ethiopia (IAFE) in 1935.[1] It focuses particularly on the Comintern's International Trade Union Committee of Negro Workers (ITUCNW), based in Hamburg, of which Padmore was secretary from 1931 to 1933. While future members of the International African Service Bureau (IASB) – variously operating in Hamburg, London, Lancashire, the United States and West Africa – had little face-to-face contact with each other at this time, through the ITUCNW many of them developed political relationships both with

1 The organisation was founded as the International African Friends of Abyssinia. At some point, it changed its name to the International African Friends of Ethiopia. For the sake of consistency I use the latter, unless quoting from another source.

each other and with the British and international socialist movements. The chapter begins with a discussion of Communist anti-imperialism during the late 1920s and 1930s. It then examines how Padmore was drawn into the movement, and the ways in which he both embraced and resisted Comintern orthodoxies, culminating in his break from the organisation in 1934. It thereby challenges historians who have suggested a more fundamental distinction between Padmore's pan-Africanism and his Communism. We will see that Padmore and other Black activists, while occasionally frustrated by the Communist movement, were convinced of Leninism's rectitude, and appreciated the Comintern's material and political support for African anti-imperialism. When, during the mid 1930s, the Comintern began to compromise its anti-imperialism, Black radicals did not denounce their old political philosophies, but rather upheld Leninism to explain the errant ways of the Comintern.

The chapter then considers in turn Kenyatta's and C. L. R. James's activism during the same period. Kenyatta came within the orbit of British Communism in London, while James was part of the networks of the Labour left in Nelson, and eventually of the British Trotskyist movement in London. Both men were in contact with Padmore during this period, and looked to him as the leading Black anti-imperialist in Europe. These activists all later worked together in the IAFE and IASB. We can detect the seeds of these organisations in the period before 1935, as Padmore, Kenyatta and James adopted Leninist understandings of imperialism and embraced the necessity of working within the British socialist movement. At the same time, they were acutely aware of the movement's deficiencies. The alliances and debates of this earlier period, hinging on varying understandings of the relationships between capitalism, imperialism, fascism and war, prefigured those of subsequent years. They thus help us to understand everything from responses to the 1935 Italian invasion of Ethiopia to the 1945 Pan-African Congress. Furthermore, examining the nature of British anti-imperialism before 1935 allows us to understand how the IAFE and IASB reshaped the politics of British socialism in later years, challenging the longstanding paternalism of many of their comrades.

## The Communist International and the League Against Imperialism

In the late 1920s, the most potent expression of Communist anticolonialism was the League Against Imperialism and for National Independence (LAI). The LAI was initially a broad left-wing anticolonial organisation established, but not dominated, by Communists. It was founded at a February 1927 congress in Brussels, and declared that all 'who are fighting . . . for the self-determination of all nations, for the national liberty of all people, for the equal rights of all races, classes and individuals shall be allowed to affiliate to the League'.[2] The German Communist Willi Münzenberg initiated the congress. He ensured collaboration with social democrats, such as the Labour Party's George Lansbury, and anticolonial nationalist organisations, such as the Indian National Congress and the Kuomintang. The British Section of the LAI held its first conference in July 1928, which was dominated by members of the Independent Labour Party and Communist Party of Great Britain.[3]

But 1928 proved to be a turning point in the history of the Comintern. The Sixth Congress of the Comintern, held that summer, declared that capitalism was entering a 'Third Period' since the First World War, in which economic crisis was imminent. Revolutionary class struggle by the proletariat against the bourgeoisie ('Class against Class') was now the only acceptable form of socialist activity. Social democrats, who did not support this revolutionary strategy, were regarded as 'social fascists' – as great an enemy as the bourgeoisie. Another aspect of Third Period policy was the demand for the immediate national independence of colonial peoples and increased support for anticolonial struggles. The social-democratic parties of the Labour and Socialist International (LSI, commonly referred to as the Second International) were largely equivocal about, if not hostile to, these struggles, so the Comintern attacked them on this front. The LSI had already forbidden its members from affiliating to the LAI on the grounds that it was a Communist front organisation. The ILP's Fenner

---

2 International Institute of Social History (IISH), Amsterdam, League Against Imperialism archives, ARCH00804, 'Resolution on the Organisation of the League', p. 1.

3 IISH, LAI archives, 'Report on the First Conference of the British Section of the League Against Imperialism'.

Brockway was the original chair of the LAI, but at a meeting of the LSI's International Executive he was given the option of resigning from his LAI posts or resigning from the LSI International Executive.[4] This resulted in the ILP MP James Maxton replacing Brockway as chair of the LAI.

Meanwhile, by the time of the LAI's Second Congress, held in Frankfurt in July 1929, the LAI had become increasingly dominated by the Communist 'Class against Class' thesis. The Congress's manifesto proclaimed: 'To fight effectively against imperialism means also to wage a relentless fight against its agents in the labour movement, against international Social Democracy, the Amsterdam Trade Union International, and the most brazen of all – the British Labour Party and the American Federation of Labor.'[5] There was therefore hostility to ILP involvement in the LAI from both the Second and Third Internationals. This meant that even those who were critical of the Labour Party's imperialism, such as Brockway and Maxton, were gradually forced out of LAI work by the early 1930s as a result of their unwillingness to break completely with the Labour leadership.[6]

Another important decision was reached at the Sixth Congress of the Comintern. The prominent African American Communist, James Ford, and the general secretary of the Red International of Labour Unions (RILU, or Profintern), Solomon Lozovsky, criticised the Communist parties of the United States, South Africa, France and Britain for their neglect of the 'Negro question' (the liberation of Africa and its diaspora). The congress led to the creation of the International Trade Union Committee of Negro Workers, whose leadership was drawn predominantly from the ranks of the CPUSA. Through the ITUCNW, the Comintern, whose only national party in Africa or the Caribbean was the Communist Party of South Africa, for the first time began to make serious attempts to organise among Black workers in countries and regions without Communist parties. Comintern concerns about White chauvinism and neglect of the colonial question in its parties coalesced

---

4 Fenner Brockway, *Inside the Left: Thirty Years of Platform, Press, Prison and Parliament* (Leicester, 1947 [1942]), p. 168.

5 IISH, LAI archives, ARCH00804, 'Manifesto of the Second World Congress, July 20 to July 31, Frankfort-am-Main, Germany', p. 3.

6 League Against Imperialism, *The Colonies and Oppressed Nations in the Struggle for Freedom: Resolutions Adopted by the Executive Committee of the League Against Imperialism and for National Independence* (Berlin, 1931), p. 4.

in the formation of the ITUCNW. Hakim Adi has called the organisation 'a communist organisation with a Pan-Africanist orientation', and Holger Weiss has located it in 'an overlapping space' of the 'African Atlantic' and the Comintern.[7] The formation of the ITUCNW was closely followed by the creation of a Negro Bureau, which had a brief to 'conduct research, propaganda, and agitation, as well as the building of connection with the Negroes'.[8]

## Padmore and the First International Conference of Negro Workers

Malcolm Nurse, who would later become famous as George Padmore, was born in Arouca in Trinidad's East-West Corridor in 1903. Leslie James has argued that the distinctive historical mix of the Caribbean – slavery, the plantation and ethnic heterogeneity – produced people with 'a strikingly modern perspective'.[9] Padmore's career certainly attests to the contradictions and struggles of twentieth-century modernity: between human rights and racial oppression, between self-determination and imperialism, and between socialism and capitalism. His father was a schoolmaster and agricultural instructor, but the Nurses' professional ambitions were hindered by the island's racism and colourism.[10] Malcolm Nurse's childhood friend, C. L. R. James, later recalled the barriers faced by young men like them:

> Socially racial lines were clear. The whites, the browns and the blacks each kept their own company. The best positions were shared (very unequally) by the first two . . . It was on the black as opposed to the

---

7 Hakim Adi, *Pan-Africanism and Communism: The Communist International, Africa and the Diaspora, 1919–1939* (Trenton, NJ, 2013), p. xxi; Holger Weiss, *Framing a Radical African Atlantic: African American Agency, West African Intellectuals and the International Trade Union Committee of Negro Workers* (Leiden, 2014), p. 9.

8 Russian State Archive of Socio-Political History (RGASPI), Moscow, 495/155/54, Draft Resolution on the Organisation of a Negro Bureau attached to Eastern Secretariat, 22 November 1928.

9 Leslie James, *George Padmore and Decolonization from Below: Pan-Africanism, the Cold War, and the End of Empire* (Basingstoke, 2015), p. 17.

10 James R. Hooker, *Black Revolutionary: George Padmore's Path from Communism to Pan-Africanism* (London, 1967), p. 2.

brown middle class that the discrimination fell hardest and George was a member of that class.[11]

James remembered that the young Nurse 'was very sensitive to all this', and was appalled by the racism to which he was subjected when working as a journalist for the *Trinidad Guardian*.[12] Nurse married Julia Semper in September 1924, before leaving to study in the United States by the end of the year while his wife and newborn daughter remained in Trinidad. He enrolled at Fisk University in Nashville to study medicine but did not graduate, and soon moved to Howard University in Washington, D.C. to study law, all while developing a reputation for his anticolonial activism. It was at Howard that Nurse, in 1927, became a member of the CPUSA. In order to mask his activities, he adopted the name George Padmore.

One of his earliest acts using the pseudonym was to protest the visit to Howard of a British ambassador who had allegedly played a role in the deportation of the Jamaican pan-Africanist and leader of the Universal Negro Improvement Association, Marcus Garvey. By 1928, Padmore was writing for the CPUSA's *Daily Worker* and editing its *Negro Champion*.[13] The CPUSA had provided a home for radical Black activism since its collaboration with Cyril Briggs's African Blood Brotherhood during the early 1920s, and included prominent Black members such as James Ford, Harry Haywood and Otto Huiswoud. Padmore fitted well into this movement, and was soon recruited to work for the Comintern's Negro Bureau in Moscow, arriving – highly recommended by Ford – in late 1929.[14]

Once in Moscow, Padmore was immediately thrust into the task of helping to organise the ITUCNW's most ambitious project: an international conference of Black workers to be held in London in 1930. The African labour movement had seen marked growth in the 1920s.[15] Communists saw in the continent parallels with the development of the

---

11 Rare Book and Manuscript Library, Columbia University, New York, C. L. R. James papers, box 5 folder 21, C. L. R. James, 'Notes on the Life of George Padmore', p. 5.

12 C. L. R. James, 'George Padmore: Black Marxist Revolutionary – A Memoir' (1976), in C. L. R. James, *At the Rendezvous of Victory* (London, 1984), p. 253.

13 Hooker, *Black Revolutionary*, pp. 4–8.

14 RGASPI, 534/3/450, James Ford to George Slayin, 23 December 1929.

15 Barbara Bush, *Imperialism, Race and Resistance: Africa and Britain, 1919–1945* (London, 1999), p. 109.

European proletariat during the nineteenth century. The ITUCNW therefore desired to help build this nascent movement and draw it into revolutionary and internationalist channels.

A conference of Black workers had been proposed at the Comintern's Sixth Congress. The plans stalled, but at the Second Congress of the LAI in Frankfurt, in July 1929, the ten-strong Negro Delegation met with a small number of British, Chinese and Indian delegates concerned with the 'Negro question'. Shapurji Saklatvala, a British-Indian Communist, suggested 'that an effort should be made to hold such a conference in London, pointing out the large number of Negroes under the British Empire, and the fact that as the Labour Government was in power the question of holding such a conference could be put squarely before them'.[16]

From the conference's inception, then, it was conceived by CPGB anti-imperialists as a provocative challenge to the Labour government's 'social fascism' in the British Empire. Maxton, as an MP, 'promised to assist all he could in parliament', and the LAI's Reginald Bridgeman was nominated as the main point of contact for the ITUCNW in Britain.[17] This was the situation when Padmore arrived in Moscow in late 1929. Along with the Americans Ford and William Patterson, and the Surinamese CPUSA member Otto Huiswoud, he became one of the four principal organisers of the conference. As the conference was due to be held in Britain, Padmore also had his first contact with the British socialist and anticolonialist movements during the preparation for it. Although he did not know it at the time, within just a few years he would become a central figure in these movements.

Padmore's first contact with these movements, however, was inauspicious. With the conference planned for July 1930, Patterson arrived in Berlin in April to meet Edward Small, a Gambian trade unionist. He found that Small was, despite contact with the British LAI and the British RILU section, the National Minority Movement (NMM), 'totally ignorant' about the coming conference. As a result, Patterson and Padmore travelled to London, only to find there '[n]othing being done' to prepare for the conference. They met with the CPGB's Colonial Commission, and their intervention shook CPGB and LAI members into action.

---

16  RGASPI, 534/3/450, Ford, Report on the Negro Question at the LAI Congress, 3 October 1929.

17  Ibid.

Patterson and Bridgeman visited the House of Commons in an attempt to find the sympathetic Labour MPs W. J. Brown and James Marley, but saw 'only' Maxton. Maxton, though marginalised by the 'Class against Class' policy, was at this point still a member of the British LAI Executive Committee, and immediately drafted a letter to the Labour home secretary, J. R. Clynes. Patterson assured the Comintern Negro Bureau that he had 'not been won at all by [Maxton's] honied words'. Voicing his frustration with the British Communist movement, he observed that, due to the presence of Black workers in port cities, Britain was an 'Objectively good field for Negro work. Subjectively extremely bad.'[18] It soon became apparent that the Labour government, hostile to the Comintern, would not permit the conference to be held in Britain. The location was ultimately changed to Hamburg.

The conference organisers saw in the Labour government's repression of a meeting of Black trade unionists a validation of the Third Period concept of 'social fascism'. A Negro Bureau report after the conference stated: 'We encountered the most hostile reaction of the capitalists and imperialists and their agents, especially the British "Labour" Government.'[19] However, the ITUCNW also concluded:

> One of the most important shortcomings in the preparatory work was the lack of attention on the part of the NMM of G.B. or the Unitary Confederation of France towards the Conference. These organisations not only showed lack of any initiative of their own to popularise the Conference in the respective British and French colonies, but were very slow in carrying out the directives of the RILU.[20]

The passivity of the CPGB and NMM in organising the conference set a precedent for Padmore's relationship with the British Communist movement. He no doubt remembered these episodes when debating with the CPGB later in the decade – debates in which he produced balanced criticism of the Comintern but was vituperative in his denunciations of the CPGB.

---

18  RGASPI, 534/4/330, Padmore to 'Comrades', 15 April 1930; W. W. to Profintern Negro Bureau, 18 April 1930.

19  RGASPI, 495/155/87, The International Conference of Negro Workers, 29 July 1930.

20  RGASPI, 534/3/546, Resolution on Negro Work, 27 August 1930.

The First International Conference of Negro Workers was held in Hamburg on 7 and 8 July 1930. There were only seventeen delegates (plus three fraternal delegates), partly as a result of poor organisation, but also because colonial governments prevented certain activists from travelling.[21] The proceedings were thus dominated by CPUSA members. Ford held true to the Third Period theory of social fascism. On the subject of the 'reformist organizations' (including the ILP, despite Maxton's interventions during the planning of the conference), he remarked: 'as they do in the imperialist countries, the same they do in the colonies – help the imperialists in the exploitation of the colonial workers'.[22]

The conference was pan-Africanist in outlook. Black people throughout the world were understood as suffering under a common imperialist oppression. The conference declared that the 'class education of the Negro workers must be carried through by assimilation of the lessons of their struggles and the utilisation of the lessons of the struggles of the working class as a whole', thereby stating the necessity of revolutionary alliances between African and European workers.[23] But ITUCNW members, like the ABB before them, made it clear that Black people were also the victims of a particular racial oppression, and that an understanding of exploitation that failed to take race, as well as class, into account was inadequate. Ford stated that the delegates must discuss issues such as lynching, pass laws and forced labour.[24]

The conference also led to the foundation of the ITUCNW headquarters in Hamburg, to be led by Ford. Padmore served on the Executive Committee from Moscow. Despite the general passivity of the British Communist movement in the organisation of the conference, the British LAI's 1931 conference consciously echoed the Hamburg conference in calling 'for the complete independence from imperialism of all Negro workers and peasants in whatever country they reside' and for closer cooperation of British workers with Black workers and peasants.[25]

---

21 International Trade Union Committee of Negro Workers, *A Report of the Proceedings and Decisions of the First International Conference of Negro Workers* (Hamburg, 1931), p. 40.

22 Ibid., p. 7.

23 Ibid., p. 32.

24 Ibid., p. 5.

25 LAI (British Section), *Report of the National Conference of the League Against Imperialism (British Section), February 1931* (London, 1931), p. 21.

## Padmore's Political Thought in the ITUCNW

Minkah Makalani has argued that the Comintern during the Third Period 'was both an ally and an albatross to Padmore and the ITUCNW', giving 'unequivocal support to Negro work', but also restricting the ITUCNW's theory and practice to 'reductive notions of class struggle'.[26] This is undoubtedly true, but it should be added that the Comintern was more ally than albatross. More objectionable is the work of historians who attempt to explain away Padmore's Communism because they see it as incompatible with pan-Africanism. Padmore regularly attacked Garvey, accusing his 'Back to Africa' programme of simply being a means for the Black bourgeoisie to exploit Black workers and peasants.[27] He subjected W. E. B. Du Bois and Mohandas Gandhi to similar attacks, creating a dilemma for those who wish to situate Padmore in a pan-Africanist pantheon in which his tension with Garvey or Du Bois is resolved. Vincent Thompson dismisses Padmore's Communist career as 'aberrant', distinguishing his 'positive contributions' (pan-Africanist activism) from his 'negative actions' (criticising Garvey), and thereby portraying Padmore as a pan-African Jekyll and Hyde.[28]

Taking a different tack, Jerome Teelucksingh argues that Padmore 'was a supporter of the vibrant Pan-Africanist ideology promulgated by Garvey. Subsequent criticisms of Garvey by Padmore can be traced to the latter's involvement in the Comintern.'[29] He therefore makes no attempt to reconcile Padmore's Marxism with his pan-Africanism. Padmore may have moderated his criticisms of Garvey after his departure from the Comintern, but he was a consistent critic of Garveyism nonetheless.[30] Similarly, Rodney Worrell has argued that 'the communists

---

26  Minkah Makalani, *In the Cause of Freedom: Radical Black Internationalism from Harlem to London, 1917–1939* (Chapel Hill, NC, 2011), pp. 166–7.

27  See, for example, George Padmore, *The Life and Struggles of Negro Toilers* (London, 1931), pp. 125–6.

28  Vincent B. Thompson, 'George Padmore: Reconciling Two Phases of Contradictions', in Fitzroy Baptiste and Rupert Lewis, eds, *George Padmore: Pan-African Revolutionary* (Kingston, 2009), p. 134.

29  Jerome Teelucksingh, 'The Immortal Batsman: George Padmore the Revolutionary, Writer and Activist', in Baptiste and Lewis, *George Padmore*, p. 16.

30  George Padmore, *Pan-Africanism or Communism? The Coming Struggle for Africa* (London, 1956), pp. 87–104.

used Padmore and Padmore used the communists to further his object-ive of carrying out the African liberation project' – the implication being that Padmore's pan-Africanism remained untainted by Communism.[31]

While ITUCNW members undoubtedly had their problems with the rigidity and hierarchy of the Comintern, they were more concerned with the White chauvinism of the national parties. Indeed, the Comintern was seen as a valuable ally in this struggle, allowing the ITUCNW to pull rank behind a powerful authority. Moreover, most ITUCNW members embraced the revolutionary zeal of the Third Period. In the years immed-iately following his break with the Comintern, Padmore was a vocal critic of the Popular Front strategy, but rarely spoke ill of its 'Class against Class' phase. He was not an uncompromising Stalinist, but his analysis of imper-ialism meant that during the Third Period the Comintern was the most appropriate antiracist and anticolonialist organisation for him to join.

The ITUCNW expressed its political philosophy through its monthly journal, the *Negro Worker*, which came under the editorship of Padmore upon his move from Moscow to Hamburg in late 1931, and also through Padmore's *The Life and Struggles of Negro Toilers* (1931). The brand of pan-Africanism expressed in these texts would later be echoed in the IASB's publications. Brent Hayes Edwards, attuned to Padmore's agency within the structures of the Comintern, has commented on 'Padmore's determination to make the *Negro Worker* a space for the "points of view" and "daily life" of workers of African descent, rather than a place for the Communist hierarchy to debate the "Negro question"'.[32] *Life and Strug-gles* was the most thorough expression of Padmore's political philosophy. His use of the word 'toilers' strategically encompassed both the small African proletariat and the much larger peasantry, extending Lenin's analysis that the peasantry could constitute a historically progressive class. While the White, metropolitan, industrial worker continued to animate the revolutionary imaginaries of most European Communists, Padmore reconceptualised the revolutionary subject. This allowed him to position the 'Negro toilers' as an important plank of a future world socialist revolution.

---

31  Rodney Worrell, 'George Padmore: Pan-Africanist Par Excellence', in Baptiste and Lewis, *George Padmore*, p. 28.

32  Brent Hayes Edwards, *The Practice of Diaspora: Literature, Translation, and the Rise of Black Internationalism* (Cambridge, MA, 2003), p. 257.

Front cover of the *Negro Worker*
Public domain

Central to the brand of Marxist pan-Africanism expressed in *Life and Struggles* was the idea that the most oppressed people in the world were the 'Negro toilers'. Padmore explained that 'on the one hand they are oppressed as a class, and on the other as a nation. The national (race) oppression has its basis in the social-economic relation of the Negro under capitalism.'[33] Three things are apparent from this formulation. First, Padmore's theory of oppression was one in which race and class could not be disentangled; his subjects were oppressed as 'Negro toilers'. Second, race and nation were deeply connected, in such a way that anticolonialism and the demand for national self-determination had to be at the centre of the ITUCNW's activity. Third, Black people were

---

33  Padmore, *Life and Struggles*, p. 5.

oppressed because of capitalism. This was true even of instances of racism not directly related to labour conditions and economic oppression, such as in the case of the Scottsboro Nine.[34]

For Padmore and the ITUCNW, following Lenin's ideas, imperialism (of which colonialism was one feature) was a stage of capitalism. Lenin had argued that it was the growth of monopoly capitalism in the nineteenth century that had led to the carving up of the world between the European powers, driven by the impulse to find new markets and cheap labour. He stated that capitalists created 'super-profits' through this cheap labour, which were subsequently used '*to bribe* the labour leaders and the upper stratum of the labour aristocracy' in the metropole.[35] This extraction of super-profits had implications for the prospect of anti-imperialist solidarity between colonial and metropolitan workers. Padmore used Lenin's theory to denounce the labour aristocracy of the LSI-affiliated International Federation of Trade Unions. But for Lenin and Padmore the majority of European workers had an interest in combating imperialism. Padmore aimed his book not just at 'Negro toilers' but also at the European working class. He stated that the use of super-profits as bribes led the self-serving labour aristocracy 'to betray the struggles of the workers'.[36] Borrowing a quotation from Marx, Padmore reminded his White socialist readers that 'labour in the white skin cannot free itself while labour in the black is enslaved'.[37] Padmore was not using this language simply to appease the Comintern, but out of a genuine concern that the European proletariat should accept this political mission. Writing to Arnold Ward, a Barbadian activist in Britain, he implored Ward to 'push sales [of the *Negro Worker*] as much as possible, especially among the white workers. You comrades must let the British workers understand that we are fighting.'[38]

---

34  The Scottsboro Nine were a group of African American teenagers and young men falsely accused of raping two White women. In Padmore's analysis, the racism of the criminal justice system could not be separated from the class position of Black people, as the American ruling class attempted to divide the proletariat along racial lines. See George Padmore, 'Lynch Law: The Class Weapon of the American Bourgeoisie', *Negro Worker*, September 1931, pp. 12–14.

35  Vladimir Lenin, *Imperialism: The Highest Stage of Capitalism* (London, 1996 [1917]), p. 7. Emphasis in original.

36  Padmore, *Life and Struggles*, p. 6.

37  Ibid., p. 124.

38  RGASPI, 534/3/755, Padmore to Arnold Ward, 20 June 1932.

Padmore, informed by Lenin, formulated a pan-Africanist Marxism in which White proletarian consciousness was measured by a desire to aid the struggles of 'Negro toilers'. Lenin had analysed super-profits to explain the retardation of workers' struggles in Western Europe; Padmore elaborated on this to demonstrate the effect that this process had on Black workers in particular. Worrell argues that it was not until after Padmore's break from the Comintern that he 'began to advance the thesis that the liberation of colonial peoples was their own responsibility'.[39] But Padmore's pan-Africanist Marxism, whether as a member of the ITUCNW or later, hinged on the idea that revolutions in the metropole and the colonies would be interdependent. *Life and Struggles* was well received by the British Communist press. Reginald Bridgeman and Hugo Rathbone both reviewed the book for CPGB publications, and emphasised the necessity of British workers forging links with the 'Negro toilers'.[40]

## Padmore and the CPGB

The CPGB's Tenth Congress, held in January 1929, endorsed the decisions of the Sixth Congress of the Comintern and elected Harry Pollitt as the party's new general secretary. The colonial resolution conceded the Comintern's criticism that inadequate connections had been made with mass organisations in the colonies, pledged that colonial work would not simply be seen as a 'special task' separate from the 'everyday tasks of the class struggle', and declared that 'the overthrow of the capitalist class in Great Britain and the victory of the social revolution are only possible with the co-operation of the oppressed masses in the colonies'.[41] The CPGB therefore declared for a theory of interdependent metropolitan and colonial revolutions entirely consistent with that of the ITUCNW. A Colonial Commission was established to put these theories into practice. The Comintern's Negro Bureau sent a letter to the CPGB Central Committee in which it voiced approval of the colonial resolution

---

39  Worrell, 'George Padmore', p. 31.

40  Reginald Bridgeman, 'The Life and Struggle of the Negro Toilers', *Weekly Worker*, 30 January 1932, p. 7; Hugo Rathbone, 'Book Reviews', *Labour Monthly*, April 1932, pp. 249–51.

41  CPGB, *The New Line* (London, 1929), pp. 110–13.

and gave a series of concrete proposals for how the CPGB might achieve its tasks.[42]

However, Marika Sherwood has criticised the CPGB's anticolonial activism in the interwar period, calling it a 'sorry tale' marked by 'indifference'.[43] Responding to these charges, John Callaghan argues that the supposed revolutionary movements in Africa with which the CPGB was urged to make links were 'wholly fictitious', and that a party of 3,000 working-class people in Britain could not be expected to stimulate these movements even if they did exist.[44] Callaghan's argument about the material limitations of the CPGB should be taken seriously, but the shortcomings in the CPGB's anticolonial work were as much the result of attitudes as of resources. The ITUCNW's reconceptualisation of the revolutionary subject in the form of the 'Negro toiler' clearly did not resonate with large swathes of the CPGB. While British Communists no doubt felt an ethical sympathy towards emancipatory struggles in the colonies, there was limited theoretical engagement with the idea that colonial peoples, and especially Africans, could be conceived of as 'workers' in the same way as the European proletariat. Without a fundamental change in outlook, this sympathy could never translate to true solidarity. CPGB members with a commitment to anticolonialism, such as Robin Page Arnot, Willie Gallacher and Shapurji Saklatvala, consistently protested that colonial work was not taken seriously enough.[45] At the party's Twelfth Congress, held in 1932, Pollitt acknowledged shortcomings in the party's colonial work.[46] However, this began a pattern that would continue throughout the party's congresses: an acknowledgement of the party's weaknesses, a mea culpa, and a largely unfulfilled promise to do better.

It was in this context, and amid their disappointment over the Hamburg conference, that Padmore and the ITUCNW continued to

---

42  RGASPI, 495/155/67, Negro Bureau, Draft Letter on Negro Work to the CC of the CPGB, 11 March 1929.

43  Marika Sherwood, 'The Comintern, the CPGB, Colonies and Black Britons, 1920–1938', *Science & Society* 60 (1996), p. 160.

44  John Callaghan, 'Colonies, Racism, the CPGB and the Comintern in the Inter-War Years', *Science & Society* 61 (1997), p. 519.

45  RGASPI, 495/100/593, Monday morning session, p. 80; RGASPI, 495/100/599, Minutes of Central Committee Meeting, 7 December 1929; RGASPI, 495/100/938, Shapurji Saklatvala, 'A Few Thoughts on Party Work', 1934, p. 9.

46  Harry Pollitt, *The Road to Victory* (London, 1932), p. 33.

relate to the CPGB. The relationship was characterised by a theoretical consonance but a practical dissonance. Nonetheless, Padmore's belief in the necessity of forging links between African and European revolutionary movements meant that the CPGB remained central to his activism. Setting out the work to be done in late 1930, he said that one of the four general tasks of the ITUCNW was to 'closely cooperate with and give directions to the American, English, French, Belgian, Latin-American and South American sections of the RILU in order that the Negro workers might be able to organise themselves'. To this end, material should be sent to the National Minority Movement and other Communist organisations in Britain.[47] Padmore was frequently granted space in the *Labour Monthly*, edited by R. P. Dutt, a CPGB intellectual of Indian descent, to reach a British Communist audience. These articles were often tailored to the British working class, frequently attacking the 'social fascism' of Ramsay MacDonald's Labour government, but without sacrificing the pan-Africanist perspective of the ITUCNW.

However, beneath the surface was dissatisfaction with the CPGB's anticolonialism, and particularly that of its RILU sections, the National Minority Movement and the Seamen's Minority Movement (SMM). The SMM was especially important because many Black people in Britain were seafarers. The lack of assistance given by the British and French parties to the ITUCNW in preparing the 1930 conference became tied into wider fears that these parties – importantly, those operating in countries with colonial empires – were not taking African anticolonialism seriously. The ITUCNW's Report on Negro Work in France and England (August 1930) bluntly began: 'It is impossible to make a report on the Negro work of our French and British Parties. To attempt this would be to infer that concrete work in this sphere of Party activity had been accomplished.' Significantly, this report aligned itself with the Comintern and against the British and French parties by recommending Stalin's writings on colonial liberation.[48]

---

47  RGASPI, 534/1/164, Padmore, Plan of Work of the Negro Bureau of the RILU, 20 October 1930.

48  RGASPI, 495/155/87, Report on Negro Work in France and England, 4 August 1930.

## Reginald Bridgeman and Arnold Ward

But there were some sections of the British Communist movement on which Padmore felt able to rely. Reginald Bridgeman was secretary of the British Section of the LAI, and ran the organisation without ever formally joining the CPGB. Bridgeman was born in 1884 and educated at Harrow, working as a high-ranking diplomat before quitting his career to become an anticolonial activist. Although Reginald Reynolds, a fellow anti-colonialist and sometime ILP member, fiercely opposed Bridgeman's Communist sympathies, he later remembered that if Bridgeman 'was intellectually dishonest himself I could never see what he had to gain by it, compared with what he had thrown away'.[49]

Bridgeman wrote a glowing review of Padmore's *Life and Struggles*. This was not simply a Communist formality, but part of a great comradeship between the two. Bridgeman wrote privately to Padmore that he found the book 'excellent', and told him that the British LAI was 'sending out the advertisement card of it on every possible occasion'.[50] Padmore responded by expressing his appreciation of the review, and asking Bridgeman to help him find out the addresses of West Indians in London.[51] Bridgeman had been one of the few Communist-aligned activists to offer energetic support to the ITUCNW in the planning of the 1930 conference, and Bridgeman and Padmore continued to collaborate closely during Padmore's time in the Comintern. When the *Negro Worker* was banned in Trinidad and Nigeria in 1932, Padmore turned to Bridgeman to ask for assistance in having the matter raised in the House of Commons. Bridgeman successfully lobbied for Maxton to ask a question, and publicised the campaign.[52]

Padmore was also in touch with several Black activists based in Britain, including SMM member Harry O'Connell, based in Cardiff, and James Headley, secretary of the SMM's Negro Workers Committee.[53]

---

49  Reginald Reynolds, *My Life and Crimes* (London, 1956), p. 99.

50  RGASPI, 534/3/754, Reginald Bridgeman to Padmore, 17 February 1932.

51  RGASPI, 534/3/754, Padmore to Bridgeman, 26 February 1932.

52  RGASPI, 534/3/754, Padmore to Bridgeman, 7 January 1932; RGASPI, 534/3/755, Padmore to Bridgeman, 2 June 1932; Ward to Padmore, 6 June 1932; Bridgeman to Padmore, 14 June 1932.

53  Of course, Padmore offered advice not only to Black activists in Britain, but to those throughout the African diaspora. See RGASPI, 534/3/754 and 534/3/755.

Because of their mobility and ability to distribute literature, African and Caribbean seafarers – including British-based activists like O'Connell (from British Guiana), Headley (from Trinidad), Chris Jones (from Barbados) and Ronald Sawyer (from Sierra Leone) – were crucial in developing transnational Black radical networks. These activists also challenged the racially exclusionary practices of the National Union of Seamen. They were, like Padmore, staunch Communists and admirers of the Soviet Union who nevertheless expressed frustrations with the failure of some Communist institutions to recognise the particularities of Black workers' struggles.[54] Contact with these activists reinforced Padmore's general disillusionment with the British Communist move-ment. In April 1932, Headley wrote to Padmore to tell him that 'the state of affairs' was 'very unsatisfactory'.[55] One of these Communist seafarers – Chris Jones – later became the International African Service Bureau's organising secretary. Born in 1885, Jones had left Barbados after finding employment in the merchant navy. He settled in Chicago and then, after the First World War, in London. The SMM attracted him to Communism, and he joined the CPGB around 1931. Like Padmore, he later broke from the Comintern, and the pair developed a strong political relationship during the second half of the 1930s.[56]

Beyond Britain, Padmore formed connections with another activist who later played an important role in the IASB. From November 1931, Padmore was in correspondence with I. T. A. Wallace-Johnson, a Sierra Leonean trade unionist, at that time organising in Lagos as the general secretary of the African Workers' Union.[57] In the middle of the decade, Wallace-Johnson founded the West African Youth League (described by Adi as 'perhaps the most radical and active of all the anti-colonial organ-isations of this period'), before arriving in Britain in 1937 and forming the IASB with Padmore.[58] Wallace-Johnson contributed a lengthy article, 'British Oppression in West Africa', to the *Negro Worker*. His criticism of

54 David Featherstone, 'Harry O'Connell, Maritime Labour and the Racialised Politics of Place', *Race & Class* 57 (2016); David Featherstone, *Solidarity: Hidden Histories and Geographies of Internationalism* (London, 2012), Chapter 3.

55 RGASPI, 534/3/755, James Headley to Padmore, 2 April 1932.

56 Christian Høgsbjerg, *Mariner, Renegade and Castaway: Chris Braithwaite: Seamen's Organiser, Socialist and Militant Pan-Africanist* (London, 2014).

57 Weiss, *Framing a Radical African Atlantic*, p. 476.

58 Hakim Adi, *West Africans in Britain, 1900–1960: Nationalism, Pan-Africanism and Communism* (London, 1998), p. 78.

'African capitalists' as well as British imperialism certainly chimed with Comintern and ITUCNW thinking.[59]

Padmore's – and Bridgeman's – closest Black comrade in Britain was Arnold Ward. Ward was born in Bridgetown, Barbados in 1886. He lived in Trinidad between 1903 and 1906, and in Germany between 1907 and 1915. As a British subject, he was interned in Germany during the First World War, and sent to Britain in 1915. He formed the Negro Welfare Association (NWA) in London in early 1931.[60] C. L. R. James, who worked with Ward in the IASB, later remembered him as 'a slow speaking working class type' who was 'utterly devoted to the cause'.[61] The NWA, of which Hugo Rathbone was treasurer and Bridgeman chair, was affiliated to the British LAI. It was Ward, the NWA's secretary, who moved the 'resolution on the Negro question', which praised the Hamburg conference, at the British LAI's annual conference in February 1931.[62] Ward and Bridgeman frequently spoke on platforms together on a plethora of issues encompassing Africa and its diaspora, as well as the wider colonial world, and were both central to the British Scottsboro campaign.[63] Bridgeman encouraged correspondence between the NWA and ITUCNW in order that the NWA maintain '[c]lose contact with the Negro workers', illustrating his sympathy for Padmore's pan-Africanist orientation.[64]

Indeed, the impetus for the creation of the NWA came from the British Communist movement rather than from Hamburg. It was not until December 1931 that Padmore and Ward struck up a regular correspondence. Padmore praised the militancy of the NWA, and told Ward not to worry about the 'Negro lackeys' like Harold Moody and the League of Coloured Peoples. Padmore wanted, through Ward, to 'build a strong organization of all the Negro workers in England, as a part of the revolutionary movement'. Padmore associated himself with Ward both personally and politically by declaring:

---

59 'British Oppression in West Africa', *Negro Worker*, December 1931, p. 23.

60 Featherstone, *Solidarity*, p. 70.

61 James, 'Notes on the Life of George Padmore', p. 37.

62 'Good-bye to Sham Leaders', *Daily Worker*, 17 February 1931, p. 3.

63 RGASPI, 534/3/754, Seamen's Minority Movement meeting report, 23 February 1932; RGASPI, 542/1/60, Kenya and the Gold Rush; Labour History Archive and Study Centre (LHASC), Manchester, LP/ID/CI/36/34, LAI British Section, Report of Second Annual Conference, May 1932, p. 2.

64 LAI British Section, Report of Second Annual Conference, p. 2.

I am from the West Indies and only last year I was in Africa, and I
know what I am talking about. That is why we have a duty to help our
black brothers back home. If you agree to my proposition to build up
a strong movement in England, as I am a British subject then I will try
to come over as you suggest.[65]

Padmore used autobiography to appeal to Ward not simply as a member
of the international proletariat, but as a Black man whose life had been
structured by British colonialism. Ward was extremely receptive to
Padmore's suggestions, and the pair soon developed a relationship in
which Padmore was the master and Ward the apprentice. Ward was
intellectually impressed by Padmore, and wrote to Padmore that *Life and
Struggles* 'is a masterpiece and a good many negroes buy it from [the
CPGB headquarters on] King Street here'.[66] Many of Padmore's letters to
Ward had a pedagogic and instructional quality, whether addressing
theories of oppression ('It is quite true that the oppression of the Negro
masses assumes outrageous forms, but in the main our oppression is
class oppression') or practical interventions (advising Ward to sell the
*Negro Worker* to both Black and White workers, or to work with the
International Labor Defense on a Scottsboro Nine protest).[67] Of course,
as is clear from these examples, the theoretical and the practical informed
one another, but Padmore also tutored Ward on the more mundane
elements of political organising, such as building up a reserve fund.[68]

Padmore travelled to London in May 1932 during the height of the Scottsboro campaign, and this was the first time he met Ward in person. Makalani has noted that 'London must have left [Padmore] with mixed feelings',
as Ward implored Padmore to relocate to London. This revealed Padmore's
'stature as an international revolutionary' but also 'the depth of black
Communists' dissatisfaction'.[69] Two years after his first visit to London to
plan the ITUCNW conference, Padmore found that little had changed in
the British Communist movement, barring the self-activity of organisations like the NWA. Writing to the LAI International Secretariat, Padmore

---

65  RGASPI, 534/3/668, Padmore to Ward, 17 December 1931.

66  RGASPI, 534/3/754, Ward to Padmore, 3 February 1932.

67  RGASPI, 534/3/754, Padmore to NWA, 14 February 1932; Padmore to Ward,
26 February 1932; Padmore to Ward, 21 March 1932.

68  RGASPI, 534/3/755, Padmore to Ward, 1 April 1932.

69  Makalani, *In the Cause of Freedom*, p. 186.

declared: 'I want to say that it is a damned disgrace that there are so many colonial Negroes in England, some of them even in the Party and it is only by accident that I happen to discover this fact during my recent visit to England.'[70] Ultimately, Padmore's and the ITUCNW's relationship with the British Communist movement was one that relied on the support of committed individual anticolonialists, such as Bridgeman and Ward, rather than on any institutional support. The CPGB's declared anti-imperialist theory was in line with the ITUCNW's, but in practice the ITUCNW was ignored by the wider party. For all the efforts of Padmore and the ITUCNW, they failed to make a dent in the thought and activism of the party as a whole.

## Padmore and the ILP

The Independent Labour Party was, after the formation of the IASB in 1937, the political party to which Padmore was closest; but their relationship got off to a rocky start. This was partly a result of the Comintern's Third Period policy, but also of the ILP's relatively moderate political philosophy, which would only take a revolutionary turn after its disaffiliation from the Labour Party in 1932. While the ILP had always criticised British imperialism, its anticolonialism during the 1920s was largely reformist. The ILP was founded in 1893, and in 1900 affiliated to the Labour Representation Committee (later the Labour Party). When the Labour Party began to admit individual members after the First World War, the ILP effectively became a left-wing faction within the larger party. As we have seen, the ILP was involved with the LAI from its establishment in 1927, but was forced out from the left by the Comintern and from the right by the Labour and Socialist International. Much like the CPGB, its primary colonial concern in this period was India. During the late 1920s and early 1930s, there was an article about India in almost every issue of the ILP's weekly newspaper, the *New Leader*, whereas months would pass without a feature on Africa or the Caribbean.

Stephen Howe has identified a moralistic strain of anti-imperialism that was part of the ILP philosophy from its foundation.[71] Economic analysis

---

70  RGASPI, 534/3/755, Padmore to LAI International Secretariat, 12 June 1932.

71  Stephen Howe, *Anticolonialism in British Politics: The Left and the End of Empire, 1918–1964* (Oxford, 1993), p. 46.

was eschewed in favour of arguments that made appeals about the suffering of oppressed people. James Maxton's address to the ILP's 1929 annual conference typified this approach. He offered no economic explanation of the structures of the British Empire, and argued: 'The votes of the 20,000,000 electors in this country give it the right to control the destinies of hundreds of millions of people in India, Africa and other parts of the world.'[72] While Maxton advocated self-determination for colonial peoples, it seems that freedom was something to be granted by a socialist metropole rather than taken by a national liberation movement. Padmore clearly had good reason to view the CPGB rather than the ILP as the imperfect, but greatest, British friend of the 'Negro toilers' in this period.

Sometimes imperialism would be forgotten altogether. The ILP's Socialism in Our Time programme, which dominated ILP propaganda during the late 1920s and early 1930s, was reformist and domestic in its orientation. Fenner Brockway may have moved resolutions at LAI conferences that promulgated Leninist analyses of imperialism and declared colonial liberation to be essential to international socialism, but there was no such analysis in Socialism in Our Time.[73] It is therefore difficult to ascribe a systematic analysis of imperialism to the pre-disaffiliation ILP. Its analysis was pseudo-Leninist when working with more militant comrades, and often moralistic and detached from a wider critique of capitalism in its domestic manifestos and pamphlets.

The ITUCNW was therefore highly critical of the ILP. At the Second Congress of the LAI, in July 1929, James Ford attacked the ILP's David Kirkwood 'and contended that the leftwing of the British Labour Party was most dangerous for the anti-imperialist struggle, because it only pretended to fight against imperialism and thus misled the workers'.[74] The ITUCNW and Negro Bureau confronted the LAI's inclusion of not only European social democrats but also Black liberals and reformists, treating them as two sides of the same coin. William Pickens, of the moderate National Association for the Advancement of Colored People, was expelled from the LAI in 1929 after pressure from the Negro Bureau.

---

72 James Maxton, *The Roads to Socialism: Chairman's Address at the ILP Conference 1929* (London, 1929), pp. 7–8.

73 Fenner Brockway, *Socialism with Speed: An Outline of the ILP 'Socialism in Our Time' Proposals* (London, 1928).

74 RGASPI, 542/1/87, Second Anti-Imperialist World Congress, Morning Session, 23 July 1929.

Strikingly, one of the reasons given by the Negro Bureau in recommending Pickens's expulsion was 'his relations with the Maxton group'.[75] Padmore continued these attacks in the same vein. His writings in the *Labour Monthly* frequently used Maxton's name as shorthand for the left wing of the Labour Party. He claimed that, regardless of the left-wing posturing of the ILP, all representatives of the Labour Party were 'social-imperialists' who supported the government's colonial development scheme, which would 'tighten the strangle-hold of the British imperialists on the colonies'.[76]

However, the single example of direct correspondence between Padmore and Maxton in this period was one of cooperation rather than conflict. As we have seen, when the *Negro Worker* was banned in Trinidad in 1932, Padmore asked Bridgeman for assistance, and Bridgeman in turn asked Maxton to raise the issue in the House of Commons. Maxton and R. C. Wallhead, another ILP MP, put questions on the matter to Philip Cunliffe-Lister, the colonial secretary. Wallhead asked why, considering 'that these publications circulate freely in Britain and in other parts of the Empire, including other West Indian islands', the *Negro Worker* had been prohibited in Trinidad. When Cunliffe-Lister responded that the matter was at the discretion of the colony's governor, Maxton pressed: 'Why does the Rt. Hon. Gentleman allow the Governor of this particular Colony to act differently from the Governors of other Colonies; and why should the Negroes in these particular islands be denied the right to organise in trade unions, as they do in other places?'[77]

As was to be expected, Cunliffe-Lister would not be pinned down, but Maxton's intervention was important. Padmore wrote to Maxton to extend the ITUCNW's 'warmest appreciation' to both him and Wallhead for their 'expression of international solidarity with our oppressed people'. Padmore added Maxton to the free mailing list for the *Negro Worker* and sent him a copy of *Life and Struggles*.[78] Padmore also favourably reported Maxton and Wallhead's intervention in the *Negro Worker*.[79]

75 RGASPI, 495/155/78, Harry Haywood to Communist Fraction of the LAI, 16 November 1929.

76 George Padmore, 'British Finance-Capital in West Africa', *Labour Monthly*, February 1931, pp. 108–9.

77 LHASC, WG/TRI, Walter Citrine to A. A. Cipriani, 18 June 1932.

78 RGASPI, 534/3/755, Padmore to Maxton, 17 June 1932.

79 'Colonial Dictators', *Negro Worker*, June 1932, pp. 15–16.

Maxton responded graciously to Padmore: 'Thank you very much for your kindly letter and for your book, which I shall read with very great interest. I appreciate very highly your Committee's thought in sending the message recognising our efforts in the matter of the *Negro Worker*.'[80] It is unclear if Maxton was aware of Padmore's attacks on him in the pages of the *Labour Monthly*.

Padmore portrayed the matter differently in his official ITUCNW report, saying that Communist pressure 'forced Maxton to register the protest of the Negroes against the banning of the magazine in the colonies'.[81] While Bridgeman indeed prompted Maxton to raise the issue in the House, there is no indication that Maxton was anything other than an enthusiastic recruit. Padmore's correspondence with both Maxton and Bridgeman indicates his knowledge of this. Most likely, Padmore, perhaps like Patterson making it clear that he had not been won by Maxton's 'honied words', was displaying hostility towards Maxton in order to demonstrate to the Comintern hierarchy an adherence to Third Period policy. Padmore and other ITUCNW members generally supported this policy, but perhaps saw in Maxton someone who, despite being a parliamentarian and possessing a paternalistic streak, was nevertheless genuinely opposed to colonial oppression.

## Padmore's Break with the Comintern

In February 1933, Padmore was arrested in Hamburg and deported from Germany, later settling in Paris.[82] From there, Padmore continued the work of the ITUCNW throughout the summer. But in August 1933 Padmore penned his 'Au Revoir' as editor of the *Negro Worker*, issuing an appeal for financial support to keep the journal going under a new editor.[83] In the following months, Padmore and the Comintern parted ways, and each had very different explanations of the cause. A Comintern report to the CPUSA in October 1933 accused Padmore of several 'anti-Party actions'. The two most offensive actions were writing an

---

80  RGASPI, 534/3/755, Maxton to Padmore, 23 June 1932.
81  Padmore, Report on the Hamburg Committee, p. 4.
82  RGASPI, 534/3/895, Padmore to 'Comrades', 6 March 1933.
83  Padmore, 'Au Revoir', *Negro Worker*, August–September 1933, p. 18.

article in the *Negro Worker* that was 'a clear expression of Negro national chauvinism' and publishing the 'Au Revoir' article in which he 'included a note of personal offense, concealed hints that he was being removed without sufficient grounds, and informed the readers of the financial bankruptcy of the magazine'.[84] The Comintern's International Control Commission released a statement in March 1934 in which it announced the expulsion of Padmore from the Comintern 'for contacts with a provocateur [Garan Kouyaté], for contacts with bourgeois organisations on the question of Liberia, for an incorrect attitude to the national question (instead of class unity striving towards race unity) and for not handing over the affairs of the committee on which he had worked'.[85] The charge sheet had evidently ballooned since October.

The Liberian question related to Firestone, an American company operating a large rubber plantation in the independent African republic of Liberia. Firestone was creditor to the Liberian government through a predatory loan that had drawn accusations of imperialism from the ITUCNW. In November 1933, Ward wrote a letter to Patterson in which he accused Padmore of all manner of Black nationalist sins in relation to Liberia. Ward said that Padmore had confided in him about a plan for Black people 'buying out' Firestone and migrating to Liberia. Ward compared this scheme to Garveyism, writing that Padmore 'says the [Comintern] has let down the Negroes and curses everything that is white capitalist, socialist, communist'.[86] The details of this conversation were clearly embellished, if not entirely fabricated, and it is unclear exactly why Ward wrote this letter. Susan Pennybacker has arrived at the most likely explanation: Ward heard there were charges of racial chauvinism against Padmore and 'detached himself from his friend, presumably understanding that, otherwise, the resources of the London communists would not be at his disposal'.[87] It is unclear if Padmore ever knew about the letter, and the fact that Ward and Padmore later worked

---

84 RGASPI, 495/261/1380, R. Safarov to Central Control Commission of the CPUSA, 1 October 1933.

85 RGASPI, 495/261/4718, Statement of the International Control Commission, 20 March 1934. Kouyaté was a West African anticolonialist and one of Padmore's collaborators. He had been suspended from the French Communist Party in 1933. For more on Padmore and Kouyaté's political relationship, see Edwards, *Practice of Diaspora*, Chapter 5.

86 RGASPI, 534/3/895, Ward to William Patterson, 14 November 1933.

87 Susan D. Pennybacker, *From Scottsboro to Munich: Race and Political Culture in 1930s Britain* (Princeton, 2009), p. 85.

with each other in London suggests that there was no major falling out between them.

The *Negro Worker* relaunched in May 1934 with Huiswoud (using the pseudonym Charles Woodson) as editor and Ward as a contributing editor. Huiswoud published a statement about Padmore's expulsion, and later a parting shot from Helen Davis stating: 'Padmore doesn't want to stop and teach the white workers', and: 'What he really wants is free colonies but not free colonial workers.'[88] These accusations are completely inconsistent with Padmore's insistence that *Life and Struggles* and the *Negro Worker* be sold to White workers, and his criticism, both previously and subsequently, of anticolonial and antiracist movements that did not have a socialist programme.

But there was another side to the story. Padmore stayed with his friend and comrade Nancy Cunard in Réanville, Normandy, after leaving the Comintern. Cunard later remembered that Padmore was 'utterly overcome' by the attack from the Comintern.[89] In February 1934, Padmore penned a letter to the secretariat of the CPUSA saying that he found himself 'in no conflict with the fundamental principles of our movement'. However, the ITUCNW had been 'liquidated' without Padmore being able to discuss the issue with representatives in Moscow. He charged that Huiswoud had arrived in Paris in August 1933 and instructed him to shut down the committee. Padmore concluded that 'International Negro work is being sacrificed at a time when we cannot afford to weaken the Negro liberation struggles'.[90] The CPUSA publicly repudiated Padmore, so in July Padmore wrote an open letter to the CPUSA's secretary, Earl Browder. Padmore dismissed the Liberia accusations by pointing to his published output on Liberia, and charged that the ITUCNW had been shut down 'in order not to offend the British Foreign Office'.[91] Later that month, Padmore wrote to his friend, Cyril Ollivierre, again accusing the Comintern of wanting to shut down the

---

88  Charles Woodson, 'Expulsion of George Padmore from the Revolutionary Movement', *Negro Worker*, June 1934, pp. 14–15; Helen Davis, 'The Rise and Fall of George Padmore as a Revolutionary Fighter', *Negro Worker*, August 1934, pp. 15–17.

89  Harry Ransom Center, The University of Texas at Austin, Nancy Cunard collection, Nancy Cunard to Dorothy Pizer, November 1959.

90  Rare Books and Special Collections, Princeton University Library, George Padmore collection, Padmore to the secretariat of the CPUSA, 3 February 1934.

91  George Padmore collection, Padmore to Earl Browder, 9 July 1934.

ITUCNW in order to appease the British Foreign Office, thereby prior-itising Soviet foreign policy over African anticolonialism. Padmore declared that he 'stood loyally' with the Africans, and presciently stated that, based on its trajectory, the Soviet Union's next move would be to join the League of Nations.[92] With the Nazis' rise to power in Germany in 1933, the Soviet Union became increasingly concerned about its national security, and thus began to seek alliances with Britain and France, which, while 'democracies' at home, held the world's largest colonial empires. When Padmore arrived to live in London in 1935, he told C. L. R. James that he had been ordered by the Comintern to distin-guish between 'democratic' and 'fascist' imperialism. Padmore apparently retorted that Germany and Japan had no colonies in Africa, whereas the United States was the 'most racially-minded country' and 'Britain and France are the ones with the colonies in Africa'.[93] In Padmore's view, the Comintern sacrificed anti-imperialism for the sake of antifascist unity, which was guided by the demands of Soviet national security.

The episode has divided historians. James Hooker judges that Padmore's explanation of the break is 'most likely', and is completely uncritical of Padmore's version of events.[94] Given Hooker's anti-Communist slant, this is both unsurprising and unsatisfactory. Hakim Adi, however, force-fully argues against Padmore's account of the break. He states that Huiswoud did not come to 'liquidate' the ITUCNW, but instead spoke about the 'financial viability' of the *Negro Worker* and how the ITUCNW could be funded. But he does concede that 'the RILU took some time to make its decision and temporarily suspended the activities of the ITUCNW'. He further adds that there was no indication of a change in Soviet foreign policy towards Britain and France in August 1933 (the policy of collective security was adopted in December 1933, and the Soviet Union joined the League of Nations in September 1934), and that therefore this could not have been a factor in Padmore's initial protests.[95] Jonathan Derrick's account is more sympathetic to Padmore. He notes that Padmore may have suspected, perhaps correctly, that the Comintern had 'ulterior reasons' for the lack of funding of the *Negro Worker*. Yet he

92 Schomburg Center for Research in Black Culture, New York, George Padmore letters, Padmore to Cyril Ollivierre, 28 July 1934.

93 James, 'George Padmore', p. 255.

94 Hooker, *Black Revolutionary*, p. 31.

95 Adi, *Pan-Africanism and Communism*, pp. 156–61.

concludes that there is 'no reason to doubt that the reasons given for the Communist excommunication of Padmore were the real ones'.[96]

However, Adi's and Derrick's accounts are not entirely convincing. Huiswoud may not have told Padmore that the ITUCNW was being 'liquidated', nor may anyone have told Padmore to differentiate between 'democratic' and 'fascist' imperialism. But it is equally apparent that some of the charges against Padmore were fabricated, most clearly in the case of the Liberian question. We should not take Communist explanations of the expulsion at face value. Earlier in 1933, the Parti Communiste Français (PCF) had suspended funding for Kouyaté's journal, *Le Cri des Nègres*. Kouyaté protested, stopped attending PCF meetings, and was suspended from the party. Padmore worked closely with Kouyaté after his move to Paris, and was appalled by his comrade's treatment.[97] It should therefore come as no surprise that, when Huiswoud arrived from Moscow to discuss the 'financial viability' of the *Negro Worker*, Padmore was instantly suspicious of Communist suppression, and feared that the journal and committee were being closed altogether. Similarly, Padmore's continued commitment to Marxism counters any accusation that he put 'race unity' before 'class unity'. While the softening of Soviet and Comintern attitudes towards Britain and France had not yet become official policy, Padmore, as a Comintern insider, may well have sensed a change in the political direction of the movement. Indeed, his suggestion that the Soviet Union would soon join the League of Nations as part of an antifascist and pro-'democratic' realignment, months before it actually happened, reveal him to be an astute reader of the political stars. His subsequent explanations of the break were attempts to impose narrative smoothness, and a little self-aggrandisement, on an essentially accurate story.

After his break with the Comintern, Padmore stayed in Paris and continued to collaborate with Kouyaté. They planned a Negro World Unity Congress, but this was abandoned.[98] By the summer of 1934, Padmore was staying with Cunard in Réanville. A member of the family that had made its wealth through the famous shipping line, Cunard was

---

96  Jonathan Derrick, *Africa's 'Agitators': Militant Anti-Colonialism in Africa and the West, 1918–1939* (New York, 2008), pp. 291, 302.

97  Makalani, *In the Cause of Freedom*, p. 189; Weiss, *Framing a Radical African Atlantic*, p. 596.

98  Edwards, *Practice of Diaspora*, p. 275.

born in Leicestershire in 1896 to an English baronet and a glamorous American mother. She had had a rebellious youth, and was drawn to Communism in the 1920s through her association with the surrealists in Paris, becoming a tireless antiracist campaigner in the same period.[99] She closely followed the Communists' line on Scottsboro, positioning herself with them and against the liberal NAACP. She was elected to the Executive Committee of the NWA, appeared on platforms with Ward in 1932 and 1933, and offered important financial aid to the NWA and the Scottsboro campaign.[100] Communist sensibilities also informed her collection of texts for her *Negro* anthology (1934). For instance, Jenny Greenshields has noted how Cunard's writing followed Padmore's thought when she referred to Garveyism as a 'sort of Zionism' and 'a race pride which stopped at that'.[101] Padmore assisted Cunard with the compilation of *Negro* by putting her in touch with writers from across the African diaspora. He also contributed some of his own writing to the anthology.[102] Greenshields has highlighted the 'cosmopolitan' nature of Cunard's activism. She observes that, by working with Padmore and other Black anticolonialists, 'Cunard contributed to a wide-reaching network of black diasporic intellectuals working to counter ideologies of racism and colonialism'.[103]

Cunard was a valuable ally in the summer of 1934. Despite her immense sympathy for the Communist movement, she instantly sided with Padmore – although, as Anne Chisholm notes, 'it did not cause her to reconsider her allegiance' to Communism.[104] It was to Cunard that Padmore dictated his open letter to Earl Browder, which Cunard remembered as being 'well worded' and 'dignified'.[105] In August, she wrote to Huiswoud to complain about the unsubstantiated accusations against Padmore.[106]

---

99  For a biography of Cunard, see Anne Chisholm, *Nancy Cunard* (London, 1979).

100  The National Archives (TNA), London, MEPO 38/9 (Cunard), Special Branch reports on 13 December 1932, 26 April 1933, and 1 June 1933.

101  Jenny Greenshields, 'Nancy Cunard: Collector, Cosmopolitan', doctoral thesis, University of Sussex, 2016, p. 175.

102  Cunard to Pizer, November 1959.

103  Greenshields, 'Nancy Cunard', p. 181.

104  Chisholm, *Nancy Cunard*, p. 225.

105  Cunard to Pizer, November 1959.

106  Nancy Cunard collection, Cunard to the editor of the *Negro Worker*, 7 August 1934.

Padmore, meanwhile, focused on writing his new book, *How Britain Rules Africa*, before re-emerging in the British socialist movement in 1935. His years of activism for the Comintern had granted him an invaluable political education, both theoretical and practical. For the remainder of his activist career, he continued to draw on his Leninism, his organisational savvy, and his web of Comintern contacts. To Padmore, his break from the Comintern had not been signalled by any change in his own political philosophy, but rather by the changing priorities of the Comintern – he left the organisation to retain his Marxism rather than to denounce it. He was also not the only member of the IASB whose early activism was shaped by both productive and frustrating encounters with the organised Communist movement.

## Kenyatta: Communism, Liberalism, Nationalism

Johnstone Kenyatta, as he was known when he arrived in London in 1929, was born sometime during the 1890s in rural Kenya, north of Nairobi. Kenyatta, who later became the first president of Kenya, was of humble origin – his parents cultivated the land and bred livestock. He adopted the name Johnstone (in place of his given name, Kamau) at a mission school, combining the names of John and Peter.[107] Kenyatta was a Kikuyu, the largest of the ethnic groups in the British colony of Kenya. In the mid 1920s, he became active in the Kikuyu Central Association (KCA), a political association founded to voice the concerns of the Kikuyu community. Kenya was a settler colony, and the most pressing Kikuyu grievance was the appropriation of the most fertile land by British settlers – though there were also protests against forced labour and lack of political representation. Kenyatta became increasingly prominent in the KCA in 1928, editing its journal, *Muigwithania*. He was selected to present a KCA petition to a royal commission, arriving in London on 8 March 1929. Throughout the late 1920s and early 1930s, Kenyatta acted as spokesperson for the Kikuyu before several commissions and committees.[108]

---

107 For an account of Kenyatta's early life, see Jeremy Murray-Brown, *Kenyatta* (London, 1972), Chapters 3–4.

108 Jomo Kenyatta, *Facing Mount Kenya: The Tribal Life of the Gikuyu* (London, 1938), pp. xix–xx. For a detailed discussion of these petitions, see W. O. Maloba, *Kenyatta and Britain: An Account of Political Transformation, 1929–1963* (Cham, Switzerland, 2018), Chapter 2.

During these early years in London, Kenyatta would be torn between Kikuyu nationalism, the respectable liberalism and social democracy of his early patrons, and the militant revolutionary socialism of the Comintern.

Kenyatta arrived in London three months before the formation of the second minority Labour government – the same government that the following year denied the ITUCNW permission to host its conference in Britain. Kenyatta was frustrated by the government's gradualism, and received even less contact with the Colonial Office after the formation of the National Government in 1931. This has led W. O. Maloba to argue convincingly that it was Kenyatta's poor level of contact with the British state that led to his political radicalisation in London.[109]

One of Kenyatta's most enduring contacts in his early years in Britain was the liberal Labour Party member William McGregor Ross. McGregor Ross had been director of public works in Kenya, and his experiences in the colony made him sympathetic to the grievances of colonised peoples. However, Paul Rich has observed that this sympathy was informed by 'a deep sense of moral outrage', and did not lead McGregor Ross to develop 'any coherent ideological base' for his anti-imperialism. His political philosophy remained moderate.[110] McGregor Ross and Kenyatta met regularly during 1929 and 1930, and Kenyatta spent many hours at McGregor Ross's home in Hampstead, where he befriended the family. The family saw him off from Victoria Station when he returned to Kenya in September 1930, and greeted him upon his return in May 1931.[111] Kenyatta also met Drummond Shiels, Labour's under-secretary of state for the colonies, in January 1930. Shiels, aware of a trip to Moscow taken by Kenyatta in the autumn of 1929, advised him to guide the KCA's policies into constitutional channels.[112] But Kenyatta's relationship with McGregor Ross and other moderate members of the Labour Party soured as the 1930s progressed, partly as a result of Kenyatta's involvement with the Communist movement.

Kenyatta attended the Second Congress of the League Against Imperialism, held in Frankfurt in July 1929, as the Comintern consolidated its power in the LAI on the basis of its 'Class against Class' policy. In

---

109  Maloba, *Kenyatta and Britain*, p. 47.
110  Paul B. Rich, *Race and Empire in British Politics* (Cambridge, 1986), p. 71.
111  Murray-Brown, *Kenyatta*, pp. 118–52.
112  Ibid., p. 124; Maloba, *Kenyatta and Britain*, pp. 22–7.

meetings of the Negro Delegation, Kenyatta reported on conditions in East Africa, emphasising that the LAI needed to make 'direct contact with Africa'. James Ford reported that, during one Negro Delegation meeting, the drafting of the Negro resolution 'took several hours because Pickens opposed any attack on the British Labour Party'.[113] This implied by omission that Kenyatta had no qualms about such an attack, covertly thumbing his nose at people like McGregor Ross.

Kenyatta also came into contact with the CPGB. He gave a statement to the *Sunday Worker* in October 1929 in which he voiced the grievances of the Kikuyu, particularly emphasising the land question. Kenyatta accused the British government of attempting to 'divide and sow antagonism between the tribes', and compared this to divide-and-rule tactics in India and Ireland. Through this comment, Kenyatta revealed his understanding of Kenya as part of a wider imperial system. This was a developing anticolonial trend in the interwar period, and one that the LAI had helped to foster. Previously, anticolonial struggles had generally been isolated in single colonies, rather than spanning imperial systems as a whole. Kenyatta concluded by arguing that repressive measures had been 'introduced by British Governments, Conservative, Liberal, and Labour alike', calling for self-government, and saying that he expected 'even greater assistance from those British workers who realise that Imperialism is the common enemy of the oppressed throughout the world'.[114] The call for independence, criticisms of the Labour Party, and the appeal to the British working class as natural allies were hallmarks of the Comintern's Third Period. Kenyatta went far beyond the reformist petitions with which he had arrived in London.

In January 1930, Kenyatta published two articles in the CPGB's *Daily Worker*. He detailed the 1922 arrest in Nairobi of Harry Thuku, founder of the East African Association, and the revolt that followed. Kenyatta appealed to European Communist sensibilities by calling the uprising a 'general strike', and reminding his readers: 'Neither the Labour Government of 1924 nor the present Labour Government have listened to the

---

113 Ford, Report on the Negro Question. Kenyatta was also placed on the provisional Executive Committee of the ITUCNW conference, but was unable to attend the conference in Hamburg. ITUCNW, *A Report of the Proceedings and Decisions of the First International Conference of Negro Workers*, p. 1; Weiss, *Framing a Radical African Atlantic*, pp. 246–7.

114 'Extra Armed Forces for Kenya', *Sunday Worker*, 27 October 1929, p. 3.

demand of the Africans to release Thuku.'[115] Kenyatta caught the eye of the Comintern, and in February 1930 the Negro Bureau identified the reformist KCA, inaccurately, as the single 'revolutionary nationalist organisation' in East Africa.[116]

Bruce Berman has identified a tension between Kenyatta's ethno-nationalist focus on the particularities of the Kikuyu and the Communist demand that he agitate for a national Kenyan movement as part of a global struggle against imperialism.[117] This tension was undoubtedly real, and consistently plagued Kenyatta's political relationships – but Communists in fact showed a remarkable patience for what they regarded as Kenyatta's parochialism. It was Kenyatta's strategic realignment to make appeals to the British ruling class, rather than his Kikuyu nationalism, that first drew the ire of Communists. In March 1930, Kenyatta had identical letters to the editors published in *The Times* and the *Manchester Guardian*. Kenyatta identified himself as the secretary of the KCA and a 'public-spirited' man, and made suggestions for reform within a capitalist colonial system. He said he wanted to 'remove all lack of understanding between the various peoples who form the population of East Africa, so that we may all march together as loyal subjects of his Britannic Majesty along the road of Empire prosperity.'[118]

Kenyatta's appeal to liberal morality and fair-mindedness could not have been further from his writing in the Communist press. The following year, he gave an interview to *East Africa*, the organ of White settlers. He stated that the KCA 'is a moderate body' seeking 'co-operation' with White settlers, denied that he had had 'any communication' with Communist organisations, and said that his visit to Moscow in 1929 had been 'purely for sight-seeing purposes.'[119] Kenyatta's February 1932 memorandum to the colonial secretary hinged on the liberal principle

---

115 Johnstone Kenyatta, 'An African People in Revolt', *Daily Worker*, 20 January 1930, p. 4; Johnstone Kenyatta, 'A General Strike Drowned in Blood', *Daily Worker*, 21 January 1930, p. 10.

116 RGASPI, 495/155/87, Proposals in Regard to Sending Instructors to the Negro Colonies, 6 February 1930.

117 Bruce Berman, 'Ethnography as Politics, Politics as Ethnography: Kenyatta, Malinowski, and the Making of *Facing Mount Kenya*', *Canadian Journal of African Studies* 30 (1996), p. 325.

118 Johnstone Kenyatta, 'Unrest in Kenya', *Manchester Guardian*, 18 March 1930, p. 6 and *The Times*, 26 March 1930, p. 12.

119 'Johnston (*sic*) Kenyatta Interviewed', *East Africa*, 18 June 1931.

of no taxation without representation.[120] Perhaps the meeting with Drummond Shiels in January 1930, around the time of his final Communist publication for three years, had convinced Kenyatta that a shift in tone was needed if he was to bend the ear of the Colonial Office.

But while Kenyatta avoided writing in Communist publications from 1930 until 1933, he did not break off contacts with Communist organisations during this time. We must ask, therefore, how much of Kenyatta's Communist involvement was based on ideological consonance, and how much was the result of opportunism. Woodford McClellan argues that 'Kenyatta made use of the Soviet Communists. Bourgeois nationalist to the core, he achieved his purposes and left their care.'[121] However, this fails to explain Kenyatta's continued association with Marxist anticolonialists in the IASB when larger, better-connected, 'respectable' (albeit not explicitly anticolonial) organisations like the League of Coloured Peoples existed. The explanation is more nuanced. Kenyatta was undoubtedly drawn to the anti-imperialist militancy of the Communist movement at a time when he was being rebuffed by a gradualist Labour-run Colonial Office.

At the same time, Kenyatta was always more of an anticolonial nationalist than he was a Marxist. This caused friction with Communists in the early 1930s, and with the Trotskyist C. L. R. James later in the decade. Kenyatta's articles in the Communist press were radical in that they demanded self-government, rather than petitioned for reform, but nowhere was there a discussion of African socialism or a dissection of class forces in Kenya. During his early years in Britain he tried to be everything to everyone – a respectable petitioner to liberals, and a revolutionary to Communists. In the mid 1930s, however, when he began to rein in this tendency to be a political chameleon, he fashioned himself as a revolutionary nationalist with socialist sympathies.

Nevertheless, many Communists began to treat Kenyatta with suspicion in 1930. Weiss observes that he was generally distrusted and seen as a deviationist, and Adi notes that he 'was seldom relied upon by his comrades and even the security services distrusted his statements.'[122] William

---

120  RGASPI, 495/155/99, Memorandum of the KCA to the Secretary of State of the Colonies, February 1932.

121  Woodford McClellan, 'Africans and Black Americans in the Comintern Schools, 1925–1934', *International Journal of African Historical Studies* 26 (1993), p. 380.

122  Weiss, *Framing a Radical African Atlantic*, pp. 234–5; Adi, *Pan-Africanism and Communism*, p. 271.

Patterson, on his April 1930 visit to London to organise the ITUCNW conference, confronted Kenyatta about his letter to the *Manchester Guardian*. He reported that Kenyatta 'pleads coercion', concluding that Kenyatta was 'an unsafe element'.[123] Two years later, in a letter to Padmore, Ward said: 'Kenyatta is around like a dog lost his tail'.[124] One of the few sources of support for Kenyatta was the CPGB. In July 1930, responding to the concerns of the LAI International Secretariat, the CPGB's Colonial Committee announced that it was 'of the opinion that he is not a potential enemy'.[125] Padmore likewise supported Kenyatta in a dispute with the LAI International Secretariat in June 1932.[126] Days earlier, Kenyatta had written to Padmore to express his grievances with the CPGB, LAI and NWA. He argued that he had played a part in founding the NWA, but that this was not acknowledged by Ward and Rathbone. He stated that his articles for the *Daily Worker* had led to the imprisonment of his comrades in the KCA (explaining his interventions in *The Times*, *Manchester Guardian* and *East Africa*), and that he had put this matter before the LAI. Yet Bridgeman and others had 'left me alone without giving me any moral support or otherwise'.[127] Ward and Kenyatta briefed Padmore against each other, and Padmore endeavoured to keep both men in the Communist movement.

Padmore's complicated relationship to Kenyatta's politics is exemplified in the January 1933 issue of the *Negro Worker*. Kenyatta contributed an article in which he demanded 'the restitution of [Africans'] land' and appealed to 'the working class of Great Britain and elsewhere to work with us hand in hand that we may overthrow our common enemy – British Imperialism'. These were the same notes he had struck in his earlier Communist writings. Padmore appended a long editor's note to the article, in which he praised Kenyatta's militancy but chided him for speaking in 'general terms': 'We must not only demand the return of the land but must immediately apply ourselves to a radical improvement of the living conditions of the masses' through the organisation of workers and peasants.[128] Here, Padmore picked up on the tensions in all of Kenyatta's previous

---

123  W. W. to Profintern Negro Bureau, 18 April 1930.

124  RGASPI, 534/3/756, Ward to Padmore, 16 July 1932.

125  RGASPI, 495/100/699, Minutes of Colonial Committee meeting, 21 July 1930.

126  Padmore to LAI International Secretariat, 12 June 1932.

127  RGASPI, 534/7/74, Kenyatta to Padmore, 9 June 1932.

128  Kenyatta, 'An African Looks at British Imperialism', *Negro Worker*, January 1933, pp. 18–23.

Communist writings – Kenyatta made bold calls for independence or self-government and appealed to the British proletariat for support, but did not develop a vision for a socialist postcolonial Kenya. James would make similar criticisms of Kenyatta's *Facing Mount Kenya* in 1938.[129]

Kenyatta's return to open Communist and socialist activity was probably motivated by the lack of receptivity of the National Government. Unfortunately for Kenyatta, it also coincided with Padmore's break with the Comintern. After being sent by Padmore to study in Moscow, he returned to London later in 1933, where Ward continued to denounce him.[130] Kenyatta's funds from the Comintern had dried up since the Western Bureau in Germany had closed due to the Nazi ascent, and he was clearly under pressure from hostile elements both in Britain and the Comintern apparatus. When the Comintern expelled Padmore, Kenyatta, who had also begun to meet with Cunard, visited Padmore in Paris and was inclined to side with him, but did not immediately break off all Communist associations.[131] Unlike many Black radicals, Kenyatta was never a Marxist, but neither did he explicitly challenge the Marxism of activists like Padmore. He was pulled in various directions by the Communist movement and his liberal patrons during his early years in Britain. Throughout the rest of his time in Britain, he retained what could generously be termed philosophical eclecticism, or more harshly political opportunism. But a relatively consistent thread of revolutionary nationalism can be discerned. His own break from his early liberal philosophies and patrons, however, did not mirror that of C. L. R. James. Kenyatta's lack of sympathy with Marxism would shape conflicts between the two over the years that followed.

## C. L. R. James, Nelson, and the Path from Liberal to Trotskyist Anti-Imperialism

Cyril Lionel Robert James was born in Tunapuna, Trinidad, on 4 January 1901. Throughout a varied career he established himself as an activist, journalist, historian, playwright and cultural critic. His pan-Africanist

---

129  This episode is discussed in Chapter 3.

130  TNA, KV 2/1787 (Kenyatta), Ward to Padmore, 13 September 1933.

131  TNA, KV 2/1787 (Kenyatta), Colonel Sir Vernon Kell to Nairobi Commissioner of Police, 18 January 1934.

Marxism informed this vast output. After spending the first thirty years of his life in Trinidad, he lived in Britain from 1932 to 1938. He then emigrated to the United States, where he stayed for the next fifteen years. Those who knew James during the 1930s describe him as physically attractive ('very tall, lean, handsome'), a captivating speaker with a 'wonderful voice', and an immensely impressive intellectual who 'could think mightily for himself'.[132]

Like Padmore, James belonged to the Trinidadian Black middle class. The complex racial and class formations of the Caribbean played an important role in his political development.[133] James came from an intellectual family that aspired to Victorian values of respectability, and he was deeply influenced by the poet and moralist Matthew Arnold. A devoted cricketer, James opted to join Maple (the club of the brown-skinned middle class) over Shannon (the club of the dark-skinned lower-middle class). He later wrote: 'My decision cost me a great deal . . . Faced with the fundamental divisions in the island, I had gone to the right and, by cutting myself off from the popular side, delayed my political development for years.'[134] James devoured English literature, such as Shakespeare and Thackeray (he was particularly fond of *Vanity Fair*) and was so moulded in that culture that he later remembered his journey from Trinidad to Britain in 1932 as a case of the 'British intellectual . . . going to Britain'.[135] The accuracy of this statement is attested to in *The Life of Captain Cipriani*, written in his last years in Trinidad. James assured his audience that 'what the stranger unacquainted with these islands must get very firmly into his head before he goes any further is that these [Caribbean] people are not savages, they speak no other language except English, they have no other religion except Christianity, in fact, their whole outlook is that of Western civilisation modified and adapted to their particular circumstances.'[136] But this passage also points

---

132 Louise Cripps, *C. L. R. James: Memories and Commentaries* (New York, 1997), p. 11; Fredric Warburg, *An Occupation for Gentlemen* (London, 1959), p. 214; Harry Wicks, *Keeping My Head: The Memoirs of a British Bolshevik* (London, 1992), p. 182.

133 For more detailed accounts of James's youth in Trinidad, see Høgsbjerg, *C. L. R. James in Imperial Britain* (Durham, NC, 2014), Chapter 1; Kent Worcester, *C. L. R. James: A Political Biography* (Albany, NY, 1996), Chapter 1. For James's own account, see C. L. R. James, *Beyond a Boundary* (London, 1963).

134 James, *Beyond a Boundary*, p. 59.

135 Ibid., p. 114.

136 C. L. R. James, *The Life of Captain Cipriani: An Account of British Government in the West Indies* (Durham, NC, 2014 [1932]), p. 49.

to a tension within James's sense of his Britishness. Arguing the case for the Caribbean's cultural sophistication – albeit one based on an approximation of British culture – James could see no reason for the continued imperial dominance of Britain over the Caribbean. Although James spent much of the 1920s concerned with cultural pursuits, as the decade progressed he became increasingly political. He was galvanised by the activities of the Trinidad Workingmen's Association, led by Arthur Cipriani. Inspired by Cipriani's moderate social democracy, his 'hitherto vague ideas of freedom crystalized around a political conviction: we should be free to govern ourselves'.[137]

James therefore arrived in Britain in March 1932 as a liberal or social democrat. He had come to the mother country primarily concerned with furthering his literary career; in that respect he serves as a counterpoint to Padmore and Kenyatta, who arrived in Europe as political activists. James spent two months on a whirlwind tour of London, before moving to Nelson, Lancashire, where he remained until March 1933.[138] This was an early example of a lack of money having a material impact on James's activity, as he only decided to leave London when his 'money began to give out'.[139] James stayed with Learie Constantine, the Trinidadian cricketer and professional in Nelson's Lancashire League team, and helped Constantine to write his book, *Cricket and I*. Nelson had a proud history of class struggle, earning itself the nickname 'Red Nelson', and was gripped by a weavers' strike during James's time in the town. Christian Høgsbjerg has noted that 'lively stories of working-class history therefore directly challenged James's moralistic and elitist Fabian vision of social change from above'.[140] James was exposed to a vibrant socialist culture. As he later recalled, 'My Labour and Socialist ideas had been got from books and were rather abstract. These humorously cynical working men were a revelation and brought me down to earth.'[141]

James became particularly good friends with Harry Spencer, a left-wing Labour Party member and proprietor of a bakery in Nelson. James described Spencer as 'a man of sterling English character, an intellectual

---

137   James, *Beyond a Boundary*, pp. 119.

138   For the fullest account of James's time in Nelson, see Høgsbjerg, *C. L. R. James*, Chapter 2.

139   James, *Beyond a Boundary*, p. 119.

140   Høgsbjerg, *C. L. R. James*, p. 46.

141   James, *Beyond a Boundary*, p. 122.

of the first order and a man of great generosity', with whom he shared an interest in books and music.[142] James spent much time at Spencer's home and in his bakery, and went on several walks with him. He recalled that it was Spencer who encouraged him to pursue his interest in writing a book about Toussaint Louverture (the Haitian revolutionary leader) and gave him a cheque for £90 to visit the archives in Paris.[143] The resulting book, *The Black Jacobins*, was dedicated to Harry and his wife, Elizabeth.[144]

James joined the Labour Party shortly after arriving in Britain. The atmosphere in Nelson helped to ensure his place on the left of the party. He later remembered that 'Harry and all the Labour Party members and supporters with whom I became friendly, always made it clear to me that they expected nothing serious from . . . the leaders of the Labour Party'.[145] However, James gained in Nelson an understanding of the emotional and political affinity that the British working class felt for the Labour Party. He remembered that many people in Nelson attributed the rise in living standards over the previous generation to the party, and he also garnered 'an understanding of the attitude of the majority who voted for it in elections'.[146] Later, James and other Black radicals continued to recognise the mass appeal of the Labour Party, but also that members and supporters could be cynical about the leadership and sympathetic to their pan-Africanism. In Trinidad, James had by his own admission been detached from the nascent labour movement – a movement that in a matter of years would forcefully express itself. It was James's time in Nelson and his encounters with the organised British proletariat that convinced him of the importance of class struggle, rather than moralism and gradualism, in achieving political change.

He became a well-known and regular speaker at meetings in Nelson; but he was not yet a revolutionary. At a meeting in the ILP Rooms in January 1933, James, focusing on Kenya, Burma and the West Indies, made the case for colonial independence. But he said that independence should be 'granted' by Britain, offering no prospect of colonial peoples winning their own independence. Nevertheless, this was a radical

---

142 C. L. R. James papers, box 4 folder 7, C. L. R. James, 'Autobiography, 1932–38', p. 12.

143 Ibid., p. 18.

144 C. L. R. James, *The Black Jacobins: Toussaint L'Ouverture and the San Domingo Revolution* (London, 1938), p. v.

145 James, 'Autobiography, 1932–38', p. 22.

146 Ibid., p. 23.

argument to be making in 1933. The attention paid to three regions of the British Empire demonstrates that he, like Padmore and Kenyatta, had begun to think of imperialism as a global system. According to the *Nelson Leader*, 'the audience very much appreciated the striking and interesting manner in which the address was presented'.[147]

As well as providing James with the opportunity for personal encounters with the British working class and practical lessons in class struggle, Nelson also presented him with intellectual stimulation. Frederick Cartmell, the owner of a small publishing firm, lent two influential books to James: Spengler's *The Decline of the West* and Trotsky's *The History of the Russian Revolution*.[148] James was drawn more to Trotsky's philosophies than to Spengler's, but both books instilled in him a global and epic sense of history that would become his own hallmark.

James left Nelson in March 1933, but returned a year later to give a lecture on 'The Negro', which Høgsbjerg has described as illustrating his 'new, militant Pan-Africanist politics'.[149] James attacked scientific racism, before discussing colonial oppression in South Africa and Kenya and lynching in the southern United States. James's developing Marxism was illustrated when he remarked: 'Although it is a racial question on the surface, it is a political and economic question below.'[150]

His rapid political development was evident. James arrived in Britain having already written *The Life of Captain Cipriani*. This text is the most thorough expressions of James's political philosophy in the early 1930s. Høgsbjerg notes that James, like Cipriani, did not call for West Indian independence, but rather autonomy in line with the Dominions. He calls the work 'essentially a moral appeal to the British government's better conscience'.[151] Kent Worcester has similarly observed the 'limitations of its author's analysis of colonialism', as James paid no mind to the effects of slavery on the Caribbean, and rather rested his argument for self-government on the 'Westernness' of the Black middle class.[152]

James concluded the book with a final appeal for self-government: 'Democracy, dictatorship, of a group or of the proletariat, it does not

---

147  'Coloured Peoples Under British Rule', *Nelson Leader*, 27 January 1933, p. 11.
148  James, 'Autobiography, 1932–38', p. 10.
149  Høgsbjerg, *C. L. R. James*, p. 86.
150  'Racial Prejudice in England', *Nelson Leader*, 16 March 1934, p. 5.
151  Høgsbjerg, *C. L. R. James*, p. 53.
152  Worcester, *C. L. R. James*, p. 24.

matter; a people like ours must be free to make their own failures and successes, and develop themselves in their own way.'[153] This was a liberal Caribbean nationalism, couched in language to appeal to European nationalisms, much as Kenyatta's non-Communist writings had mostly been. James had written the book during his last years in Trinidad, and these elitist and gradualist ideas were being challenged during his time in Nelson. Still, James was eager to have the book published. Through an introduction from Cipriani, he was in regular correspondence with William Gillies, the Labour Party's international secretary, who displayed a tremendous concern with warding James away from the CPGB. Through Gillies, James was introduced to Leonard Woolf, who agreed in November 1932 to consider a 10,000-word abridgement of James's text. The resulting pamphlet, *The Case for West Indian Self-Government*, was published in March 1933.[154] News of the pamphlet's publication was received positively in Nelson, from where James had recently departed.[155]

Upon his return to London in 1933, James heard that Padmore, the man who was 'organising black people all over the world', was speaking in London – but it was only when Padmore walked into the room that he recognised his friend Malcolm Nurse. The two talked long into the night. James later recalled: 'I was a Trotskyite and he was a Stalinist but that didn't bother us. We were both concerned with the emancipation of Africa.'[156] This was to become a recurring theme of James's memories of the British pan-Africanist movement – an insistence that his Trotskyism, and various other forms of Marxism and socialism, were compatible with pan-Africanism and caused no friction between members of the movement.[157]

James, if he really identified as a Trotskyist by 1933, was an extremely fresh recruit to the cause. He had read Trotsky's *History of the Russian Revolution* in Nelson, but it was only on his return to London that he started to immerse himself in Trotskyist theory. Throughout late 1933 and early 1934, James, living near Grays Inn Road, was a frequent visitor to Charlie Lahr's bookshop on nearby Red Lion Street. Lahr was an

---

153  James, *Life of Captain Cipriani*, p. 159.

154  A stream of letters between James, Gillies and Woolf can be found in LHASC, WG/TRI.

155  Pertinax, 'Random Remarks', *Nelson Leader*, 7 April 1933, p. 8.

156  James, 'George Padmore', p. 254.

157  The accuracy of James's claim will be examined more thoroughly in subsequent chapters.

anarchist who had been a member of the CPGB in the early 1920s. He was sympathetic to James's burgeoning anti-Stalinism, regularly recommending and ordering books and pamphlets for him.[158] Trotsky's theory of uneven and combined development (which held that regions of the world would develop at an uneven pace while remaining part of a single global capitalist system) and his theory of permanent revolution (which held that, because of this uneven and combined development, working classes in the colonial periphery did not have to go through the long development of working classes in the advanced capitalist countries) allowed James to understand proletarian struggle in the colonies as central to a world socialist transformation.[159]

Trotskyism also entailed opposition to Stalinism. During the 1930s, Trotsky railed against the Soviet bureaucracy, which he argued had brought about the degeneration of the Soviet state. The Soviet Union could be redeemed only through a 'political revolution', to be led by a revolutionary party. This Soviet political revolution could be aided by advances made by revolutionaries in other countries, such as Britain, where James encountered activists who followed Trotsky's vision and analysis.[160] After reading Marx, Lenin, Stalin and Trotsky, James concluded that the Stalinists were 'the greatest historical liars that I had ever met or ever heard of'.[161] He also believed that, while the Bolshevik Revolution had 'wiped away any gross forms of prejudice against colour', a 'racial prejudice of a particularly dangerous and subtle kind' remained: 'Communists . . . believed themselves to be the chosen leaders. They thought they were the chosen leaders in Moscow, in London and in New York.'[162] The attempted Communist direction of anticolonial struggles was unacceptable to him.

James became formally involved with Trotskyist politics in London during the second half of 1934. There were probably fewer than one hundred Trotskyists in Britain at the time, and James periodically went to Paris, the centre of the movement, as the representative of the British section.[163] Harry Wicks, a CPGB member turned Trotskyist, recalled that

158  James, 'Autobiography, 1932–38', pp. 31–3.

159  Trotsky's influence on James is discussed in Høgsbjerg, *C. L. R. James*, pp. 75–7.

160  John Callaghan, *British Trotskyism: Theory and Practice* (Oxford, 1984), Chapter 1.

161  James, 'Autobiography, 1932–38', p. 33.

162  James, 'Notes on the Life of George Padmore', p. 24.

163  James, 'Autobiography, 1932–38', pp. 37–9.

he was attracted to James because of his ability to give Trotskyism a national presence, whereas the British Trotskyists in London were primarily concerned with internal issues.[164] Louise Cripps, who became James's lover, first met him at a dinner party at the home of Israel and Esther Heiger, at which James 'monopoliz[ed] the conversation'. He told his fellow guests 'about Trotsky and the perfidies of Stalin; also, how the Communists in Great Britain were telling lots of lies and pursuing wrong policies'.[165]

James was a member of the Marxist Group, a faction of Trotskyists that had joined the ILP. In 1933, Trotsky argued that the British Trotskyist movement should join the newly disaffiliated ILP in order to steer the party in a revolutionary direction, but this was opposed by the majority in Britain's largest Trotskyist group, the Communist League. However, a minority followed Trotsky's advice and joined the party.[166] The Marxist Group dominated a few branches in London, and Cripps believed that Fenner Brockway was friendly with James and other Trotskyists because they aided him in his struggle against the ILP's Stalinist members.[167] In a short time, James had been transformed from a liberal Caribbean nationalist to a Marxist anti-imperialist. By 1935, he was one of the leading figures of Britain's small Trotskyist movement, and also began to gain a national profile within the ILP. The anticolonial indignation of Trinidad's Black middle class had merged with the proletarian rebelliousness of a Lancashire mill town to create one of the twentieth century's most important Marxists.

In the few years prior to the Italian invasion of Ethiopia in 1935, James, Padmore, Kenyatta and Ward all migrated from the colonial empire to Britain (though Padmore took a slightly circuitous route). They came to Europe already distrustful of the supposed benefits of colonial rule, and this feeling was duly fortified. Moreover, they all became increasingly critical of the moderate and paternalistic anti-imperialism they encountered in Britain's liberal and social-democratic movements. While their

---

164  C. L. R. James papers, box 28 interior box 4, James remembered by Harry Wicks, 30 April 1985.

165  Cripps, *C. L. R. James*, p. 11.

166  Wicks, *Keeping My Head*, pp. 170–1; Sam Bornstein and Al Richardson, *Against the Stream: A History of the Trotskyist Movement in Britain, 1924–38* (London, 1986), p. 138.

167  Cripps, *C. L. R. James*, p. 29.

relationships to Marxism and the organised Communist movement varied, encounters with the British and European proletariat instilled in all of them a model for struggling against the capitalism that ravaged their homelands. These Black radicals all insisted – sometimes with support from the British left, sometimes with resistance from it – that Africans would play an active part in their own liberation. They looked to the European working class for assistance, not leadership.

This was a period of rapid development in the political thought of all of these activists. Encounters in the metropole strengthened the resolve of their anti-imperialism. These encounters also shaped ideas about how capitalism – and, increasingly important as the 1930s progressed, its corollaries, fascism and war – was inseparable from colonialism, and how they must be overthrown together. Such ideas, forged during the early 1930s, prefigured the debates in which the IAFE and IASB intervened in the subsequent years. Understanding imperialism as central to capitalism, Black radicals rejected forms of socialism that limited themselves to a simple antifascism or pacifism, and made alliances with those who made anti-imperialism central to their politics. With several Black radicals making their home in London, and tensions mounting between Benito Mussolini's expansionist Italy and Haile Selassie's independent Ethiopia, the stage was set for these solidarities and theories to be tested.

# 2

# Ethiopia and the Question of Sanctions, 1935–1936

On 3 October 1935, after almost a year of tension, fascist Italy invaded Ethiopia. Ethiopia was one of only two independent Black-ruled states in a continent otherwise partitioned into European colonies, mandates and protectorates. As such, it functioned as an important pan-Africanist symbol, a demonstration of the possibility of Black sovereignty. It was also a member of the League of Nations. The League responded to the invasion by imposing limited sanctions on Italy, but influential League members Britain and France were compromised when the Hoare–Laval Pact, which proposed the partition of Ethiopia, became public knowledge in December 1935. Italy proclaimed victory in May 1936, merging Ethiopia with its other East African colonial territories, although resistance to the occupation continued until Ethiopia's liberation in 1941.

The episode provoked a crisis in the British socialist and anticolonial movements. It therefore serves as an illuminating case study of the fissures within the movement. Would socialists support a policy of League of Nations sanctions, workers' sanctions, or no sanctions at all against Italy? Several Black activists gathered in London at this time to form the International African Friends of Ethiopia (IAFE), soon gaining a profile in British socialist and anti-imperialist circles. Ras Makonnen, who arrived in London during the Italo-Ethiopian War and collaborated with C. L. R. James and George Padmore in the IAFE, remembered: 'People began to look at you to see if you had something to say.' Makonnen, who, like his Black radical comrades, was disillusioned with

Communist anticolonialism, added that 'the best place to say it outside the liberal element was with the Independent Labour Party . . . especially if you didn't want to risk the disgrace of being a CP-er'.[1]

However, after much infighting and deliberation, the Independent Labour Party (ILP) settled on a policy of no sanctions against Italy, out of fear that sanctions would lead to war between the imperialist powers. Conversely, almost every Black radical in Britain supported either workers' sanctions or League of Nations sanctions against Italy. The official IAFE position was to support League sanctions, although there was disagreement within the group – James resigned because he believed the League of Nations to be an instrument of imperialist power. James, a member of the Trotskyist faction inside the ILP, also protested the ILP leadership's opposition to *any* form of sanctions. He was joined by prominent party figures such as Fenner Brockway, the ILP's general secretary, but ultimately defeated. Rodney Worrell has highlighted this 'failure of proletarian internationalism' as leading to Padmore's 'lost faith in the proletarian revolution' and the decision to form the Black-led International African Service Bureau (IASB) in 1937.[2]

But British Black radicals in fact recognised the need for their own autonomous organisations prior to the failure of sections of the British left to support sanctions against Italy. The IAFE formed in the summer of 1935, several months before the ILP leadership voted to advocate against sanctions. The West African Students' Union (WASU) and the League of Coloured Peoples (LCP) had been founded in the previous ten years; while they were more moderate than the IAFE, they provided models for Black-led organisations. Yet even with the formation of autonomous organisations, the IAFE and the International African Service Bureau still valued political alliances with the British socialist movement. The Italo-Ethiopian War should not be thought of as a watershed event that alone attuned people of African descent to the need to form their own organisations, independent from the 'White' socialist movement. Far more important in this respect was Black radical disillusionment with the Communist movement, illustrated by Padmore's

---

1 T. Ras Makonnen, *Pan-Africanism from Within*, ed. Kenneth King (London, 1973), p. 112.

2 Rodney Worrell, 'George Padmore: Pan-Africanist Par Excellence', in Fitzroy Baptiste and Rupert Lewis, eds, *George Padmore: Pan-African Revolutionary* (Kingston, 2009), pp. 29–31.

acrimonious break with the Comintern, and exacerbated by the turn to the Popular Front strategy in 1935. Furthermore, there is nothing to suggest that the war caused anything more than a small and momentary dent in Padmore's or James's faith in proletarian revolution.

Importantly, James initially managed to win a majority of ILP conference delegates to his position on Ethiopia. The party's parliamentary group then threatened to resign from their leadership positions in protest. This prompted a compromise resolution that the policy be decided by a party-wide plebiscite (eventually decided in the parliamentary group's favour). But the fact that an ILP conference would back James's position against the leadership's, effectively censuring the latter for a lack of commitment to anti-imperialist principles, shows that anti-imperialism was not just a marginal concern of the British left, but one that ran deep within it.

Responses to the Italian invasion were clearly shaped by race and colonial status. Black socialists saw the invasion as yet another tile within the mosaic of European violence and oppression that had shaped their lives – one that threatened to destroy a potent symbol of African sovereignty. Even those critical of the Ethiopian emperor, Haile Selassie, generally regarded the protection of Ethiopia's sovereignty as the paramount concern. White socialists appreciated the significance of this concern to varying degrees (and more abstractly than their Black comrades), and were more likely to think of the invasion's implications for European fascism and war. But the positions taken and alliances formed by activists were not *determined* by race. James's pan-Africanist understanding of the invasion may have caused him to feel vitriolic anger towards the ILP parliamentary group, and only a respectful difference of opinion with his pro-League sanctions comrades in the IAFE. But his greatest political allies were those White socialists in the ILP and the Trotskyist movement who advocated workers' sanctions. Black and White socialists were not divided along simple racial lines when proposing responses to the invasion. Black radicalism needs to be integrated into the history of British socialism not as a discrete force, but as one whose concerns overlapped with those of the broader movement.

The Ethiopian crisis and war did surprisingly little long-term damage to Black radicals' relationship with the ILP. It is a case study of political disagreements and competing priorities, but not of ruinous discord. By the end of the 1930s, the ILP, largely as a result of Black radical influence, had become the most militantly anti-imperialist political party in Britain. At the same time, while the Popular Front was undermining the CPGB's anti-imperialist activism and damaging its relationship with Black radicals, the nature of the Ethiopian crisis (a fascist power invading an independent African nation) in fact allowed antifascism and anti-imperialism to converge in the Communist movement. While some Black activists, such as James, were critical of Communist appeals to the League of Nations, the CPGB unambiguously opposed Italy's invasion of Ethiopia (although, as Padmore later noted, the international Communist movement did far more to oppose the fascist threat materially during the Spanish Civil War than it did in Ethiopia).[3] The IAFE included in its ranks Johnstone Kenyatta and Arnold Ward, whose ideas both continued to find expression through CPGB channels. Examining the crisis therefore allows us to tease out some of the nuances of British left-wing anticolonialism in the 1930s.

This chapter surveys the debates over Ethiopia and the question of sanctions within the IAFE, and then between IAFE members and the ILP and CPGB. It then goes on to discuss the manner in which James's Trotskyism shaped his criticisms of these two parties in a way that extended beyond his pan-Africanist comrades' anticolonialist concerns. Finally, it examines the ways in which IAFE members continued to think beyond Ethiopia in this period, leading to the formation in 1937 of the IASB.

## The International African Friends of Ethiopia

There has long been historiographical recognition of the impact of Italy's invasion of Ethiopia on the people of Africa and its diaspora. S. K. B. Asante calls it 'a second invasion of their homelands'; Neelam Srivastava argues that it 'enabled many blacks . . . to identify with a black sovereign state'; and Kevin Yelvington observes that the war helped to define and transform ideas of who was 'Black' across the diaspora.[4]

---

3 George Padmore, *Africa and World Peace* (London, 1937), pp. 153–5.

4 S. K. B. Asante, 'The Impact of the Italo-Ethiopian Crisis of 1935–1936 on the Pan-African Movement in Britain', *Transactions of the Historical Society of Ghana* 13 (1972), p. 217; Neelam Srivastava, *Italian Colonialism and Resistances to Empire, 1930–1970* (London, 2018), p. 68; Kevin A. Yelvington, 'The War in Ethiopia and Trinidad

Kwame Nkrumah, during a brief stay in London while completing his journey from the Gold Coast to the United States, famously declared that, when he had seen the headline that Mussolini had invaded Ethiopia, 'it was almost as if the whole of London had suddenly declared war on [him] personally'.[5] More than anything, this quotation points to the manner in which the invasion was seen as inseparable from the wider system of European imperialism in Africa. Padmore at the time wrote of the 'tremendous feeling of racial solidarity among Blacks' that transcended national borders, and Hakim Adi has observed how Black and anticolonial organisations in Britain (such as the League Against Imperialism, the LCP and WASU) achieved greater unity with each other as a result of the invasion.[6] One notable exception to this unity was Marcus Garvey, who lived in London during the last five years of his life, between 1935 and 1940. In a debate with Padmore, he blamed the invasion on Selassie's cowardice.[7] During the latter years of the 1930s, Garvey again clashed with James and Padmore when he condemned the growing militancy of Caribbean trade unions.[8]

It was this mood of racial solidarity transcending national borders that led James and Amy Ashwood Garvey to form the International African Friends of Ethiopia in July 1935, three months before the impending invasion. The stated goal of the organisation was 'to assist by all means in their power in the maintenance of the territorial integrity and political independence of Abyssinia'.[9] Ashwood Garvey was born into a middle-class Jamaican family in 1897. After meeting Marcus Garvey in 1914, she became his first wife in 1919. She was one of the secretaries of the Universal Negro Improvement Association and a

---

1935–1936', in Bridget Brereton and Kevin A. Yelvington, eds, *The Colonial Caribbean in Transition: Essays on Postemancipation Social and Cultural History* (Mona, 1999), pp. 189–90.

5  Kwame Nkrumah, *The Autobiography of Kwame Nkrumah* (Edinburgh, 1957), p. 27.

6  George Padmore, *How Britain Rules Africa* (London, 1936), p. 363; Hakim Adi, *West Africans in Britain, 1900–1960: Nationalism, Pan-Africanism and Communism* (London, 1998), p. 68.

7  Charles E. Young Research Library, University of California, Los Angeles, Ralph J. Bunche papers, box 279 folder 1, Ralph Bunche, 1937 Annual Diary, 3 June.

8  Bill Schwarz, 'George Padmore', in Bill Schwarz, ed., *West Indian Intellectuals in Britain* (Manchester, 2003), p. 137.

9  George Padmore, *Pan-Africanism or Communism? The Coming Struggle for Africa* (London, 1956), p. 145.

director of the Black Star Line, until she and Marcus separated in the early 1920s. She first arrived in London in 1922, and in 1924 helped to establish the Nigerian Progress Union with Ladipo Solanke. In 1934, after a decade away, Ashwood Garvey returned to London with her partner, the Trinidadian musician and activist Sam Manning.[10] James later remembered her as 'a very powerful personality' who had gained much political experience working with Marcus Garvey, and Peter Abrahams recalled her being 'a gay spirit filled with pealing laughter'.[11] The officers of the IAFE were Peter Milliard, a Guianese physician, T. A. Marryshow, a Grenadian journalist and trade unionist, Kenyatta, Ashwood Garvey, and, once they had arrived in Britain later in the summer of 1935, Makonnen and Padmore.[12] The group also included Manning and Mohammed Said from Somaliland, and was sponsored by George Moore and Samuel Wood of the Gold Coast Aborigines' Rights Protection Society.[13] Its headquarters was Ashwood Garvey's International Afro Restaurant on New Oxford Street. At meetings there the IAFE would decide when and where to hold public events. Minkah Makalani has noted the 'heavy lifting' done by Ashwood Garvey to nurture the IAFE's politics, most notably in creating 'centers of activism' in her establishments.[14] The creation of spaces for intellectual activity is the kind of under-acknowledged intellectual labour often performed by Black women.

---

10  Keisha N. Blain, *Set the World on Fire: Black Nationalist Women and the Global Struggle for Freedom* (Philadelphia, 2018), pp. 13–19; Tony Martin, *Amy Ashwood Garvey: Pan-Africanist, Feminist, and Mrs Marcus Garvey No. 1: Or, A Tale of Two Amies* (Dover, MA, 2007).

11  Rare Book and Manuscript Library, Columbia University, New York, C. L. R. James papers, box 4 folder 7, C. L. R. James, 'Autobiography, 1932–38', p. 51; Peter Abrahams, *The Coyaba Chronicles: Reflections on the Black Experience in the Twentieth Century* (Kingston, 2000), p. 36.

12  James, 'Autobiography, 1932–38', p. 51.

13  Padmore, *Pan-Africanism or Communism?*, p. 145.

14  Minkah Makalani, 'An International African Opinion: Amy Ashwood Garvey and C. L. R. James in Black Radical London', in Davarian L. Baldwin and Minkah Makalani, eds, *Escape from New York: The New Negro Renaissance Beyond Harlem* (Minneapolis, 2013), p. 86. Makalani has further analysed the intellectual labour of Black women in creating social spaces conducive to the development of Black radical thought in Minkah Makalani, 'Black Women's Intellectual Labor and the Social Spaces of Black Radical Thought in Harlem', in Andrew M. Fearnley and Daniel Matlin, eds, *Race Capital? Harlem as Setting and Symbol* (New York, 2018).

James described the group's main strategies as speaking 'in Hyde Park, in Trafalgar Square and in other public locations. We distributed pamphlets on the crisis and I published various articles through Brockway in the ILP newspaper, *New Leader*.'[15] We can see from these strategies that the group was keen to maintain independence from British socialist groups, but also placed value on alliances, particularly where propaganda and publishing were concerned. Makonnen recalled that the invasion of Ethiopia made Black people realise that 'the stories of Lenin and Trotsky, or Sun Yat-sen, must have their African counterparts'. But while the IAFE would not have European leadership, they would collaborate with White socialists and anticolonialists.[16]

Makonnen was born George Griffith in British Guiana around 1909. He adopted the name Ras Makonnen at the time of the Italian invasion, expressing a perhaps apocryphal claim to Ethiopian ancestry. Like Padmore, he left the Caribbean to study in the United States as a young man and became involved in Black radical politics, but was drawn to the cooperative movement rather than to organised Communism. He knew Padmore when they were at Howard together, and called Padmore's later publication, *Life and Struggles*, 'a revelation to me with its new approach'. However, he said of the CPUSA, 'I borrowed a lot from them, just as they had from Marx and others, but I felt I could do this without carrying the magic party card.'[17] Unlike James and Padmore, Makonnen was a socialist but not a Marxist. He described himself as a 'blatant nationalist' on the Ethiopian question, offering uncritical support to the emperor Haile Selassie in a way that Marxists could not.[18] Makonnen stumbled across the IAFE when he was passing through London on his way to Denmark and saw the group holding a rally in Trafalgar Square. He soon returned to London and became a prominent member of the group.[19]

The IAFE held its first public meeting in Farringdon Memorial Hall on 28 July 1935. The broadness of the IAFE's politics became apparent when Marryshow remarked that the 'British Empire is only safe and prosperous . . . so long as the coloured people are safe and prosperous.'[20] This kind

15  James, 'Autobiography, 1932–38', p. 52.
16  Makonnen, *Pan-Africanism from Within*, pp. 116–17.
17  Ibid., pp. 102–3.
18  Ibid., p. 114.
19  Ibid., p. 113.
20  'Africans' Pride in Abyssinia', *Manchester Guardian*, 29 July 1935, p. 13.

C. L. R. James giving a speech in Trafalgar Square, 1935
Getty Images

of moderate statement, endorsing a reformed empire, would find no place in the IASB, which formed out of the remnants of the IAFE two years later. It was James's speech, however, that captured most press attention. James detailed the recent history of Ethiopia, urged the formation of African battalions drawn from across the diaspora, and advocated a scorched-earth policy in the event of Ethiopian military defeat, so that, using the language of the African American abolitionist Frederick

Douglass, Ethiopians would 'die free rather than live enslaved!' Importantly, he also observed that the recent Peace Ballot had shown that '11,000,000 people in England were devoted to League ideals. Of these a large number were in favour of sanctions against an aggressor nation.'[21] Indeed, the meeting as a whole demanded 'that the League of Nations take measures to restrain Italy from this gross infringement of international law'.[22]

The IAFE followed this on 25 August with a large meeting in Trafalgar Square. Speakers included Ashwood Garvey, James, Chris Jones, Kenyatta, Padmore and Ward – the involvement of the latter belying Makonnen's statement that 'any black man coming into our camp who had one foot in the communist camp, we would deal with ruthlessly'. At the rally, Ashwood Garvey declared: 'No race has been so noble in forgiving, but now the hour has struck for our complete emancipation. We will not tolerate the invasion of Abyssinia.'[23] The *Manchester Guardian* estimated that a crowd of 200 swelled to 500 within an hour of the beginning of the meeting.[24] It was at this meeting that Makonnen introduced himself to the IAFE. He later recalled:

It was after [Kenyatta] and a few others had spoken for a time, that I passed my card forward saying that I was an Ethiopian and would welcome an opportunity to speak . . . I linked up the struggle in Ethiopia with the larger struggle against imperialism in Africa. Across the square I pointed to South Africa House and linked its significance with the present conflict . . . I proceeded to show that it was not in Britain's interest to assist Ethiopia, and pleaded the supreme necessity of sanctions against Italy.[25]

After the meeting, Makonnen went for tea with the IAFE, before departing three days later for Denmark. But he was in Britain long enough 'to see that the Left was in some difficulty over the attitude to intervention

---

21  'Coloured Friends of Abyssinia', *News Chronicle*, 29 July 1935, p. 2.

22  International African Friends of Ethiopia, 'An Appeal for Funds', 1935, in possession of Marika Sherwood.

23  Hannen Swaffer, 'I Heard Yesterday', *Daily Herald*, 24 August 1935, p. 8; Ritchie Calder, 'Trafalgar Sq. Warning against Invasion', *Daily Herald*, 26 August 1935, p. 3; TNA, KV 2/1787 (Kenyatta), 26 August 1935; Makonnen, *Pan-Africanism from Within*, p. 117.

24  'Friends of Abyssinia', *Manchester Guardian*, 26 August 1935, p. 8.

25  Makonnen, *Pan-Africanism from Within*, p. 113.

in the Italo-Ethiopian War'.[26] In fact, this 'difficulty' also permeated the IAFE, and was shaped by differing attitudes to the application of sanctions against Italy. James later remembered the sanctions debate within the IAFE as follows: 'I got myself into a blunder. Being a Marxist I was naturally opposed to the League of Nations, but in the excitement of forming the organisation we passed a resolution demanding or supporting, I cannot remember which, those who were urging that the League of Nations take steps against the Italian Government.'[27]

Official IAFE policy, and the majority of the group's members, supported League of Nations sanctions against Italy in order to maintain Ethiopian independence. However, James, in accordance with many of his Trotskyist and ILP comrades, believed that League sanctions would be used as an excuse by Britain and France to gain an advantage in their imperialist rivalry with Italy. He instead advocated workers' sanctions, arguing that it was only if workers themselves stopped the shipments of supplies to Italy that the sanctions movement could be genuinely anti-imperialist. While there is no record of James repeating the appeal for League of Nations sanctions that he made at the 28 July meeting, there is also no record of his directly contradicting the official IAFE position over the remainder of the summer – perhaps out of a desire to maintain a united front of Black people against Italian aggression. His recollection that the IAFE was mostly focused on organising a detachment of Black troops in Britain (a plan rebuffed by the Ethiopian ambassador in London), and that they later 'made it quite clear that we were not looking to the League of Nations to give any assistance to Ethiopia', is a misleading account of events.[28]

While most IAFE members remained sceptical of the League of Nations, dominated as it was by Britain and France, the largest colonial powers, most saw it as a useful tool in the struggle against Italian aggression. This was to be expected of reformist members like Moore, Wood and Marryshow (none of whom would feature prominently in the more militant IASB). But, though it was not central to his strategy, even the more radical Makonnen saw merit in appealing to the League. Padmore did not voice an opinion on League sanctions during the war; he saved most of his

---

26  Ibid., p. 114.

27  C. L. R. James, 'Black Intellectuals in Britain', in Bhikhu Parekh, ed., *Colour, Culture and Consciousness: Immigrant Intellectuals in Britain* (London, 1974), p. 158.

28  Ibid., p. 159.

criticism for those who opposed any form of sanctions, indicating a level of consonance with Makonnen's position. However, at the 1937 ILP summer school, he insisted that, in the event of future imperialist attacks, 'it is the duty of the British working class not to advocate League of Nations sanctions but organised refusal by the working class to provide war materials to the Imperial power concerned' – a position identical to James's.[29]

James, unable to square his anti-League position with the position of the IAFE, ultimately resigned from the group in October 1935.[30] The account that seems most accurate, therefore, is the one that appears in James's unpublished autobiographical notes. In his own words, 'Marxism clashed with the IAFE . . . and therefore I broke with it. I broke with it and went with the Marxists, but I did not quarrel or otherwise denounce the IAFE.'[31] The sanctions debate, and the interwar socialist movement in general, should therefore not be understood as a series of uneasy alliances and open conflicts between two essentialised blocs: Black and colonial radicals on one side, Eurocentric White Marxists on the other. Figures such as James drew on the heritage of Marx and Lenin as much as they drew on strategies of Black self-organisation. In 1937, Padmore advocated a sanctions policy identical to that supported by a majority of delegates to the 1936 ILP annual conference. Kenyatta's views on the crisis were promoted by the CPGB. Conflicts over the correct strategy for opposing imperialism were influenced by race and colonial status, but not determined by them, and divided White socialists as much as they did pan-Africanists. At the time of his amicable split from his comrades in the IAFE in the autumn of 1935, James became a central figure in a much fiercer debate about sanctions in the ILP.

## The ILP and the Sanctions Debate

After disaffiliating from the Labour Party in 1932, the ILP moved significantly to the left. This was partly the result of members looking to the global depression, the betrayal of Ramsay MacDonald's National Labour,

---

29  'Socialist Issues Discussed at the ILP Summer School', *New Leader*, 13 August 1937, p. 3.

30  TNA, KV 2/1824 (James), Vernon Kell to General MacBrien, 23 December 1936.

31  James, 'Autobiography, 1932–38', p. 53.

and the rise of fascism, and concluding that a predominantly parliamentary strategy would be insufficient to achieve socialist change. But it was also the result of the loss of members on the right of the ILP – in particular to the newly formed Socialist League (SL), which remained in the Labour Party. This led to greater ideological consonance among those who remained. The ILP now declared itself a revolutionary party, with direct implications for its anti-imperialism. While membership declined considerably after disaffiliation, the ILP remained relatively strong in London, where the IAFE was based, and in Glasgow, which provided all of the party's MPs after the 1935 general election. During the second half of the 1930s, the party had between 3,000 and 4,000 members and four MPs, remaining a small but potent force in British politics.[32]

By 1935, interpretations of imperialism that were at least nominally Leninist were dominant in the ILP. The National Administrative Council (NAC) submitted *A Socialist Policy for Britain* to the 1935 annual conference. It argued that Britain's colonial markets had allowed it to stave off the worst of the economic crisis, but that 'growing movements of revolt among the subject peoples in [capitalist powers'] Empires' threatened 'the whole system of Capitalist Imperialism', which was the primary cause of war.[33] As well as recognising the agency of colonial peoples in rebellion and eschewing paternalistic forms of anticolonialism, this statement also integrated colonialism into the ILP's conception of domestic British politics. With colonial liberation looking increasingly achievable, the ILP began to theorise what exactly 'independence' would entail. While emphasising that national independence should be unconditional, the official statement of policy in 1935 added:

At the same time the ILP does not regard political independence as an end in itself, recognising that it might be used by the owning class in India and other colonial countries to exploit the workers and peasants. It therefore supports the workers' organisations which are carrying on the class struggle in such countries and identifies itself particularly with the Revolutionary Socialist parties and groups.[34]

---

32 Gidon Cohen, *The Failure of a Dream: The Independent Labour Party from Disaffiliation to World War II* (London, 2007), Chapter 3.

33 ILP, *A Socialist Policy for Britain* (London, 1935), p. 3.

34 Ibid., pp. 13–14.

By the time of the Italian invasion of Ethiopia, after only a year of membership, James had built a significant profile within the ILP. He was chair of the Finchley and Hendon branch, and a popular speaker. He toured Britain engaging with the grassroots of the socialist movement, much as he had in Nelson. He used this immersion in the British socialist movement and working class to write articles for the *New Leader* that bore little apparent relation to pan-Africanism – one about miners' struggles in south Wales, another about the National Government's projected move towards fascism.[35]

But the Ethiopian question dominated James's ILP writings and speaking engagements in this period, especially given that the ILP was tearing itself apart over the issue. The ILP had never been a cheerleader for the League of Nations, instead criticising it as an organisation dominated by capitalist interests. But in 1928, it had advocated that the League's colonial mandate system be replaced with direct rule by the League itself, with an eye to eventual self-government.[36] However, more militant anti-League sentiments began to predominate in the 1930s. This position hardened following the Japanese invasion of Manchuria in 1931. Rather than relying on the League, workers' organisations were urged to resist 'provision of credit and the manufacture and export of arms and war materials of any kind to Japan'.[37]

When Italy invaded Ethiopia, however, the appropriate ILP response was unclear. On the one hand, the ILP had supported workers' sanctions against Japan and declared unconditional support for all anticolonial movements. On the other hand, the 1934 annual conference had declared its 'Unconditional refusal to assist any Government whatever in the prosecution of war except for the purpose of defending a Workers' Socialist Republic'.[38] Haile Selassie's monarchy was clearly not a socialist republic. That it was also an independent nation rather than a colony muddied the waters about whether or not the defence of Ethiopia could be considered an anticolonial struggle. The ILP's dilemma was later

---

35  C. L. R. James, 'How the Miners Could Win an Increase: What I Learned in Wales', *New Leader*, 1 November 1935, p. 3; C. L. R. James, 'Baldwin's Next Move: Parliament Has Become a Nuisance to the Ruling Class, Look Out for Fascist Developments', *New Leader*, 3 January 1936, p. 2.

36  ILP, *Annual Report of the NAC, 1929* (London, 1929), pp. 47–8.

37  ILP, *Annual Report of the NAC, 1932* (London, 1932), p. 70.

38  ILP, *Decisions of the Forty-Second ILP Annual Conference* (London, 1934), p. 3.

succinctly captured by Brockway: 'The problem was to work out a policy which would obstruct Mussolini's imperialist aggression without identifying ourselves with the war-like preparations and imperialist aims of French and British Capitalism.'[39] His editorial line in the *New Leader* became one of advocating workers' sanctions and opposing League of Nations sanctions.

This was a position shared by the Socialist League, a left-wing faction within the Labour Party. It drew its membership primarily from those in the ILP who had rejected disaffiliation and wished to remain in the Labour Party. From the summer of 1935, the SL argued that the League of Nations was being used to further imperialist interests. In September, it declared that socialists 'must seize the occasion not to demand international sanctions against Italy through the instrumentality of the League of Nations, but to create the will to employ working-class sanctions.'[40] The SL's chair, Stafford Cripps, even resigned from the Labour Party's National Executive Committee in September 1935 because of that body's endorsement of League sanctions.[41]

Embracing the same sentiment, the front page of the 30 August edition of the *New Leader* warned: 'Don't Trust Government!' The article urged: 'Workers must apply their own sanctions' because British prime minister '[Stanley] Baldwin wants Capitalist "sanctions" in interests of Imperialism'. It added: 'With proper leadership and organisation the working class could in their own strength stop the attack by Italy on Abyssinia. This would require no compromise with their own Capitalist class and the Imperialists . . . It would hasten the downfall of Capitalism and Imperialism. It would open the door to the social revolution.'[42]

Brockway was here echoing the position of the International Bureau for Revolutionary Socialist Unity (IBRSU). The ILP was affiliated to the Bureau, nicknamed the Three-and-a-Half International, which sought to attract revolutionary elements from both the Labour and Socialist International (LSI) and the Comintern. In a meeting chaired by Brockway, the IBRSU had reached a position on Ethiopia earlier that month. The resolution criticised both the LSI and the Comintern for supporting

39 Fenner Brockway, *Inside the Left: Thirty Years of Platform, Press, Prison and Parliament* (Leicester, 1947 [1942]), p. 325.

40 'War or Socialism', *Socialist*, September 1935, p. 1.

41 Stafford Cripps, 'Edinburgh and After', *Controversy*, November 1936, p. 18.

42 'Don't Trust Government!', *New Leader*, 30 August 1935, p. 1.

League of Nations sanctions, accusing the Soviet Union of being in thrall to French imperialism as part of a self-preserving anti-German alliance. It concluded that Ethiopia's struggle to maintain independence was one of anti-imperialism. Therefore, the three tasks of the working class were a boycott of Italy, the prevention of the transport of armaments and munitions to Italy, and the prevention of the transport of troops to Africa.[43] This statement contained a radical commitment to anti-imperialism, in which international working-class action was deemed to be the appropriate weapon.

The ILP was united in believing that League sanctions would be used merely to serve the interests of British and French imperialism. Meeting on 13 September 1935, the Executive Committee of the ILP voiced its opposition to League sanctions – but the priorities of the leadership were becoming evident.[44] On the same day, the ILP's Inner Executive (a decision-making body created in 1934 that consisted of the party's MPs, James Maxton, Campbell Stephen and John McGovern) published a resolution in the *New Leader* refusing to identify any salient difference between the regimes of Mussolini and Selassie. They argued that the efforts of the British working class should be directed towards resisting British war preparations, and declared: 'In our estimation the difference between the two rival dictators and the interests between them are not worth the loss of a single British life.'[45] This statement was indicative of the strength of anti-war sentiment on the British left during the 1930s, which was galvanised by the recent trauma of the Great War and the concomitant fear that a second world war was imminent.

James was a member of the ILP's militant London Division. Its militancy hinged on an uneasy alliance between Trotskyists and a minority of members of the Revolutionary Policy Committee (RPC), led by Jack Gaster. The RPC was a faction of the ILP, which advocated greater unity with the Comintern, and most of its members supported the Communist line of League of Nations sanctions. Gaster, however, along with the Trotskyists and John Aplin, rejected League sanctions and supported

---

43 'Act against War Danger: International Bureau's Clear Lead', *New Leader*, 16 August 1935, p. 4.

44 British Library of Political and Economic Science (BLPES), London, ILP, COLL MISC 0702/11, Meeting of Executive Committee of the NAC, 13 September 1935, p. 1.

45 James Maxton, John McGovern and Campbell Stephen, 'ILP Call', *New Leader*, 13 September 1935, p. 3.

workers' sanctions. In September 1935, the London Divisional Council wrote to the NAC:

> Only the organised forces of the workers can be relied upon. War cannot be stopped by pious resolutions. Of what use is it presenting a petition to a prowling tiger? . . . Without waiting for the League of Nations or the National Government we must follow the magnificent example of the Trade Unions in South Africa who by refusing to handle goods already have stopped supplies destined for Italy.[46]

James's hand was evident in this formulation. The 'prowling tiger' metaphor was strikingly similar to one he used the following year ('How does the lion co-operate with the lamb?'), and the reference to the struggles of African workers – and the suggestion that they set an example for British workers – resonates with James's pan-Africanist Marxism.[47]

James followed this letter with an article in the *New Leader*, written, probably not accidentally, at the time of his resignation from the IAFE. He attacked the plans of the League of Nations Committee of Five to deploy 'specialists' to help govern Ethiopia as European imperialism in another guise. With one eye on the European proletariat he saw as vital to world socialist revolution, and another on his comrades in the IAFE and other Black-led organisations, he asked: 'is there any British worker, any Negro in Africa, who, having understood this infamous document, is prepared to urge League sanctions and follow the Imperialists in their defence of the "Independence of Ethiopia"?' Instead, workers and peasants from Europe, Africa and Asia should work together to assist the Ethiopians 'by [their] own sanctions'. In doing so, they would simultaneously challenge British and French imperialism.[48]

The ILP NAC's manifesto was decided at its meeting on 9 October 1935, six days after the Italian invasion and two days after the

---

46 BLPES, ILP/7/11/9, London and Southern Counties Divisional Council to ILP Head Office, September 1935. For more on the RPC, see Cohen, *Failure of a Dream*, Chapter 5. The ILP's anti-sanctions position led to most RPC members resigning from the ILP in October 1935, the vast majority joining the CPGB.

47 C. L. R. James, '"Civilising" the "Blacks": Why Britain Needs to Maintain Her African Possessions', *New Leader*, 29 May 1936, p. 5.

48 C. L. R. James, 'Is This Worth a War? The League's Scheme to Rob Abyssinia of Its Independence', *New Leader*, 4 October 1935, p. 5.

announcement of limited League of Nations sanctions. The battle lines had already been drawn. The Inner Executive declared that ' "working-class sanctions" could not be distinguished publicly from League sanctions and would help to create a psychology for war against Italy'.[49] It therefore rejected the stance of Brockway, the London Divisional Council (represented on the NAC by Gaster) and the IBRSU. At the meeting of the NAC – a slightly larger body than the Inner Executive – Brockway, under pressure from the MPs who constituted the Inner Executive, reluctantly redrafted his manifesto to remove the paragraph advocating working-class sanctions against Italy.[50] The new manifesto declared: 'the conflict . . . is not worth the life of a single worker' – wisely, and in contrast to the Inner Executive's resolution, omitting the word 'British'.[51] However, no alternative policy to secure Ethiopia's continued independence was produced. The avoidance of a European war was evidently the priority. The word 'British' may still have been visible to the discerning eye.

The opposition got its chance to challenge the NAC's position at the annual conference, held in Keighley on 11–14 April 1936. In what was described by Brockway as 'a typically torrential speech', James moved reference back on the NAC's 'Report on Activity Against War' on the grounds that the party had a 'do-nothing policy on the Abyssinian war'. James's motion was carried by sixty-six votes to sixty-five, prompting further discussion on the issue.[52] However, James's speech was used by the MPs who opposed sanctions to support the argument that he was a nationalist rather than a socialist. Nationalism was considered the ultimate sin in the ILP, and some members made no distinction between an anticolonial nationalism and an expansionist European nationalism. John McGovern, one of the party's MPs, insisted that Selassie was 'as much a dictator as Mussolini'.[53] But the opposition was in the ascendant. Representatives of the Lancashire and London divisions moved a resolution stating: '[This conference] congratulates Cmde. Brockway, and endorses the line adopted by him on the sanctions issue. Conference

---

49  Brockway, *Inside the Left*, p. 326.

50  BLPES, ILP, COLL MISC 0702/11, Meeting of NAC, 9 October 1935, p. 2.

51  ILP, *Annual Report of the NAC, 1936* (London, 1936), pp. 15–16.

52  Brockway, *Inside the Left*, p. 326; ILP, *Official Report of the 44th Annual Conference, 1936* (London, 1936), p. 3.

53  Brockway, *Inside the Left*, pp. 326–7.

disassociates itself from the declaration of the Inner Executive of the NAC as published in the *New Leader* of September 13th, 1935. It considers this declaration to be in direct conflict with declared Party policy.'[54]

The resolution was carried by seventy votes to fifty-seven. It appeared the leadership had been defeated. But later that evening, Maxton, in Gidon Cohen's words, 'effectively blackmailed' the conference, tendering his resignation as party chair and as a member of the NAC. He said that fellow MPs McGovern and Campbell Stephen would follow him.[55] He insisted that 'the Parliamentary Group was unable conscientiously to carry out the policy endorsed by Conference'.[56] Brockway feared a split, and predicted that most of the party would rally to Maxton. He later remembered:

> I decided on a compromise and when James Carmichael proposed a ballot of the membership I agreed at once, though without any illusions about the result. I knew it was inevitable that the vote would be influenced more by the desire to retain Maxton and his colleagues than by the political issue. I myself drafted the compromise resolution and moved it at the conference the next day.[57]

Brockway and Carmichael's new statement carried the following day at conference by ninety-three votes to thirty-nine. It reaffirmed the ILP's 'opposition to capitalist and imperialist war', and prompted a ballot vote of the membership on the issue of working-class sanctions.[58] James later remembered that Brockway had come to talk to him about his suggested compromise. He supported the resolution, calling it his 'first experience of big politics'.[59] Within the following month, the ILP published a pamphlet containing the arguments for and against sanctions, with contributions from six prominent ILP members. In his contribution, James appealed to the anticolonial policy decided at the ILP's 1935 annual conference as well as the IBRSU's resolution on Ethiopia. He

---

54  ILP, *Official Report of the 44th Annual Conference, 1936*, p. 3.

55  Cohen, *Failure of a Dream*, p. 121.

56  Brockway, *Inside the Left*, p. 327.

57  Ibid., p. 327. Cohen also convincingly argues that Maxton's position was further strengthened by the fact that the immediate crisis had passed. Cohen, *Failure of a Dream*, p. 175.

58  ILP, *Official Report of the 44th Annual Conference, 1936*, p. 5.

59  Al Richardson, Clarence Chrysostom and Anna Grimshaw, *C. L. R. James and British Trotskyism* (London, 1987), p. 3.

repudiated the most popular arguments of his opponents, arguing that the primary conflict was between Italy and Ethiopia, and not between Italy and Britain. He asserted that Ethiopia was feudal rather than capitalist, and should therefore be treated as a '*colonial* nation' rather than a 'small nation'. He wrote that the ILP leadership, by pretending there existed an equivalence between capitalist-imperialist Italy and feudal Ethiopia, and therefore declaring neutrality, 'justif[ied] every past, present and future raid by capitalism against a colonial people'.[60]

James's position was supported in the pamphlet by Brockway and Bob Edwards of the NAC. Edwards also appealed to existing ILP and IBRSU policy. He turned McGovern's accusations of nationalism against James around on him, stating that McGovern had himself declared a duty to the British working class. But McGovern had failed to realise that the interests of the British working class were 'inseparably linked with those of the colonial and exploited peoples of the world'.[61] Like James, Brockway urged the distinction between capitalist Italy and feudal Ethiopia. He stated that the implementation of workers' sanctions 'would not be anti-Italian and pro-British. It would be anti-Imperialist'.[62]

The opposing view was presented by Maxton, McGovern and Joseph Southall. Of the two MPs, Maxton took the more diplomatic approach. He acknowledged that his 'natural sympathies' were with Ethiopia. If the aggression had been that of Britain rather than Italy, the ILP's task would have been 'to try in every way possible to overthrow capitalist power in Britain'. However, in this instance, it was in the interest of British imperialism that Italian imperialism be defeated. In this case, the Inner Executive 'could not see the distinctions' between the different forms of sanctions. Maxton added, revealing that his greatest motivation for opposing sanctions was fear of another European war: 'It is regrettable that numbers of Abyssinians have died in anguish, it is equally regrettable that numbers of Italians have also lost their lives. It would not have been any less regrettable if numbers of Britons had died alongside of them, and it would have been criminal if Europe had been allowed to become again one vast battlefield'.[63]

---

60  ILP, *Italy and Abyssinia: Should British Workers Take Sides?* (London, 1936), pp. 13–15. Emphasis in original.

61  Ibid., pp. 3–5.

62  Ibid., pp. 8–10.

63  Ibid., pp. 5–7.

McGovern's intervention was more heavy-handed. He again compared Mussolini and Selassie, this time adding: 'in my estimation the rule of the Negus is the more brutal one'. He appealed to precedent by citing the ILP's decision not to support imperialist war in the name of defending Belgium from German aggression at the outbreak of the First World War. He even added that the case for defending Belgium was stronger than the case for siding with Ethiopia, 'due to [Belgium's] people being more civilised'. He urged the ILP membership to concentrate on ending the system of capitalist rivalry rather than being 'diverted by sentimental hysteria'.[64]

The wording of the plebiscite was decided in May 1936 at a meeting of the Executive Committee, to which six branches sent protests against the leadership's refusal to accept the conference decision.[65] But the matter was somewhat academic by now; an Italian victory had already been declared. Party members were asked two yes-or-no questions. The first asked: 'Should the ILP have declared against Italy and in favour of Abyssinia by advocating the refusal of War Materials to Italy?' The second asked: 'Should the ILP have refused to back either Italy or Abyssinia and opposed the sending of War Materials to either side?'[66] The party leadership had seemingly compromised its position on refusing to send war materials to Italy, but now advocated a position that also sanctioned Ethiopia. The results of the ballot were announced in July 1936. Question 1 was answered in the negative by 734 votes to 576, while Question 2 was answered positively by 809 votes to 354. Protests against the 'form of the questions' were sent by twenty-one branches, including James's branch of Finchley and Hendon. The Gateshead and Watford branches even refused to vote at all. Nevertheless, the ballot granted the NAC a mandate to adopt a statement of war policy based on Maxton's position, which was adopted unanimously.[67]

The Ethiopian question is a useful case study in examining what Anne-Isabelle Richard calls 'the limits of solidarity'.[68] While Richard

---

64  Ibid., pp. 11–13.

65  BLPES, ILP, COLL MISC 702/12, Meeting of Executive Committee, 23 May 1936.

66  ILP, *Annual Report of the NAC, 1937*, p. 21.

67  BLPES, ILP/3/74, Brockway, 'An Urgent Call to the Party', 8 July 1936.

68  Anne-Isabelle Richard, 'The Limits of Solidarity: Europeanism, Anti-Colonialism and Socialism at the Congress of the Peoples of Europe, Asia and Africa in Puteaux, 1948', *European Review of History* 21 (2014).

uses the phrase to refer to disagreements between European and colonial activists at a 1948 congress in Paris, it also taps into a recurring phenomenon of metropolitan and colonial socialists adopting divergent political positions. But it should be noted that James took with him a majority of delegates at the 1936 ILP conference – the 'limits of solidarity' crossed metropolitan and colonial divides, and James found himself in greater political agreement with Brockway than with Makonnen. The Ethiopia crisis provoked particularly fierce debates, but was not the only occasion in this period in which tensions between socialism, anticolonialism, nationalism and anti-war principles led to conflict, even within the ILP itself. Also at the 1936 conference, James moved an addendum to the Basic Resolution on Imperialism, India and the Colonies. It stated: 'British workers must realise the necessity of helping to foster revolutionary movements in the colonies, and the formation of principled united fronts with nationalist movements of a bourgeois character, because these movements represent a step towards the achievement of Workers' Power in these countries.' The delegates were again split down the middle, and James's addendum was carried by sixty-three votes to sixty.[69]

The vote points to the divisions within the ILP about whether anticolonialism that was not strictly proletarian should be embraced. During the sanctions debate, Maxton seemingly contradicted the position he had taken in a 1934 *Labour Monthly* questionnaire. He had responded to the question, 'What is your attitude towards a war of a colonial people for liberation from British Imperialism?' with 'Support for the people who are fighting for liberation.'[70] Perhaps he differentiated between British and Italian imperialism – or, more likely, did not have in mind a war for colonial liberation that had the potential to spill over into Europe. At the following annual conference, the NAC reaffirmed its position in the Resolution to Resist War, which advocated 'Opposition to sanctions imposed for Imperialist purposes and involving the danger of war'.[71] But it would be a mistake to characterise large swathes of the ILP in this period as unconcerned with African liberation in particular. Maxton later revealed his consistency when he expressed great relief at

---

69  ILP, *Official Report of the 44th Annual Conference, 1936*, p. 9.

70  Glasgow City Archives, Mitchell Library, James Maxton papers, TD/956/7/23, Maxton to R. P. Dutt, 1 July 1934.

71  ILP, *Final Agenda of Resolutions and Amendments: Forty-fifth Annual Conference, 1937* (London, 1937), p. 18.

the Munich Agreement – which saw war averted through the sacrifice of a European nation's sovereignty.[72]

One of the most enduring arguments about the ILP's decision to reject sanctions is that it was motivated by pacifism. Minkah Makalani, Marc Matera and Susan Pennybacker make this case, despite the ILP's unequivocal support for armed conflict in Spain only months later.[73] Maxton's response to the *Labour Monthly* questionnaire suggested support for anticolonial armed struggle, at least in theory. As William Knox has observed, what distinguished the Spanish Civil War from the Italo-Ethiopian War for Maxton was that 'this was a workers' fight'.[74] The ILP leadership's anti-war position was grounded in opposition to *imperialist* war, rather than a nebulous pacifism. Figures like Maxton and McGovern may not have appreciated the anti-imperialist significance of the Ethiopian struggle, but their opposition to sanctions was couched in opposition to British imperialism. They did not decry anti-imperialist armed struggle in general, but rather preferred to see Ethiopia as a 'small' nation rather than a colonial nation. Furthermore, defending Ethiopia meant in practice defending an authoritarian emperor, rather than a workers' movement, as was the case in Spain.

In 1935 and 1936, therefore, the ILP was undergoing a clash of priorities and analyses. Brockway prioritised his anti-imperialism over other concerns, but compromised to keep Maxton in a leadership position. James soon left the ILP with his Trotskyist comrades. Even then, he was able to cooperate closely with the ILP, indicating that the differences were not as fundamental as they might have appeared. Maxton was always less theoretically engaged with the ILP's new militant anti-colonialism than figures like Brockway. He and the parliamentary group desired colonial liberation, but, perhaps pessimistically or cynically, argued that they could envisage no way in which Ethiopia's independence could be maintained. Either way, African liberation was the first principle to be sacrificed. An inter-imperialist war was to be avoided at

---

72  James Maxton, *Maxton's Speech in Parliament* (London, 1938).

73  Minkah Makalani, *In the Cause of Freedom: Radical Black Internationalism from Harlem to London, 1917–1939* (Chapel Hill, NC, 2011), p. 201; Marc Matera, *Black London: The Imperial Metropolis and Decolonization in the Twentieth Century* (Oakland, CA, 2015), p. 79; Susan D. Pennybacker, *From Scottsboro to Munich: Race and Political Culture in 1930s Britain* (Princeton, 2009), p. 88.

74  William Knox, *James Maxton* (Manchester, 1987), p. 125.

almost all costs; a colonial conquest was not. But the ILP now integrated anti-imperialism into its broader political philosophy, as it had failed to do with the Socialism in Our Time programme. If five years earlier anti-imperialism had been a minor concern, now it had come closer than any issue, barring the ILP's relationships with the Labour and Communist parties, to splitting the party in two.

There was also no neat cleavage between 'British' socialism on one side and Black radicalism on the other. Black activists were more likely to prioritise Ethiopian sovereignty while White activists were more likely to be concerned with avoiding an inter-imperialist war. Yet James's position shows a deep overlap between the concerns of pan-Africanism and socialism in Europe, predicated on the idea of international revolution. Furthermore, before Maxton's threatened resignation, James had managed to win more than half the annual conference delegates to his position – had the question of sanctions been a practical and not a theoretical one at the time of the plebiscite, the opposition might well have won that vote. James distanced himself from the IAFE when intervening in the ILP sanctions debate. This was partly because he realised that his association with that group would strengthen accusations of nationalism from the ILP leadership, but also because of a genuine political disagreement with its position on League of Nations sanctions. It was no accident that James broke with the IAFE in October 1935: the moment of Italy's invasion of Ethiopia, but also of his first public statement of support for workers' sanctions. He found greater political kinship with the Trotskyists and Brockway's group in the ILP than he did with his pan-Africanist comrades. But this did not lead to a fundamental rupture. His fiercest criticisms were reserved for those in the ILP who, like Maxton, opposed all sanctions. But again, this did not cause a permanent rift. While Black radicals continued to criticise the ILP's Ethiopia position, there was a continued recognition on both sides that metropolitan and colonial workers should continue the fight against capitalist-imperialism together.


## Padmore, James, and the British Left after the Italo-Ethiopian War


James was not the only member of the IAFE to be frustrated by the ILP's position on Ethiopia. George Padmore, who in a matter of years would be editing the ILP's journal, reacted fiercely to the ILP's opposition to sanctions. In *How Britain Rules Africa*, the book on which Padmore was working during the crisis, he complained: 'There are many socialists in Britain, like Sir Stafford Cripps of the Socialist League, James Maxton and Fenner Brockway, leaders of the Independent Labour Party, who are also opposed to the application of sanctions against the fascist warmongers.' It seemed that Padmore had misunderstood Cripps's and Brockway's position, treating their opposition to League of Nations sanctions as identical to Maxton's opposition to all sanctions. He further misrepresented Brockway by attributing the ILP's October 1935 statement that the conflict was 'not worth the life of a single worker' solely to Brockway, rather than to the NAC collectively (Brockway had only reluctantly redrafted the manifesto).[75] Interestingly, Padmore's source for this attack on Brockway was the CPGB's *Daily Worker*. The *Daily Worker* claimed that Brockway believed Ethiopian independence to be of 'no concern for the British working-class', and that he had dismissed the issue 'as merely a quarrel between British and Italian imperialism'. Padmore then lifted this Communist analysis of Brockway and quoted it in *How Britain Rules Africa*.[76] There is an irony that, despite recent Communist slanders against him, Padmore in 1935 still took Communists at their word when discussing Brockway. His alignment in this instance with the CPGB against the ILP should further dispel any notion of an abrupt rupture in Padmore's relationship with organised Communism.

Despite Padmore's hostility (albeit based on a misunderstanding), Cripps wrote the foreword to Padmore's next book, *Africa and World Peace* (1937). Padmore here showed a clearer understanding of Brockway's and the Socialist League's position of support for workers' sanctions. He instead attacked the ILP's parliamentary group for 'declaring that Haile Selassie and Mussolini were no different'. Observing the lack of unity within the British left, Padmore called the situation 'revolutionary comic-opera'.[77] Reginald Reynolds, in his review for the *New Leader*, pointed to the section on Ethiopia as the weakest in an otherwise strong book: 'Padmore shows us the failure of "Collective Security" and its causes. He fails, however, to examine the nature of the League and its "security" in relation to Socialism.'[78]

---

75  Padmore, *How Britain Rules Africa*, pp. 15–16.

76  'The ILP Leaders' Role', *Daily Worker*, 11 October 1935, p. 2; Padmore, *How Britain Rules Africa*, pp. 15–16.

77  Padmore, *Africa and World Peace*, p. 154.

78  Reginald Reynolds, 'Skeletons of Empire', *New Leader*, 2 July 1937, p. 5.

In the book, Padmore also criticised H. N. Brailsford's writing on Ethiopia. Brailsford was a journalist and Socialist League member. Before the invasion he expressed sympathy for Ethiopia and criticised League of Nations manoeuvres against Ethiopian sovereignty.[79] However, the following year he made the case for the Spanish Civil War being worthier of British workers' attention than the Ethiopian war had been. Spanish workers were fighting against two dictatorships 'planning to enslave Europe', whereas 'Abyssinians had a claim to our help and our fellow-feeling, but this backward country had nothing to give to civilisation; it was a feudal kingdom outside the fraternity that links workers the world over.'[80] Brailsford, like Maxton, distinguished between Ethiopia and Spain in a way that was unacceptable for pan-Africanists. In *Africa and World Peace*, Padmore retorted:

> When one reads such utterances as those by Mr. Brailsford . . . one cannot help feeling that had it been Abyssinians raining death from the air upon a white people – even if these white folks were among those 'outside the fraternity that links workers the world over' – that European Socialists would not merely have passed pious resolutions on behalf of the victim, but would have aroused the working classes into action.[81]

Padmore viewed the ILP sanctions decision and Brailsford's depiction of Ethiopians as betrayals. However, contrary to Worrell's claim, this did not lead him to abandon faith in the European proletarian revolution. In fact, Padmore reacted so strongly against this betrayal precisely because he viewed the European revolution as an essential element within his projected world revolution. Padmore concluded his attack on Brockway in *How Britain Rules Africa* by stating: 'So far as the Africans are concerned, Mr Brockway and other advisers of the British working class can rest assured that while they regret to learn that "Abyssinia's independence is no concern of the British working class", the Blacks will fight for their country's independence so as not to involve "the life of a single

<hr>

79  H. N. Brailsford, 'International Notes', *Socialist Leaguer*, 15 February 1935; H. N. Brailsford, 'International Notes', *Socialist Leaguer*, March–April 1935, pp. 155–6.

80  H. N. Brailsford, 'Must Europe Play the Coward?', *Reynolds News*, 16 August 1936, p. 4.

81  Padmore, *Africa and World Peace*, p. 155.

worker".[82] Here Padmore continued to recognise the agency of African peoples struggling against European imperialism. But his bitterness towards Brockway betrayed his view that the British working class, were they not misled by their leaders, would have been an invaluable ally in the struggle. This analysis was a continuation of Padmore's theory of interdependent metropolitan and colonial revolutions, which he had followed since his Communist days.

James continued his attack on the ILP's Ethiopia position from inside his Trotskyist faction, the Marxist Group. In the first issue of the group's journal, *Fight*, published in October 1936, the ILP's MPs were branded 'opportunists'. The article, likely written by James as the journal's editor, argued that Brockway had originally taken the correct line, but 'climbed down' because he 'preferred peace to principle'.[83] There was a degree of political dishonesty here, as James had also supported Brockway's compromise at the annual conference. For James and the Marxist Group, however, Brockway's equivocation over Ethiopia raised questions about his political reliability.

But James was also not completely at home within the British Trotskyist movement. He later claimed that Padmore had been accused of racial chauvinism by his Communist comrades in the United States, and that he himself had been accused of racial chauvinism by certain Trotskyists during his time with the IAFE.[84] James's believed that his reading of Lenin and Trotsky supported his and Padmore's position – that a celebration of Blackness, unlike White chauvinism, was not about establishing superiority, but about establishing equality. This position was reaffirmed by his 1939 meeting with Trotsky, whom he described as sounding 'like the most extreme of the Africans'.[85] For James, then, as for Padmore, clashes with European socialists in practice were not enough to deter them from Marxism in theory, or from the necessity of working with European socialists. For every Brailsford or McGovern, there was a

---

82  Padmore, *How Britain Rules Africa*, p. 16.

83  'Will Brockway Swallow This Too?', *Fight*, 10 October 1936, p. 6.

84  C. L. R. James papers, box 5 folder 21, C. L. R. James, 'Notes on the Life of George Padmore', pp. 8, 30. F. A. Ridley also remembered that many Trotskyists disapproved of James because they saw him as a nationalist, but Harry Wicks denied that he personally believed James to be a nationalist. C. L. R. James papers, box 28 interior box 4, James remembered by F. A. Ridley, 13 August 1986; C. L. R. James papers, box 28 interior box 4, James remembered by Harry Wicks, 30 April 1985.

85  James, 'Notes on the Life of George Padmore', p. 31.

Trotsky or Cunard to reinforce the rectitude of their position as the true heirs of Marx and Lenin.

Indeed, another important ally of the IAFE was Sylvia Pankhurst, a leading suffragette who became a central figure in interwar revolutionary socialist and anti-imperialist circles.[86] During the early 1920s, she collaborated with Claude McKay, the famous Jamaican Marxist writer, granting him a platform to express his anti-imperialist ideas in her newspaper, the *Workers' Dreadnought*.[87] After the Italian invasion of Ethiopia, she launched the *New Times and Ethiopia News*, which brought together antifascist and anticolonial voices committed to defending Ethiopia's sovereignty.[88] Throughout the war and the subsequent Italian occupation, Pankhurst corresponded and shared platforms with Ashwood Garvey, Kenyatta, Makonnen and Padmore. Pankhurst, like the IAFE, believed that the Italian 'conquest' of Ethiopia did not mean that the struggle was over, and continued to agitate for Ethiopia's liberation. In 1938, Padmore wrote to Pankhurst that the *New Times and Ethiopia News* was 'more necessary now than ever to hold high the banner of Abyssinian freedom'.[89]


## A Convergence of Antifascism and Anti-Imperialism: The CPGB and Ethiopia

While the IAFE's relationship with the ILP endured an intense yet short-lived test during the Ethiopian crisis, its relationship with the CPGB and the Comintern was in the early phases of a prolonged tension. This tension originated in Padmore's discontent with the CPGB, which had emerged when he worked for the International Trade Union Committee of Negro Workers (ITUCNW), and his eventual dismissal from the Comintern, and in James's embrace of Trotskyism after his return to London from Nelson. However, it was exacerbated by the Comintern's turn to the Popular Front.

---

86  Katherine Connelly, *Sylvia Pankhurst: Suffragette, Socialist and Scourge of Empire* (London, 2013).

87  Winston James, 'In the Nest of Extreme Radicalism: Radical Networks and the Bolshevization of Claude McKay in London', *Comparative American Studies* 15 (2017).

88  Connelly, *Sylvia Pankhurst*, Chapter 7; Srivastava, *Italian Colonialism*, Chapter 5.

89  Richard Pankhurst, *Sylvia Pankhurst: Counsel for Ethiopia* (Hollywood, CA, 2003), p. 75.

During the Third Period, beginning in 1928, the Comintern had enthusi-astically if crudely supported left-wing anticolonial movements almost unconditionally. The rise of fascism, and particularly the ascent of Hitler in 1933, spooked Moscow. The Comintern, dominated by the foreign policy interests of the Soviet Union, turned increasingly to Western liberal democracies to form antifascist alliances. The Soviet Union joined the League of Nations in September 1934 and signed a treaty of mutual assis-tance with France in May 1935. As part of this realignment, the Soviet Union began to moderate its anti-imperialism in order to preserve its relationships with antifascist elements in the colonial powers of Britain and France. At the Seventh Congress of the Comintern, in the summer of 1935, the 'Class against Class' policy was officially abandoned in favour of pursuing a Popular Front of socialists and liberals against fascism. This decision plagued the relationship between Black radicals and the CPGB for the remainder of the 1930s. More immediately, it had implications for the CPGB's position on Ethiopia.

James, like Makonnen, regarded the period as one of open hostility between Black activists and the CPGB.[90] James acknowledged that, before the Popular Front period, the CPGB had taken up many colonial issues, and often granted a platform to grateful colonial nationalists.[91] Several of the IAFE's members, including Padmore and Kenyatta, were deeply involved with Communist politics before 1935, but turned away from them with the adoption of the Popular Front policy (dramatically in Padmore's case, gradually in Kenyatta's). James recalled that Chris Jones, a Barbadian activist, had previously been a Communist, but was 'very bitter' about the Popular Front strategy. He would join James and Padmore in going to Communist meetings in order to criticise it.[92]

In general terms, James was correct that Communist anti-imperialism was compromised by the Popular Front. The Comintern and CPGB

---

90  Makonnen, though, had a different emphasis to James. He was less concerned with the turn to the Popular Front, and more concerned that Black people should 'create a movement that was free from any entanglement'. Makonnen, *Pan-Africanism from Within*, p. 117.

91  James, 'Autobiography, 1932–38', pp. 48–9. But James was also critical of the effect of the Third Period on the CPGB, saying that the proclamation of 'imminent revolution' was a 'glaring absurdity'. C. L. R. James, *World Revolution, 1917–1936: The Rise and Fall of the Communist International* (London, 1937), p. 312.

92  C. L. R. James papers, box 12 folder 8, Alan J. Mackenzie, 'Marxism and Black Nationalism: A Discussion with C. L. R. James' (c. 1975), p. 5.

became willing to sacrifice aspects of their programme in the name of maintaining or creating antifascist alliances; but it is important to recognise that, where there was a confluence between anti-imperialism and antifascism, the CPGB retained much of its old militancy. The Ethiopian crisis was such a case. Large sections of the Communist movement were probably more motivated by waging an antifascist struggle against Mussolini's Italy than by concern for the sovereignty of Ethiopia. From a Communist perspective, however, these issues converged. James may have been critical of Communist appeals to the League of Nations, suspecting ulterior motives. But other members of the IAFE, such as Kenyatta, found in the Communist press an outlet to express their revolutionary anticolonialism. Thus, even though the Popular Front strained relations between Black radicals and the Communist movement, the Ethiopia crisis nevertheless demonstrates both the residual anticolonialist commitments of the Communist movement and the ongoing entanglement of pan-Africanism with Western socialism.

CPGB policy on Ethiopia followed the dictates of Soviet foreign policy. At a meeting of the League of Nations Council in September 1935, the Soviet commissar for foreign affairs, Maxim Litvinov, declared his support for the imposition of League sanctions against Italy.[93] The CPGB stated its policy in the 2 October edition of the *Daily Worker*, the day before the invasion. The statement duly called for the stoppage of all war materials to Italy and the closing of the Suez Canal to Italian transport, as well as the removal of the ban on the export of arms to Ethiopia. Furthermore, the CPGB, following its analysis that the National Government was sympathetic to fascism and becoming increasingly fascistic itself, called for a 'redoubling' of efforts to defeat the government and secure the return of Labour to power. Finally, the statement called for a nationwide programme of meetings, demonstrations and conferences to demand the maintenance of Ethiopia's independence.[94] In contrast with the situation within the ILP, where debates were taking place about the nature of Selassie's regime, there was no doubt within the CPGB that Italy was the imperialist aggressor attempting to colonise an African nation.

---

93  Paul Corthorn, *In the Shadow of the Dictators: The British Left in the 1930s* (New York, 2006), p. 49.

94  'What the Communists Stand For', *Daily Worker*, 2 October 1935, p. 1.

Indeed, as the CPGB met at a special national conference on 6 October, R. P. Dutt spelled out the CPGB's differences with the ILP and the Socialist League. He argued that their rivals' position, with its emphasis on avoiding war in Europe, had an 'imperialist basis' revealing 'a deeply British outlook' – a criticism with which many Black radicals no doubt agreed. Dutt, following Popular Front antifascist analysis, declared that the crisis was not simply a question of anticolonial struggle. Ethiopia was also 'the immediate centre of the world fascist attack', and thus a concern to all who valued world socialism in general and the Soviet Union in particular.[95] Like Maxton, Dutt made no distinction between League of Nations sanctions and workers' sanctions, but from a different perspective. In Dutt's analysis, reactionary governments like Britain's offered only minimal support to League sanctions because they did not want Italy to be defeated: 'that means a defeat and a check to reaction all over Europe'. Instead, it was the duty of the British working class to force its own government to support sanctions through collective action.[96]

The CPGB's position rested on the logic of the Popular Front, seeking collective security through the League of Nations. CPGB member Emile Burns argued that the response to the Italian invasion proved that the League had undergone a change in character. For Burns, Soviet membership of the League and its alliance with France 'to check German aggression' showed that the League was 'no longer *merely* the instrument of a few capitalist Powers whose supremacy is unchallenged'. Nonetheless, Britain's 'support of German rearmament' and its willingness to make a deal with Italy for the partition of Ethiopia showed 'that in other respects the League of Nations has not changed'.[97] Unlike the ILP and Trotskyists, the CPGB looked to the League as an imperfect but potentially progressive force. This was because, to the Communists, the most important index of progressiveness was antifascism. Their anticapitalism and anticolonialism were significantly moderated. In their view, the Ethiopian crisis was simply a microcosm of the essential political division of the age. On one side were those who sought imperialist war and rejected collective security, such as fascist governments and 'reactionaries' in liberal democracies who were sympathetic to fascism. On the other side were

---

95  R. P. Dutt, *Decisive Days Ahead* (London, 1935), pp. 18–20.
96  Ibid., p. 23.
97  Emile Burns, *Abyssinia and Italy* (London, 1935), pp. 135–7. Emphasis in original.

socialists and 'progressive' capitalists who embraced the principle of collective security.

Thus, in February 1936, Dutt wrote that, since the revelation of the Hoare–Laval Pact (a British–French plot for the partition of Ethiopia) in December 1935, 'the war-making forces in the world situation, both in Germany and Japan, and also in the dominant reactionary circles in Britain and France, are advancing their offensive in opposition to the line of collective security'. These reactionary forces were contrasted with the 'mass movement of sympathy with the Abyssinian struggle, fusing into a single force all the popular sympathies of the fight for peace, of the colonial struggle for liberation and of the fight against the hated fascist tyrannies'.[98] Dutt's article located the Ethiopian war within the broad concern of the CPGB's Popular Front: against fascism and war.[99] The colonial struggle for liberation was, in the case of Ethiopia, an important corollary of Popular Front antifascism. As we will see in subsequent chapters, however, it was a principle that would be sacrificed when it came into conflict with the CPGB's primary concerns. Within Dutt's division between progressive and reactionary forces, those on the left who undermined collective security through attacks on the League of Nations were objectively on the side of the reactionaries.

Unsurprisingly, ILP and SL members publicly criticised the Communist position. In September 1935, the SL's Barbara Betts opined that 'the Communist attitude to the Abyssinian question is dictated, not so much by the desire for Abyssinia's freedom as by fear of Fascism and particularly of Fascist aggression against the Soviet Union'.[100] The most fervent attack from the ILP came from the Trotskyist James. Writing two weeks after the ILP NAC had agreed not to advocate any form of sanctions, James argued that the CPGB, 'instead of following its own class policy, is doing exactly what Litvinov is doing at Geneva'. He declared that revolutions in other countries would be sacrificed for the sake of Soviet foreign policy, and warned his readers that there was 'no salvation in Geneva for the workers, none for Ethiopians'.[101]

---

98  Dutt, 'Notes of the Month', *Labour Monthly*, February 1936, pp. 69–81.

99  See Kevin Morgan, *Against Fascism and War: Ruptures and Continuities in British Communist Politics, 1935–41* (Manchester, 1989).

100  Barbara Betts, 'International Notes', *Socialist*, September 1935, p. 2.

101  C. L. R. James, 'The Workers and Sanctions: Why the ILP and the Communists Take an Opposite View', *New Leader*, 25 October 1935, p. 4.

R. F. Andrews responded in the *Daily Worker*, identifying the ILP's argument against sanctions as identical to that of 'National Government spokesmen in Parliament'. He observed that even arguments in favour of workers' sanctions had recently disappeared from the *New Leader* (and were also absent from James's article). He further chided James for lapsing into 'unaccountable silence' when discussing 'what Litvinov is doing at Geneva'. For Andrews, the Soviet Union's 'readiness to sacrifice trade and, maybe, diplomatic relations with a great Power in order to defend a small, semi-colonial struggling people' was 'not such a bad lead for class-conscious workers all over the world'.[102]

The CPGB's position on Ethiopia found more support from other sections of the IAFE. In September 1935, Kenyatta, as the IAFE's honorary secretary, was given space in the CPGB's *Labour Monthly* to voice his analysis of the conflict. He also attended a CPGB meeting in Clerkenwell.[103] Although Kenyatta had enjoyed a tumultuous relationship with the Communist movement, there was sufficient consonance between their ideas about the Ethiopian crisis for Kenyatta to be brought back into the fold. He identified the invasion of Ethiopia as 'the culmination of a historical process' that had begun with the partition of Africa during the 1880s. Kenyatta applied a Leninist analysis to the invasion: Italy, late to the colonial table and not a major beneficiary at Versailles in 1919, was motivated by the 'economic advantages' of capitalist-imperialism. Kenyatta's plea to save Ethiopia was pan-Africanist; a more global socialism (or at least antifascism) was for him a secondary concern: 'The honest Ethiopian has perhaps a chance of coming into his own, but only with the support, political, financial and moral, of all Africans and people of African descent as well as with the co-operation of all who are concerned with the overthrow of Fascism all over the world.' Kenyatta, retaining his chameleon-like quality, knew the right buttons to press when writing for a Communist publication ('To support Ethiopia is to fight Fascism').[104] Yet it was clear that he saw resistance in Africa and the diaspora, rather than attempts by the European working class to pressure their governments into supporting League of Nations sanctions, as the most likely salvation of Ethiopia.

---

102  R. F. Andrews, 'War and Mr James: The Muddle of the ILP', *Daily Worker*, 28 October 1935, p. 2.

103  TNA, KV 2/1787 (Kenyatta), 3 September 1935.

104  Johnstone Kenyatta, 'Hands off Abyssinia!', *Labour Monthly*, September 1935.

Of course, another associate of the IAFE who supported the Communist position, and more fully than Kenyatta, was Arnold Ward. As we have seen, Ward spoke at the IAFE's Trafalgar Square rally on 25 August 1935. This was a meeting at which IAFE members advocated League sanctions, pointing to the political affinity between the CPGB and some members of the IAFE. However, Ward's relationship with the CPGB continued to be strained by what he saw as a dissonance between its theory and practice, much as Padmore's had been before his split from the Comintern. In June 1935, Ward wrote to the Comintern that the 'inactivity' of the CPGB and League Against Imperialism on the 'Abyssinian question' had done 'a lot of harm' to the Negro Welfare Association, of which Ward was secretary.[105] Nevertheless, Ward continued to support CPGB policy, as expressed at the annual conference of the NWA in October 1935.[106]

Whether during the anticolonial militancy of the Third Period or during a moment of anti-imperialist confluence with the antifascism of the Popular Front, it seemed that, at least according to the party's Black activists, there were deficiencies in the implementation of the CPGB's anti-imperialist theories. As evidenced by the CPGB's interventions and policy on Ethiopia, its primary concern was creating a Popular Front against fascism, which in turn was motivated by the desire to defend the Soviet Union. In the Ethiopian case, there was no conflict between its anti-imperialism and its antifascism – indeed, they complemented each other. In later episodes, when British or French imperialism was under fire, the CPGB would not benefit from such a confluence, and would not be able to enjoy productive relationships with activists such as Kenyatta.

## James's Trotskyism, the Popular Front, and the Break from the ILP

The fiercest attacks on the CPGB from the British pan-Africanist movement came from James. Summarising the decisions of the 1935 Seventh Congress of the Comintern, he wrote: 'henceforth monopoly Capitalism

---

105  RGASPI, 495/155/102, Letter from Ward, 26 June 1935.
106  'Conference of the Negro Welfare Association', *Negro Worker*, December 1935, pp. 8–9.

did not lead inevitably to imperialist war, war could be prevented, the world was divided into peace-loving democratic Capitalisms like France and Czechoslovakia, and war-making Capitalisms like Japan and Germany, Russia's enemies'.[107] Much of this criticism was informed by James's Trotskyism. This meant that, unlike for most pan-Africanists, James's criticisms of Communism extended far beyond the weaknesses of the movement's anti-imperialism. While Black radical frustrations with Communist anticolonialism often led to criticisms of the Popular Front, James was particularly engaged with the broader implications of the strategy.

In Britain, the Popular Front was more aspiration than reality. In France and Spain, however, Popular Front governments were formed in 1936. This resulted in Communists siding with capitalist and imperialist governments in struggles against more revolutionary elements of the socialist movement. James and the Marxist Group insisted that the CPGB leadership was aware that it was workers' struggle, rather than the Popular Front government, that had gained 'paper concessions' for French workers in the summer of 1936. However, the CPGB leadership fought for the Popular Front 'because [Harry] Pollitt, [J. R.] Campbell and the rest of them are carrying out Stalin's orders and using the working-class movement for the benefit of Soviet foreign policy'.[108] But it is important to realise that, for James, there was no distinction between Communist errors in anti-imperialist strategy and Communist errors in other spheres of activity. The Communist who abandoned the anticolonial revolution in order to appease the French government betrayed striking French workers for the same reason.

James quickly became a leading figure in the Marxist Group. Louise Cripps remembers that the group's journal, *Fight*, was launched at James's insistence.[109] James served as editor, and wrote much of the material himself. The first edition appeared in October 1936, and opened with an attack on the Popular Front. It stated that the ongoing Spanish Civil War had proved that 'the population of the world is divided into two camps, not war-loving States and peaceful, democratic States, but the workers

107　James, *World Revolution*, pp. 385–6.
108　'The Popular Front in Britain', *Fight*, 12 December 1936, p. 2.
109　Louise Cripps, *C. L. R. James: Memories and Commentaries* (New York, 1997), p. 24.

and exploited peasants on the one side and landlords and capitalists on the other, with the lower middle classes wavering uncertainly in between'.[110]

The most thorough expression of James's Trotskyism was *World Revolution, 1917–1936* (1937). The left-wing anti-Stalinist publisher, Fredric Warburg, had approached Brockway looking for suitable writers. Brockway suggested James, who easily convinced Warburg of the necessity of the book. Harry Wicks offered James much assistance, lending him Bolshevik texts collected in Moscow and commenting on his drafts, as did Charlie Lahr, who advised James about relevant literature and the German political landscape.[111] James set out to tell the history of the origin of the Comintern, as well as 'its collapse as a revolutionary force'. He declared that the book was based on 'the fundamental ideas of Marxism', which, James argued, had since 1923 'been expounded chiefly by Trotsky and a small band of collaborators'.[112]

James praised the Leninist confluence of anticapitalism and anti-colonialism by citing Bolshevik support for 'the demands of the subject nationalities'.[113] Conversely, he railed against Stalin's purges (including the ongoing Moscow Trials), the Stalinist doctrine of Socialism in One Country, and the growing personal wealth of the Soviet bureaucracy. In a premonition of the 1937 Barcelona May Days, James remarked: 'The day is near when the Stalinists will join reactionary governments in shooting revolutionary workers.' Faced with the only choice in 'imperialist war', between capitalism and the revolutionary workers, Stalinism would side with the former.[114] James nonetheless believed that the Bolshevik Revolution, while bruised and bloodied, was still alive, and might find further expression through the Soviet proletariat, which would be buoyed by global revolutionary movements.[115]

*World Revolution*, noted Warburg, 'sold moderately well, if you apply low enough standards of sale to it'.[116] The book was the subject of a debate in *Controversy*, the left-wing discussion journal published by the ILP.

---

110 'The Need for a New International', *Fight*, 10 October 1936, p. 1.

111 Harry Wicks, *Keeping My Head: The Memoirs of a British Bolshevik* (London, 1992), p. 180; James, 'Autobiography, 1932–38', pp. 48–51.

112 James, *World Revolution*, p. xi.

113 Ibid., p. 86.

114 Ibid., p. 389.

115 Ibid., p. 421.

116 Fredric Warburg, *An Occupation for Gentlemen* (London, 1959), p. 215.

J. R. Campbell represented the CPGB, Wicks the Trotskyist movement. Campbell diagnosed James with 'political dementia', saying that he was 'the industrious apprentice who has wallowed in the literature of Trotskyism'. Branding Trotskyists 'saboteurs', Campbell cited the call of Trotskyists to form Soviets during the 1936 French general strike as evidence of their not being able to tell the 'difference between a risky strike movement and a revolutionary crisis'. Wicks, meanwhile, defended James's arguments and attacked the Popular Front: 'Lenin's banner, against national unity, against any concessions to national defence, for the revolutionary struggle against one's own government, has been uprooted.'[117]

The book was received ambivalently by Brockway in a review for the *New Leader*. This was the culmination of a year of mounting tension between the Marxist Group and the ILP; the former had been proscribed at the April 1936 conference. The October 1936 launch of *Fight* was thus a provocative act. In December, James and the Marxist Group's secretary, Arthur Ballard, addressed a statement to the NAC to announce that the Trotskyists were leaving the ILP. Ballard was, according to James, a valuable member of the British Trotskyist movement because he was a 'gifted intellectual with a proletarian base'. The pair became close friends as well as comrades.[118] James and Ballard stated that recent events had shown that the 'behaviour of the leadership on the Abyssinian question is no isolated action but marks definitely its determination to control the party in the interests of the parliamentary group and not of the Socialist revolution'. They concluded their statement with a call for 'revolutionaries' both inside and outside the ILP to collaborate with the Marxist Group 'in laying the foundation of a revolutionary party'.[119]

Brockway's review praised the boldness and scope of *World Revolution* and agreed with many of James's criticisms of the Comintern. But he accused Trotskyists of seeing 'nothing other than the mistakes of Soviet Russia and the Communist International'. For Brockway, the

---

117 'Lunacy or Logic? Two Views of One Book', *Controversy*, May 1937, pp. 36–7. The *Daily Worker* also refused to carry an advertisement for *World Revolution*, an action criticised by both *Controversy* editor C. A. Smith and publishing house Secker and Warburg as 'censorship'. C. A. Smith, 'Censorship of the Left', *Controversy*, June 1937, pp. 41–2; 'Correspondence', *Fight*, June 1937, p. 11.

118 Richardson, Chrysostom and Grimshaw, *C. L. R. James and British Trotskyism*, p. 2.

119 Arthur Ballard and C. L. R. James, 'Towards the New Workers' Party', *Fight*, 12 December 1936, pp. 5–6.

weakest argument of the book was the call for the formation of a Fourth International. Challenging James on self-declared Leninist terms, he stated that a new international must 'come from a new upsurge of the working class itself; otherwise it cannot be the instrument of the class struggle'. Brockway here declared for the policy of the IBRSU, uniting the revolutionary sections of the LSI and Comintern in preparation to form a new international when the moment was right.[120]

It is notable that the most serious conflict between Brockway and James was largely unrelated to James's pan-Africanism and anticolonialism. James did not see a distinction between his Trotskyism and his pan-Africanism, but he also viewed Brockway as a friend of the African revolution. Indeed, Brockway's review of *World Revolution* acknowledged that, when distinguishing between 'democratic' and fascist powers, the Soviet Union 'ignored such patent facts as the restriction of democracy in the British Empire . . . and the operation over the greater part of that Empire of a tyranny repeating in almost every respect the dictatorship of Fascism'.[121] This was an argument that James and Padmore had been making for the preceding two years, indicating their influence on Brockway's anticolonial thinking – or, at the very least, a confluence of ideas.

## Thinking Beyond Ethiopia

James was not the only IAFE member to have broader concerns than Ethiopia. As Makonnen made clear at the group's Trafalgar Square rally, imperialism was a global system. The IAFE was concerned with the liberation of all of Africa and the diaspora. On 29 October 1935, the National Peace Council, a loose coalition of activists and politicians advocating for peace, held a conference on Peace and the Colonial Problem at Livingstone Hall, in Westminster. Significantly, the organisers of this conference recognised that 'the war between Italy and Abyssinia and the relation thereto of the League of Nations' had drawn urgent attention to the question of a wider 'colonial problem in its bearing upon

---

120 Fenner Brockway, 'The Rise and Fall of the Communist International', *New Leader*, 16 April 1937, p. 2.

121 Ibid., p. 2.

the prevention of war and aggression'.[122] Prominent attendees included Arthur Salter, the Marquess of Lothian, Norman Bentwich, Leonard Barnes, William Macmillan, Lucy P. Mair, John Harris, William McGregor Ross, Charles Roden Buxton, Leyton Richards, Wilfred Wellock and Stanley Jevons – a veritable who's who of British peace advocates.

Salter, a professor of political theory at Oxford who in 1937 became an independent MP, opened the conference by opposing the transfer of colonies to the 'dissatisfied' powers of Germany, Italy and Japan. Instead, the mandate system should be extended so that there was a 'double trusteeship' – one to the inhabitants of the country, another to 'the world in general'. This would work in tandem with an international convention guaranteeing that 'raw materials should be supplied on equal terms to all purchasers'.[123] Salter's view was informed by a liberal pacifism and moderate anticolonialism. His suggestions that raw materials be equally available to all purchasers was an attempt to satisfy the 'dissatisfied' powers, thereby averting another world war. It was a hacking at the leaves of imperialism, rather than a tearing up of its roots. Leonard Barnes, a social democrat and anticolonialist writer, reminded the conference of the meaning of 'trusteeship'. He stated that the 'lives', 'well-being' and the 'interests' of 'native peoples' must 'overrule all other considerations in our scheme for securing world peace'. However, even Barnes advocated an international mandate system based on 'ripeness for self-government'.[124]

The IAFE was represented at the conference by Ward and Padmore.[125] Ward criticised the liberal imperialism of the conference – which, he said, in discussing issues such as access to raw materials, was 'simply

122  National Peace Council, *Peace and the Colonial Problem* (London, 1935), p. 2.

123  Ibid., pp. 5–10.

124  Ibid., pp. 30–9. For more on Barnes's anticolonialism, see Paul B. Rich, *Race and Empire in British Politics* (Cambridge, 1986), Chapter 4.

125  The official National Peace Council report, *Peace and the Colonial Problem*, reports two speeches by Ward. *East Africa*, on 7 November 1935, reported a single speech by John (*sic*) Padmore, almost identical to the second of Ward's speeches reported in *Peace and the Colonial Problem*. It is possible that Ward made the first speech and Padmore the second, or that one man made both speeches. Given that Padmore discussed Salter's speech in *Africa and World Peace* (pp. 220–1), it seems likely that Padmore was there. It is most likely that Ward made the initial intervention and Padmore the second; whoever produced the official report then assumed that the second intervention must have been made by the same dark-skinned Caribbean man. If correct, this affords an insight into the casual racism of interwar Britain.

anxious to satisfy the European nations', rather than taking colonial peoples into account:

> We would like to ask Sir Arthur Salter if he has any proof whatsoever that these black people are not capable of governing themselves. If he says they are not capable of doing so in the interests of British capitalists, then I should say he is quite right, but if he says they are not capable of governing themselves in the interests of their own people, I should say he was quite wrong.[126]

Salter then responded to Ward that he did not propose 'to inflict a new foreign tyranny'. His proposed mandates system served the purpose of allowing colonies 'to proceed as fast and as far as possible to self-governing autonomous communities'.[127] This promise of self-government at some indeterminate date was insufficient for the IAFE.

In his speech, Padmore argued that the 'dissatisfaction' of Germany and Italy, discussed by the conference, was caused by their operation 'within the sphere of imperialism' – it was this entire system of global unevenness and exploitation that needed to be removed, something an international mandate system would be unable to achieve. Returning to his leitmotif – the idea of European and African partnership and interdependence – Padmore 'declared that Africans wished to co-operate with Europeans, but the co-operation could not be of the kind as between horse and rider'.[128]

Communist opinion was represented at the conference by Shapurji Saklatvala (three months before his death) and Reginald Bridgeman. Again, opposition to colonial concessions to Germany and Italy was in harmony with Communist Popular Front antifascism. However, Saklatvala and Bridgeman, always more concerned with imperialism than other Communists, presented a sincere case against colonialism. Saklatvala remarked that colonial peoples' 'irritation is a hundred times greater than that of Germany', and that 'foreign national rule in any part of the globe should be removed immediately'. Bridgeman, meanwhile, insisted: 'We ought . . .

---

126  National Peace Council, *Peace and the Colonial Problem*, pp. 17–18.

127  Ibid., p. 22.

128  Ibid., p. 51; 'Give Away the Colonies! Cranks – and a Few Others – in Conference', *East Africa*, 7 November, pp. 185–6.

to do away with the colonial system and with the mandates system.'[129] Both men were prepared to criticise all imperialisms, including those of Britain and France (although, importantly, the French Popular Front government had not yet been formed). Accordingly, there were no reports of friction between IAFE members and Communists at the conference.

As the Ethiopian war ended, IAFE members undertook other projects – but those projects always had at their heart the goal of African liberation. James translated his research on the Haitian Revolution into a play, *Toussaint Louverture*, about the revolution's leader. It was performed twice to private audiences at London's Westminster Theatre in March 1936, with Paul Robeson in the title role. Toussaint's story, performed at the time of the ILP sanctions debate, allowed James to make a persuasive case for Black sovereignty and the revolutionary potential of colonial peoples.[130] The play was not a commercial success and did not get an extended run. Nonetheless, it was warmly reviewed in the *New Leader*. Recognising the play as a critique of contemporary imperialism, the review noted that the play 'cogently puts the problem of empire with its exploitation and slavery of the coloured people'.[131]

Padmore's *How Britain Rules Africa*, the book he began writing while staying with Nancy Cunard in Réanville, was also published early in 1936. Cunard (praised in the book as 'one of the staunchest and most trusted white friends of the black race') typed out the book for Padmore and put him in touch with various publishers.[132] As Carol Polsgrove has noted, 'For an African, writing a book – asserting his view of the world in a form that Europe had claimed as its own – was in itself a political act.'[133] Padmore began by locating Africa's 'backwardness' within a global system of capitalism and imperialism. The first source of Africa's 'backwardness' was 'its long isolation', since it had 'only come within the ambit of capitalist economy during the past half-century'. But there was a second source. Within

---

129  National Peace Council, *Peace and the Colonial Problem*, pp. 18–19, 50–1.

130  For an edition of *Toussaint Louverture* with a complete playscript and analysis, see C. L. R. James, *Toussaint Louverture: The Story of the Only Successful Slave Revolt in History*, ed. Christian Høgsbjerg (Durham, NC, 2013 [1934]).

131  'Revolt! Negroes Struggle for Freedom', *New Leader*, 20 March 1936, p. 3.

132  Padmore, *How Britain Rules Africa*, p. 17; Harry Ransom Center, The University of Texas at Austin, Nancy Cunard collection, Cunard to Pizer, November 1959; Carol Polsgrove, *Ending British Rule in Africa: Writers in a Common Cause* (Manchester, 2009), pp. 10–13.

133  Polsgrove, *Ending British Rule*, p. 6.

the global capitalist economy, Africa served as an 'agrarian hinterland' – a source of raw materials, a market for manufactured commodities, and an outlet for both 'surplus finance-capital' and European settlers.[134]

In Padmore's Marxist analysis, the original cause of Africa's backwardness was its lack of contact with Europe – Europe being the wellspring of modernity – but European exploitation exacerbated that backwardness. Europe had therefore played a contradictory role in the African modernity sought by Padmore. A socialist Europe would help to resolve this contradiction. Padmore was therefore involved in the project of what Priyamvada Gopal has called 'decolonizing' the 'logic of modernity', and 'teasing out its revolutionary promises'.[135] After discussing the most pressing contemporary African grievances and struggles, Padmore appealed to his primary audience, Britain's 'working and middle classes'. He urged them to realise that their future was 'inseparably bound up with that of hundreds of millions of coloured peoples in India, Africa, and other colonial lands'.[136] He retained the theory of metropolitan and colonial revolutionary interdependence that he had developed while working for the ITUCNW.

In fact, many of the arguments made in Padmore's 1931 book, *The Life and Struggles of Negro Toilers*, reappeared in *How Britain Rules Africa*. This reveals the continuities of Padmore's political thought after his break with organised Communism. By depicting oppression and resistance in Africa, Padmore hoped to arouse the sympathies of the British working class. He reminded them of the formation of their own workers' organisations in the nineteenth century, and staked a claim for Africans within a global proletarian solidarity. His descriptions of various colonial laws and practices as 'fascist' also implicitly challenged the Popular Front distinction between 'democratic' and 'fascist' powers, and called for colonial peoples to have their oppression taken seriously by the broader antifascist movement.

But Padmore did single out some 'exceptions' to the 'conspiracy of silence among British politicians about discussing colonial mis-rule'. He cited the Labour MP William Lunn, as well as Maxton and Saklatvala.[137]

---

134  Padmore, *How Britain Rules Africa*, p. 1.

135  Priyamvada Gopal, *Insurgent Empire: Anticolonial Resistance and British Dissent* (London, 2019), p. 26.

136  Padmore, *How Britain Rules Africa*, p. 2.

137  Ibid., p. 323.

His praise for Saklatvala illustrates his awareness that there were currents of genuine anti-imperialism within the CPGB. However, this was not enough to stop the book being poorly received in the Communist press, due to its criticisms of the Popular Front strategy and Padmore's recent political history. Bridgeman, inspired by William Patterson's review of the book, criticised Padmore's advocacy of the slogan 'Africa for the Africans': '[T]here are white Africans as well as black; there is an African bourgeoisie, African landlords, as well as an African proletariat, toilers, farmers. What Africans is Africa to be for?' He then accused Padmore of advocating a 'starkly reactionary policy' of declaring a 'race war'.[138] This was a serious misrepresentation of Padmore's argument. Padmore had stated his support for the slogan in the context of South Africa, in a bid to unite African ethnic groups suffering under a particularly brutal settler colonialism. Bridgeman either failed to notice or intentionally overlooked this nuance.

The book did not sell well. In the first six months, only 165 copies were sold, slowing to eighteen copies in the first half of 1938.[139] Makonnen, however, remembered it having an incendiary impact on those who did read it: 'I know the reaction from Africa, because letters came in from students we didn't know saying that up till their reading of this thing, they had been in darkness; but now they had a Magna Carta.'[140] But Makonnen here made no comment on the effect of the book on Padmore's explicitly intended primary audience: the British working and middle classes. The appeals of Padmore and other Black radicals to British people have been the source of much debate. Makonnen recalled that politically active Africans went to the metropole 'because they held the belief that there were two Englands – the England of the colonies, the settlers and the plantocrats, and the England of Westminster, the anti-slavery societies, and the rebel movements of the Left'.[141] This attitude has been fiercely criticised by Cedric Robinson:

> To [Makonnen and Padmore] and many of their fellows, England . . . was the embodiment of fair play and deep moral regulation . . . Not even the gross imperfections and racism they confronted in the

138  Reginald Bridgeman, 'Africa: A Confused Argument', *Labour Monthly*, September 1937, p. 577.

139  Polsgrove, *Ending British Rule*, p. 18.

140  Makonnen, *Pan-Africanism from Within*, p. 194.

141  Ibid., p. 150.

metropole dissuaded them. It was as though they had come to accept that as Black Englishmen a part of their political mission was to correct the errant motherland.[142]

Makonnen and Padmore were undoubtedly struck by the liberalism of the metropole compared to the colonies, which they regarded as a great irony. As James noted when discussing the decision not to imprison Padmore for his conscientious objection during the Second World War, the 'British in Britain are a very tolerant people'.[143] Black activists were aware that they had far greater freedom of speech and other legal protections in the metropole, and gladly exploited this fact. Winston James notes the 'political latitude' in London, while convincingly arguing that the British ruling class granted this latitude 'because they reckoned these expatriate radicals could do no harm to the sturdy social structure of metropolitan Britain'.[144] Stephen Howe has highlighted the possibilities of multiple and overlapping identities in the relationship of Black radicals – especially James – to Britishness: one could 'think of oneself as Trinidadian or Antiguan, *and* West Indian, *and* British'.[145] Kennetta Hammond Perry, in her study of postwar Caribbean migrants to Britain, makes the case that Black Britons 'made choices to exercise their imperial citizenship', and in so doing 'remapped the very boundaries of what it meant to be both Black and British'.[146]

Robinson's criticism of Black radicals' attachment to Britain is likely motivated by the broader issue of what he sees as a nagging attachment to the European proletariat, rather than an unadulterated embrace of his 'Black radical tradition'. The conclusion to *How Britain Rules Africa* is a flashpoint in this respect. Padmore wrote that Africans 'welcomed' the appeals for cooperation from 'the more enlightened and far-sighted sections of the ruling classes of Europe'.[147] They also sought support from

---

142  Cedric J. Robinson, *Black Marxism: The Making of the Black Radical Tradition* (Chapel Hill, NC, 2000 [1983]), pp. 264–5.

143  James, 'Notes on the Life of George Padmore', p. 48.

144  Winston James, *Holding Aloft the Banner of Ethiopia: Caribbean Radicalism in Early Twentieth-Century America* (London, 1998), p. 76.

145  Stephen Howe, 'C. L. R. James: Visions of History, Visions of Britain', in Schwarz, *West Indian Intellectuals*, p. 161. Emphasis in original.

146  Kennetta Hammond Perry, *London Is the Place for Me: Black Britons, Citizenship, and the Politics of Race* (New York, 2015), p. 6.

147  Padmore, *How Britain Rules Africa*, pp. 391–2.

White people who sympathised with 'subject races' out of 'religious sentiments, humanitarian reasons or political convictions'.[148] C. L. R. James was thanked by Padmore in *How Britain Rules Africa* for reading proofs and offering suggestions, but wrote an ambivalent review for the *New Leader*.[149] James acknowledged the book's importance and Padmore's breadth of knowledge, but attacked the book's praise for elements of the British ruling class, asking: 'How does the lion co-operate with the lamb?'[150] As Makalani has observed, James 'was being disingenuous' – Padmore had framed this passage with rhetorical questions suggesting there could be no 'co-operation with imperialists'.[151]

Robinson, following James, overstates his argument about Padmore's faith in the British ruling class. *How Britain Rules Africa* was probably Padmore's least radical book of the interwar period – yet it concluded that it was the 'common folks' of Britain, exploited by the 'same classes' that oppressed the colonial peoples, who should 'become a weapon in the struggle for the new social order.'[152] More problematically, however, Robinson extends James's criticisms of appeals to the European ruling class to encompass all Europeans. Discussing James's review of *How Britain Rules Africa*, he remarks that, in 'James's view, with only the most sporadic support to be expected from the European working class and the European Left, the radical Black intelligentsia was now compelled to seek the liberation of their peoples by their own means.'[153] James had in fact argued in his review for the interdependence of colonial and metropolitan struggles. He declared that Africans 'need co-operation, but that co-operation must be with the revolutionary movement in Europe and Asia.'[154] Black people would liberate themselves, and the European ruling classes were not their allies – but the European socialist movement would play a part in this global liberation. This was consistent with the Marxist pan-Africanism that James and Padmore would later apply as the theoretical bedrock of the IASB, and also with Padmore's revolutionary theory as an ITUCNW member.

---

148　Ibid., p. 395.
149　Ibid., p. 17.
150　James, ' "Civilising" the "Blacks" ', p. 5.
151　Makalani, *In the Cause of Freedom*, p. 210.
152　Padmore, *How Britain Rules Africa*, p. 395.
153　Robinson, *Black Marxism*, pp. 272–3.
154　James, ' "Civilising" the "Blacks" ', p. 5.

Contrary to Robinson's portrayal of a naive romanticism, Black radicals were as aware of racial prejudices within the British socialist movement as they were of racism within wider British society. Ralph Bunche, who visited London in 1937 and worked closely with the IASB, recorded an incident at a CPGB dance at which 'two ofay girls refused to dance with Peter [Koinange]'.[155] As we have seen, Padmore commonly attributed weaknesses in Communist anti-imperialism and the British left's responses to the Ethiopia crisis to racial chauvinism. There was nonetheless a general feeling that the British proletariat, though imperfect, had a great progressive potential. Padmore attributed working-class racism to a false consciousness instilled by the ruling class and labour aristocracy. James commented on the lack of racism in the militant working-class town of Nelson.[156] He even remembered that occasionally, at conferences at which there was competition to speak, White workers would ask that James be allowed to speak precisely because he was Black.[157] For Marxists like James and Padmore, then, it seemed that there was a direct relationship between the class consciousness and antiracism of British workers. There was no contradiction between Black radicals' critiques of British racism and a defence of the general progressiveness of, and respect for, the British proletariat.

The IAFE continued to hold public meetings until as late as April 1936, but the energy was sucked out of the organisation following the Italian capture of Addis Ababa in May 1936.[158] Of course, it did not forget about Ethiopia. Black radicals, particularly Kenyatta, continued to work with Sylvia Pankhurst, the most tenacious pro-Ethiopian voice in Britain, to promote the cause of Ethiopian liberation. Pankhurst was determined that the British government should not recognise the Italian 'conquest' of Ethiopia. In September 1937, she was joined by colonial activists – including Kenyatta, Ward, V. K. Krishna Menon, Harold Moody and I. T. A. Wallace-Johnson – to make this very demand.[159] However, the IAFE

---

155　Bunche, 1937 Annual Diary, 17 July. Koinange was Kenyatta's comrade in the KCA.

156　James, 'Autobiography, 1932–38', p. 6.

157　Mackenzie, 'Marxism and Black Nationalism', p. 7.

158　TNA, KV 2/1787 (Kenyatta), 27 April 1936.

159　'Justice for Abyssinia', *Manchester Guardian*, 10 September 1937, p. 4; Pankhurst, *Sylvia Pankhurst*, p. 61.

maintained an interest in broader questions of colonial liberation throughout the Ethiopian crisis. After Italian victory was declared, they founded a new, short-lived organisation in June 1936, the Pan-African Federation (PAF – not to be confused with the body formed in 1944).[160] The group dubiously claimed to be the 'British section' of a global federation with twenty-five sections spanning British, Dutch, French and Portuguese colonies.[161] There is no doubt that the PAF had contacts in all of these countries and regions, but there was nowhere near this level of formality to the organisation.

The PAF also continued to make use of Black radicals' increased immersion in the British socialist movement. The group organised a meeting at Memorial Hall in Farringdon for 31 July 1936, attracting a roster of British socialists to address the meeting, including even Communist-sympathising activists Krishna Menon of the India League and Bridgeman of the League Against Imperialism. Padmore chaired the meeting, and was joined on the panel by Brockway, Labour members Arthur Creech Jones and William Mellor, and Dorothy Woodman of the Union of Democratic Control.[162] Despite reservations about the Labour Party institutionally – in *How Britain Rules Africa*, Padmore had detailed how the 1929 Labour government was complicit in the suppression of African workers' struggles – the PAF also solicited commitments from Labour MPs to raise their concerns in the House of Commons.[163] These approaches, however, were rebuffed when Labour's international secretary, William Gillies, caught wind of the PAF's letters. He warned his colleagues that 'the initiative in this matter is Communist', and that they 'ought certainly to have nothing to do with the Federation'.[164]

The PAF seems to have all but disappeared by the end of the summer. Its claim of being a global federation was a fabrication. Furthermore, a coalition of Marxists and anticolonial revolutionaries, like Padmore and Makonnen, and more moderate critics of colonialism, like Moore and Wood, must have been difficult to maintain. It was simpler to achieve unity over a single issue, such as opposing the colonisation of Ethiopia

---

160  TNA, KV 2/1787 (Kenyatta), 3 July 1936.

161  LHASC, LP/ID/CI/59, Tomasa Griffith to Rhys Davies, undated.

162  'Negro Rights: Remarkable Meeting to be Held in London', *New Leader*, 31 July 1936, p. 4.

163  Padmore, *How Britain Rules Africa*, p. 356.

164  LHASC, LP/ID/CI/59, various letters.

(even then, James split from the IAFE); but unity would be difficult to sustain when diagnosing, and prescribing actions against, broader systems of imperialism. The left wing of the IAFE and PAF, always the most prominent and active, was considerably more involved with the world of British socialism than it had been at the start of the crisis. James and Kenyatta had not been permanently resident in Britain until the early 1930s, and Padmore and Makonnen not until 1935. The Ethiopia crisis inserted the IAFE into the middle of the most important issue of the day. Whether or not IAFE members agreed with members of the ILP, CPGB or other socialist parties or groups (or even with each other), pan-Africanism was now inseparable from the broader debates taking place within the British left over the futures of capitalism and imperialism. The socialists in the IAFE maintained contact with each other and with the British socialist movement, reconvening in the spring of 1937 to form the International African Service Bureau.

# 3

# Against Capitalism and Imperialism, 1937–1938

The International African Friends of Ethiopia (IAFE) was a broad church uniting those of African descent opposed to the colonisation of Ethiopia. By contrast, the International African Service Bureau (IASB) had a more thorough Marxist and pan-Africanist philosophy. This was engendered primarily by C. L. R. James and George Padmore, as a culmination of their theoretical and political work of the 1930s. The IASB's attitudes towards the various British left-wing parties are exemplified by a February 1938 article by Padmore in the *New Leader*. Padmore argued that the cause of the looming world war was the rivalry between the 'Haves' and 'Have-Nots' of European imperialism. Following Lenin, it was only through the abolition of imperialism that the 'menace of war' could be eliminated. The colonial peoples were therefore the 'potential allies of the workers against a common enemy – the British Imperialist class'. Padmore stated that Labour Party leaders 'suffer[ed] from all the illusions and deficiencies' typical of social democrats. Most of them would 'line up behind' the bourgeoisie during crises of British imperialism. The record of Labour governments and their colonial policy proved that they were 'the last people in the world to support the cause of self-determination'. While such policies were to be expected from the Labour Party, the attitude of the Communist Party of Great Britain (CPGB) to the colonial question was 'a tragedy': 'While its Moscow leaders still continue to admit that war is inevitable under Imperialism . . . the British Communist Party, in order to accommodate itself to the foreign diplomacy of the Soviet Union, pursues a policy identical with that of the Labour Party'. The Popular Front distinctions between fascist and 'democratic' powers made by the Comintern and CPGB, as well as their appeals to collective security and the League of Nations, subordinated the question of colonial self-determination.[1]

Finally, Padmore turned his attention to the Independent Labour Party (ILP). Padmore called it 'the only working-class party in Britain that has a correct theoretical approach on the questions of Imperialist war and colonies. It must be stated that the ILP has only recently arrived at this clear Marxist position, for even up to the Italo-Abyssinian War the Party displayed a lamentable confusion.'[2] Padmore's continued criticism of the ILP's Ethiopian decision is unsurprising, but this passage is indicative of the hardening of the ILP's anti-imperialism in the intervening two years, and of the IASB's vastly improved relationship with them. Padmore's statement, which positions him as a legitimate adjudicator of British socialists' Marxism and uses anti-imperialism as its key measure (all while being published in the newspaper of the party he is judging), illustrates how Black radicalism needs to be more thoroughly integrated into the history of British socialism. Padmore and other Black activists were reshaping British socialism from within, positioning themselves as the defenders of a political inheritance passed down from Marx and Lenin.

The late 1930s was a particularly productive period for British Black radicalism. Padmore later called this period 'one of the most stimulating and constructive in the history of Pan-Africanism'.[3] Accordingly, this chapter begins with an overview of the IASB's formation and activities, before discussing the group's key ideas and publications. It focuses in particular on the extent to which Johnstone (or Jomo, as he refashioned himself in this period) Kenyatta's revolutionary nationalism and Ras Makonnen's African socialism clashed with or complemented the Marxism of James and Padmore. It will be seen that Black radical ideas informed, and were informed by, the IASB's place in the British socialist movement. The chapter will then discuss the relationship between the IASB and the parties and individuals of the wider British socialist

---

1 George Padmore, 'Hands off the Colonies', *New Leader*, 25 February 1938, p. 2.
2 Ibid.
3 George Padmore, *Pan-Africanism or Communism? The Coming Struggle for Africa* (London, 1956), p. 151.

movement. It culminates in a discussion of the 1938 Conference on Peace and Empire as a case study of these relationships, and comments more generally on the forces and alignments within British anti-colonialism during the age of the Popular Front.

## The Formation and Strategy of the International African Service Bureau

On 3 March 1937, I. T. A. Wallace-Johnson arrived in Britain, settling in London. Wallace-Johnson had been in touch with Padmore since the latter's Communist days. He had recently been found guilty of sedition in the Gold Coast for his anti-imperialist article, 'Has the African a God?' Wallace-Johnson escaped with a fine and travelled to the metropole in order to continue his anticolonial agitation.[4] He appealed the guilty verdict in London, with support from Stafford Cripps and the National Council for Civil Liberties, but ultimately lost the appeal.[5] Ralph Bunche, who arrived in London the month before Wallace-Johnson, commented in his diary that Wallace-Johnson was 'a blatant "I" man. He's no shrinking violet . . . Given to exaggeration, I think.'[6] Conversely, James's memory of Wallace-Johnson was less conflicted: an 'absolutely first class man' and 'one of the greatest political leaders I have known.'[7]

Bunche was an African American political scientist and anthropologist who visited London for research from February to July 1937. During his outbound journey, he was on the same ship as Ellen Wilkinson, a Labour MP, and spent much time socialising with her.[8] A working-class socialist with a commitment to feminism and internationalism, Wilkinson soon became a patron of the IASB.[9] During his time in London, Bunche became heavily involved in the IASB's networks, mainly through

4 S. K. B. Asante, 'I. T. A. Wallace Johnson and Italo-Ethiopian Crisis', *Journal of the Historical Society of Nigeria* 7 (1975), pp. 637–8; Stephanie Newell, *The Power to Name: A History of Anonymity in Colonial West Africa* (Athens, OH, 2013), Chapter 3; TNA, CO 323/1610/2 (IASB), Wallace Johnson and the International African Service Bureau, January 1938.

5 Newell, *Power to Name*, p. 85.

6 Ralph J. Bunche, 1937 Annual Diary, 18 April.

7 C. L. R. James papers, box 12 folder 10, Interview (undated).

8 Bunche, 1937 Annual Diary.

9 For more on Wilkinson, see Laura Beers, *Red Ellen: The Life of Ellen Wilkinson, Socialist, Feminist, Internationalist* (Cambridge, MA, 2016).

meeting Kenyatta at the London School of Economics, where both men regularly attended Bronisław Malinowski's anthropology seminars. On 5 April, Bunche attended a meeting with James, Padmore, Makonnen, Wallace-Johnson and Akiki Nyabongo at which the decision to form the Bureau was taken.[10] On 29 April, a meeting of Bunche, Padmore, Wallace-Johnson, Kenyatta, Makonnen and Donald M'Timkulu decided to name the organisation the International African Service Bureau.[11]

Makonnen later explained that the impetus behind the formation of the IASB was that 'the existing African and West Indian organizations in England at the time were very mild'.[12] James remembered that 'Padmore was the chief . . . With him was Ras Makonnen, Jomo Kenyatta, myself and maybe half-a-dozen others.'[13] Padmore himself stated that the most important officers of the IASB were Wallace-Johnson, Chris Jones, James, Kenyatta, Makonnen and himself.[14]

The IASB had an informal membership structure. Many Africans 'came around simply because [the IASB headquarters] provided a base and a talking point where the coffee pot was almost always on the stove'.[15] The group's activism depended on a small core of activists who had arrived in the metropole from Africa or the Caribbean in the past decade. The first issue of their journal *African Sentinel* declared:

> Our main objective is to serve as a medium of information between the Colonial and European public – the British in particular – as well as to create a connecting link between the Africans at home (in Africa) and the Africans abroad (in the West Indies, United States of America and other Western countries) by the transmission of messages and informations, news and views, from one to another, in the most accurate and concise forms.[16]

---

10  Bunche, 1937 Annual Diary, 5 April.

11  Ibid., 29 April.

12  T. Ras Makonnen, *Pan-Africanism from Within*, ed. Kenneth King (London, 1973), p. 117. Makonnen believed WASU to be more 'outspoken' than the LCP. The IASB's relationship with the LCP 'was one of convenience', and the IASB would criticise them for being liberal 'obstructionists'. Makonnen, *Pan-Africanism from Within*, p. 127.

13  C. L. R. James, 'Black Intellectuals in Britain', in Bhikhu Parekh (ed.), *Colour, Culture and Consciousness: Immigrant Intellectuals in Britain* (London, 1974), p. 160.

14  Padmore, *Pan-Africanism or Communism?*, p. 146.

15  Makonnen, *Pan-Africanism from Within*, p. 118.

16  'Our Policy', *African Sentinel*, October–November 1937, p. 1.

Masthead of *International African Opinion*
15X/1/121/4, Modern Records Centre, University of Warwick

Many of the IASB's strategies had been forged during the IAFE days. James would speak on a Trotskyist platform in Hyde Park on Sunday afternoons before joining 'George and the others' on a different platform to speak about the colonial question. They wrote to the press, fed questions to sympathetic MPs, addressed meetings of societies and political parties, and published in the ILP's *New Leader*.[17] They also published a succession of journals (*Africa and the World*, *African Sentinel* and *International African Opinion*), launching a new journal each time one was banned in the colonies. Carol Polsgrove has asked us to 'consider the possibility' that IASB members 'wanted, simply, to write and be published'.[18] However, Leslie James argues more convincingly that, for Padmore, his 'writing and his organizing were never distinct spheres: his

17 Rare Book and Manuscript Library, Columbia University, New York, C. L. R. James papers, box 5 folder 21, C. L. R. James, 'Notes on the Life of George Padmore', pp. 32–4; Makonnen, *Pan-Africanism from Within*, pp. 118–19; IASB Executive Committee, 'A Brief Review of the Activities of the IASB', *African Sentinel*, March–April 1938, p. 14.

18 Carol Polsgrove, *Ending British Rule in Africa: Writers in a Common Cause* (Manchester, 2009), p. 169.

writing was a form of action'.[19] The value of IASB publications was measured by their impact on the struggle for colonial liberation, much as C. L. R. James celebrated the Abbé Raynal's writing for its influence on Toussaint Louverture.[20]

Each member contributed different skills. Wallace-Johnson had experience of labour organising in West Africa, and edited *African Sentinel*. Padmore and James were the most prominent writers and intellectuals, editing *International African Opinion* and contributing articles to other publications. James remembered that the IASB depended on 'Padmore's encyclopedic knowledge of Africa, of African politics and African personalities [and] his tireless correspondence with Africans in all parts of the continent'.[21] Padmore's flat on Cranleigh Street in Camden, shared with his British Jewish partner, Dorothy Pizer, became an important hub of British anticolonialism in this period. James described it as 'the acknowledged centre of fighters for the emancipation and independence of Africans and people of African descent from all over the world'.[22] Makonnen was the treasurer, securing the IASB's headquarters on Westbourne Grove in Bayswater and helping to fund the IASB's journals.[23] Jones, a seafarer and trade unionist, was particularly important in distributing pamphlets. He 'used to collect West Indian sailors on the docks to man boats and was thus well placed for getting literature into territories where they were banned'.[24] Without this help, the IASB 'were but a few intellectuals in London' – a candid acknowledgement by James of his detachment from mass movements.[25]

The IASB relied on the financial and political support of several 'patrons', mostly drawn from British socialist circles.[26] Mary Downes, a

---

19 Leslie James, *George Padmore and Decolonization from Below: Pan-Africanism, the Cold War, and the End of Empire* (Basingstoke, 2015), p. 10.

20 C. L. R. James, *The Black Jacobins: Toussaint L'Ouverture and the San Domingo Revolution* (London, 1938), p. 16.

21 C. L. R. James, *Nkrumah and the Ghana Revolution* (London, 1977), p. 65.

22 James, 'Notes on the Life of George Padmore', p. 2.

23 Padmore, *Pan-Africanism or Communism?*, pp. 146–7; C. L. R. James, 'George Padmore: Black Marxist Revolutionary – A Memoir' (1976), in C. L. R. James, *At the Rendezvous of Victory* (London, 1984), p. 260.

24 James, 'Notes on the Life of George Padmore', p. 37.

25 Al Richardson, Clarence Chrysostom and Anna Grimshaw, *C. L. R. James and British Trotskyism* (London, 1987), p. 6.

26 The intelligence agencies identified these patrons as Reginald Sorensen, Daniel Escarte, K. A. Chunchie, Ellen Wilkinson, Mary Downes, Ethel Mannin, Dorothy

Welsh schoolteacher who worked with Sylvia Pankhurst on the Ethiopia campaign, was one of these patrons. Wallace-Johnson published an article by her in the *African Sentinel*. He noted that it 'speaks much for the feeling which dominates the minds of some of our British friends and sympathisers'.[27] Nancy Cunard contributed two articles to the *African Sentinel*, one about the poor treatment of 'Moorish' soldiers in Francisco Franco's army during the Spanish Civil War, and the other a review of 'international African press publications'.[28] She also expressed eagerness to help Wallace-Johnson publicise the IASB's work, and likely donated money to the group.[29] However, the IASB always struggled financially. Bunche recorded that the IASB, from its inception, was in desperate need of money and struggled to open an office.[30] Nearly every publication or meeting featured an urgent appeal for funds.

This lack of money limited possibilities. Padmore wanted to write another book, but was unable to do so as it would prevent him from undertaking freelance journalistic work (his 'only means of keeping the wolf from the door').[31] Payment from these newspapers was irregular, and Padmore often received no payment for his work.[32] His choice of work reveals a blend of financial pragmatism and political ambition. While writing for newspapers and journals no doubt placed some constraints on Padmore's intellectual and political freedom, he decided to write almost exclusively for left-wing and African diaspora publications. Padmore knew that many of these publications operated on a shoestring, but also recognised that they played an important role in disseminating the IASB's ideas. It was Makonnen 'who got most of the money' in the early days of the IASB.[33] The same was true of the 1945

Woodman, Sylvia Pankhurst, Nancy Cunard, Geraldine Young, George Daggar, Morgan Jones, D. N. Pritt, Philip Noel-Baker, Arthur Creech Jones, E. L. Mallalieu, Victor Gollancz, F. A. Ridley, Peter Rhode and Max Yergan. TNA, CO 323/1610/2 (IASB), Wallace Johnson and the International African Service Bureau.

27  Mary Downes, 'Let's Pull Together', *African Sentinel*, October–November 1937, p. 4.

28  Nancy Cunard, '"Only a Black"', *African Sentinel*, November–December 1937; Nancy Cunard, 'The African Claims His Responsibility: A Review of International African Press Publications', *African Sentinel*, March–April 1938.

29  TNA, MEPO 38/9 (Cunard), 2 July 1937.

30  Bunche, 1937 Annual Diary, 29 April.

31  Schomburg Center, Ralph Bunche papers, box 10 folder 14, Padmore to Bunche, 13 April 1937.

32  James, 'Notes on the Life of George Padmore', p. 28.

33  Ibid., p. 37.

Pan-African Congress, when Makonnen's clubs and restaurants in Manchester proved invaluable. There was a stark difference between Makonnen and Padmore here, as Padmore was extremely reluctant to undertake work that he thought would compromise his socialist principles. Makonnen later remembered that Padmore, only part-jokingly, called him a 'damn businessman', who might have to be 'restrain[ed]'.[34]

Money problems also created tension within the group. In June 1937, Wallace-Johnson came to Bunche's house with a 'hard luck story' about having been 'put out of his digs' and needing money for the IASB. Bunche reluctantly gave him fifteen shillings.[35] In early 1938, Wallace-Johnson was accused of stealing from the IASB's funds. He was expelled and returned to Sierra Leone in April 1938, shortly thereafter founding the Sierra Leone section of the West African Youth League.[36] Wallace-Johnson was replaced as secretary by Babalola Wilkey, from Nigeria, who was himself soon expelled after accusations of stealing money from the IASB.[37] Makonnen resigned from the organisation in the autumn of 1938, retaining the offices while the IASB moved into the ILP headquarters in the City. The intelligence services speculated that Makonnen had also been stealing from the group, but given that James expressed regret at Makonnen's decision to resign, this seems an unlikely explanation.[38] The reason for his resignation remains unclear, but Makonnen continued to work with IASB members into the postwar period.

Given all this instability, it seems extraordinary that the IASB was so productive in the first two years of its existence. The tumult of the 1930s forced socialists and anti-imperialists to search frantically for diagnoses of the accumulating crises, and to prescribe actions to overcome them. As James declared of his masterpiece, *The Black Jacobins*, it contained 'the fever and the fret' of the age.[39] The Italo-Ethiopian War, the Spanish

---

34  Makonnen, *Pan-Africanism from Within*, p. 146.

35  Bunche, 1937 Annual Diary, 12 June.

36  TNA, CO 323/1610/2 (IASB), Vernon Kell to F. J. Howard, 11 April 1938; Asante, 'I. T. A. Wallace Johnson', p. 639.

37  TNA, CO 323/1610/2 (IASB), Vernon Kell to Howard, 17 June 1938; 'Expulsion Notice', *International African Opinion*, February–March 1939, p. 9.

38  TNA, KV 2/1824 (James), Vernon Kell to Captain Brodie, 5 May 1939; TNA, KV 2/1824, 11 October 1938.

39  James, *Black Jacobins*, p. ix. Christian Høgsbjerg picks up on this quotation to discuss James's response to the Spanish Civil War. Christian Høgsbjerg, '"The Fever and the Fret": C. L. R. James, the Spanish Civil War and the Writing of *The Black Jacobins*', *Critique* 44 (2016).

Civil War, the Caribbean labour rebellions, and of course the approaching Second World War provoked questions about the relationships between capitalism, imperialism, fascism and war. They forced the IASB, as well as other actors within the British socialist movement, to theorise about how capitalism and its corollaries could be defeated. The output of the IASB in this period was therefore remarkable, but necessary.

## The IASB's Political Thought

The IASB's most important theory was that of the interdependence of the metropolitan and colonial revolutions, united against the common (and hyphenated) enemy: 'capitalist-imperialism'. This was particularly evident in the writings of James and Padmore, the latter having espoused this theory since his Communist days. There were some differences in the ways James and Padmore conceptualised these interdependent revolutions – James drew on Trotsky's theory of permanent revolution, while Padmore's Marxism was Stalinist-inflected – but these differences were relatively insignificant.

The theory of interdependence had been strengthened through contact with the British working class. While the IASB had been formed partly to shift debates about colonialism within the British socialist movement, the group also acknowledged the importance of the British working class in shaping the Bureau's ideas about liberation. We have already seen how crucial James's time in Nelson was to the development of his Marxism. Makonnen, although he was one of the IASB members most sceptical of collaboration with White socialists, noted that Africans were inspired by British trade unionism: 'you saw that along with it went a whole machinery for dealing with grievances. At a stroke you got removed from a world that talks about the *ju-ju* into one of ideas and movements'.[40] The editorial in the first issue of *International African Opinion* argued that Black people must win their own freedom, and criticised European organisations for ignoring the African struggle. But it also noted that the IASB, through the pages of their journal, could give Africans 'the benefit of our daily contact with the European movement'.[41]

---

40  Makonnen, *Pan-Africanism from Within*, p. 151.
41  'Editorial', *International African Opinion*, July 1938, p. 3.

The IASB attempted to turn these linkages into a practical strategy for liberation.

In *The Black Jacobins*, James observed: 'If [Toussaint Louverture] failed, it is for the same reason that the Russian socialist revolution failed . . . – the defeat of the revolution in Europe.'[42] But he also argued: 'The part played by the blacks in the success of the great French Revolution has never received adequate recognition. As Franco's Moors have once more proved, the revolution in Europe will ignore coloured workers at its peril.'[43] Similarly, Padmore wrote that 'the colonial peoples might be the decisive factor in the coming struggle for power, just as the peasantry and the national minorities of the Czarist Russian Empire were the decisive factors in consolidating the victory of the October Revolution.'[44] This theory of interdependence was influenced by the Comintern's theses on the national and colonial questions, which argued that anticolonial revolutionary movements challenged the foundations of European capitalism. They should therefore be supported, as colonial revolution would accelerate the collapse of capitalism in the metropole.[45] The IASB used this theory to argue that colonial peoples therefore had a role to play not only in destroying the British Empire, but also in defeating European capitalism.

This theory was the basis of the group's appeals to the British working class. In September 1938, the IASB sent a message to the British Trades Union Congress (TUC) about the ongoing Caribbean labour rebellions. It declared: 'At the present moment Africans and West Indians are struggling for their elementary democratic rights. What are you going to do about it?'[46] The same month, the IASB published a 'Manifesto Against War', stating that the coming war was one of rival imperialisms. It said to the 'workers of Britain': 'Though you have neglected us in the past, today in this hour of common crisis, we want you to know that we Blacks bear you no ill-will. The imperialists are the common enemy. Our freedom is a step towards your freedom.'[47] These writings therefore

---

42  James, *Black Jacobins*, p. 237.

43  C. L. R. James, *A History of Negro Revolt* (London, 1938), p. 13.

44  George Padmore, *Africa and World Peace* (London, 1937), pp. 265–6.

45  Vladimir Lenin, 'Report of the Commission on the National and the Colonial Questions' (1920), at marxists.org.

46  IASB Executive Committee, 'To the Delegates of the Trades Union Congress at Blackpool', *International African Opinion*, September 1938, p. 2.

47  TNA, MEPO 38/91 (IASB), IASB, 'Manifesto Against War', September 1938.

contained not only an awareness of historical precedents (the Haitian and Bolshevik revolutions), but also 'the fever and the fret' of the age (the Spanish Civil War, Caribbean labour rebellions, and the imminent Second World War). Black radicals challenged the idea that the metropolitan revolution was more important than the colonial revolution. Instead, James and Padmore theorised that these revolutionary movements were interdependent, thereby decentring Europe. The IASB yearned for a 'world socialist commonwealth', in which a socialist alliance between Britain and its former colonies would be achieved.[48]

In his unpublished biography of Padmore, James unequivocally stated the centrality of the interdependent revolutions to the IASB's political theory: 'Between 1930 and 1945 all of us saw African emancipation as dependent upon the breakdown of imperialist power in Europe. Armed rebellion was sure to be crushed unless the imperialist powers were impotent, and this could only be the result of revolutions within the metropolitan powers themselves.'[49] But James's insistence on the centrality of the metropolitan proletariat to the political thought of all members of the IASB before 1945 is overstated. The IASB was not a uniformly Marxist organisation. James himself remembered that Kenyatta was 'always vigilant for any suspicion that the African cause might be contaminated or manipulated by a Marxist, even though that Marxist was a Negro'.[50] This is consistent with observations in Bunche's diary. Bunche noted Kenyatta's distrust of almost all White men, and that Kenyatta's advice about White people was 'value them but don't "trust them"'.[51] Kenyatta was therefore less wedded to the idea that the African revolution would rely on revolution in Europe. As discussed in Chapter 1, he was more comfortable expounding nationalism than Marxism.

Makonnen was also unconvinced by Marxism. He was unmistakably a socialist, arguing that the pan-Africanist movement should 'adopt the high British ideal of morality in the co-operative movement and link this with our traditional African form of co-operation in the *osusu*'.[52] But he

---

48  IASB Executive Committee, 'An Open Letter to West Indian Intellectuals', *International African Opinion*, May–June 1939, p. 3.

49  James, 'Notes on the Life of George Padmore', p. 40.

50  Ibid., p. 31.

51  Bunche, 1937 Annual Diary, 7 April and 22 April.

52  Makonnen, *Pan-Africanism from Within*, p. 135. An *osusu* is a traditional form of cooperative capital accumulation used in Africa.

was more sceptical than James and Padmore of the role that the European proletariat would play in the creation of African socialism. It should nonetheless be noted that, due to Padmore's efforts, all of the IASB's collective statements and policies were Marxist in nature. James later recalled his frustration in attempting to convince Kenyatta of Marxist policies, whereas Padmore would have Kenyatta 'nodding his head' within two minutes of discussion.[53]

The idea of interdependent revolutions also began to find regular expression in the ILP. For instance, a 1939 ILP statement argued that the victory of 'the struggle of the colonial people against British and other Imperialism . . . hastens the day of our emancipation'.[54] Such claims about the symbiotic relationship between the metropolitan and colonial revolutions were a new development in the previously paternalistic ILP. It is difficult to ascertain whether this development was a result of the direct influence of the IASB or simply inspired by the upsurge of colonial revolt in the 1930s. But it is noteworthy that the ILP's new emphasis on the agency of colonial peoples coincided with Black radicals' increased immersion in ILP networks.

While the IASB's theory was influencing, or at least converging with, that of the ILP, it was far removed from Communist Popular Front thinking. In April 1936, Hugo Rathbone wrote in *Labour Monthly*: 'it may very well happen that the backward nature of Negro African economy *may* result in African independence being achieved *only parallel* with the revolution in imperialist countries'.[55] In Rathbone's analysis, metropolitan countries, after their own socialist revolutions, would end the exploitation of African countries. However, African countries would play no part in securing the liberation of either themselves or the European proletariat.

Indeed, Minkah Makalani has observed (contra Hakim Adi, who argues that the CPGB inspired unity between Britain's Black organisations in the late 1930s) that 'the Comintern's Popular Front policy seemed to vindicate Padmore'.[56] Padmore continued to criticise the

---

53 James, 'Notes on the Life of George Padmore', p. 32.

54 ILP, *War? Democracy? Czech Independence? Where Do the Workers Come In?* (London, 1939), p. 8.

55 Hugo Rathbone, 'The Problem of African Independence', *Labour Monthly*, April 1936, p. 247. Emphasis in original.

56 Minkah Makalani, *In the Cause of Freedom: Radical Black Internationalism from Harlem to London, 1917–1939* (Chapel Hill, NC, 2011), p. 194; Hakim Adi,

Popular Front, with its faith in alliance with capitalists and the collective security of the League of Nations. In *Africa and World Peace*, Padmore reminded his readers that 'Lenin described the League as a Thieves' Kitchen. A characterization which the communists have completely forgotten.'[57] The IASB was joined in its criticisms of the Popular Front by the ILP, which in 1937 declared that the tactic 'ignore[d] the fact that Fascism and Reaction are inseparable from Capitalism and can only be defeated by the overthrow of Capitalism.'[58] The International Bureau of Revolutionary Socialist Unity (IBRSU), at its February 1938 congress, passed a resolution asserting that the Popular Front 'leads to the abandonment of support to colonial peoples and proletarians struggling for their emancipation, and in consequence it becomes a bulwark of Imperialism.'[59]

Opposition to the Popular Front prompted the development of another major IASB theory: that of the equivalence of colonialism and fascism. The comparison was not without precedent. It had been made by socialists such as Fenner Brockway and Reginald Reynolds at the time of Hitler's rise to power in 1933.[60] The argument was also made by Black radicals. In November 1933, Arnold Ward addressed the Southgate Labour Party branch to condemn British rule in Africa. He concluded his speech by saying that 'Fascism was nothing new to Africa.'[61] The idea also had precedent in Communist Third Period rhetoric, in which the word 'fascist' was applied quite freely, including to imperialists. Bill Schwarz notes that it was in 1933 that Padmore began to think seriously about fascism, 'draw[ing] out the centrality of race to the Nazi order'.[62] The Ethiopian crisis led to fascism acquiring 'a broader meaning for him',

---

*Pan-Africanism and Communism: The Communist International, Africa and the Diaspora, 1919–1939* (Trenton, NJ, 2013), pp. 290–1.

57  Padmore, *Africa and World Peace*, p. 47.

58  ILP, *Final Agenda of Resolutions and Amendments: Forty-fifth Annual Conference, March 1937* (London, 1937), p. 9.

59  *Resolutions Adopted at the Revolutionary Socialist Congress, 1938* (London, 1938), p. 15.

60  Fenner Brockway, 'The Next Step: Towards Workers' Unity', *New Leader*, 21 April 1933, p. 8; Reginald Reynolds, 'Social Democracy and Empire', *Twentieth Century*, August 1933, p. 347; Reginald Reynolds, 'An Introduction to War Resistance', *Friendship*, November 1934, p. 6.

61  'A Native Speaker Addresses Southgate Labour Party: British Imperialism in Africa', *Wood Green Sentinel*, 23 November 1933.

62  Bill Schwarz, 'George Padmore', in Bill Schwarz, ed., *West Indian Intellectuals in Britain* (Manchester, 2003), p. 138.

in which systems of racial domination, such as colonialism, could be characterised as fascist.[63] In *How Britain Rules Africa*, Padmore argued that the colonies were 'the breeding-ground for the type of fascist mentality which is being let loose in Europe to-day'.[64] In September 1938, the IASB argued: 'The Kenya African has been deprived of his land by stealing infinitely more criminal than anything Nazism has done to the Jews.'[65] As Schwarz has observed, 'fascism for Padmore represented state-directed racial supremacy, in which a dominant ethnic group enslaved a subordinate ethnic group (by employing extra-economic means, including terror, to compel it to labour) on the sole basis of its putative racial identity'.[66]

Moreover, European fascism was the result of the frustrations of the 'have-not' powers of Europe. Britain and France drew super-profits from their colonies, allowing metropolitan governments to implement a limited democracy at home – a luxury not available to Germany or Italy. Padmore therefore argued: '"Democratic" Imperialism and "Fascist" Imperialism are merely interchanging ideologies corresponding to the economic and political conditions of capitalism within a given country on the one hand, and the degree to which the class struggle has developed on the other.'[67] Colonialism acted as a safety valve against fascism at home, but also as a prop to capitalism and as the primary cause of war. Therefore, the struggle against colonialism and for socialism was central to the struggles against fascism and war.

The IASB postulated an equivalence between colonialism and fascism, and even a causative relationship between the two. As a result, it dissolved Popular Front distinctions between fascist powers, such as Germany and Italy, and 'democratic' imperialist powers, such as Britain and France. As Priyamvada Gopal has observed, 'the false binary between freedom-loving democracies with colonies and tyrannical fascism had to be put

---

63  Ibid., p. 139.

64  George Padmore, *How Britain Rules Africa* (London, 1936), pp. 3–4.

65  'Politics and the Negro', *International African Opinion*, September 1938, p. 9. The IASB was neither oblivious nor indifferent to Nazi antisemitism. The same article declared the struggle against antisemitism to be part of the struggle against imperialism. Two months later, Kenyatta was part of a deputation 'to protest the German Ambassador against the persecution of the Jews in Germany'. TNA, KV 2/1787 (Kenyatta), 14 November 1938.

66  Schwarz, 'George Padmore', p. 142.

67  Padmore, *Africa and World Peace*, p. 252.

under scrutiny'.[68] British liberals and Communists who criticised the brutality of fascism while overlooking the analogous brutality of British imperialism were accused of double-standards. Those whose antifascism omitted or subordinated the anticolonial struggle were accused of ignoring both the root cause of fascism and the millions of Africans who suffered under the same tyranny as the Jews and workers of Germany.

### *Africa and World Peace, Facing Mount Kenya* and *The Black Jacobins*

The late 1930s saw the IASB's theories appear in a plethora of books. *Africa and World Peace*, published around the time of the IASB's formation, was Padmore's most significant statement of his Marxist pan-Africanism. It was published, like James's *World Revolution*, by Secker and Warburg. The primary intended audience for the book was the British working class. Padmore believed that they had shirked their anticolonial responsibilities for too long, but would still be an essential component in the defeat of capitalist-imperialism. Although James's criticisms of *How Britain Rules Africa* as appealing to the British ruling class were somewhat exaggerated (see Chapter 2), they contained a degree of truth. But there could be no mistaking Padmore's militancy in *Africa and World Peace*. If the proletarian revolution had flitted upstage in *How Britain Rules Africa*, frequently disappearing behind the curtain, in *Africa and World Peace* it was in the spotlight. Capitalism had decayed to the point that the world stood 'at the crossroads between Socialism and Fascism'. The proletariat was the only hope of leading civilisation down the path to the former.[69]

Anti-imperialism was central to the tasks that Padmore foresaw for the proletariat. Supporting his claim by quoting Lenin and Grigory Zinoviev's *Socialism and War* (1915), he argued: 'Regardless of the attitude of the middle class liberals and other advocates of Popular Fronts, the workers must demand the complete independence of the colonial peoples, which alone can guarantee world peace'.[70] Updating the logic

68 Priyamvada Gopal, *Insurgent Empire: Anticolonial Resistance and British Dissent* (London, 2019), p. 378.

69 Padmore, *Africa and World Peace*, p. 8.

70 Ibid., p. 206.

of Marx, Padmore argued that 'another spectre which haunts [the bour-geoisie] is the revolt of the colonial peoples'.[71] If imperialism was an outgrowth of capitalism, then the spectre of colonial revolt haunted Europe just as much as the spectre of European communism did.

However critical Padmore was of the Comintern's Popular Front strategy, he retained an ambivalent attitude towards the Soviet Union. He argued that it was still a revolutionary force, but that, for its self-preservation, it was making manoeuvres with imperialist powers. He called it 'the only great Power whose foreign policy is motivated by a genuine desire for peace and not merely by political expediency'.[72] Padmore understood why socialists were disturbed by the Moscow Trials, but urged loyalty to the Soviet Union. He declared that, in the event of an imperialist invasion of the Soviet Union, the proletariat should rally to its defence, which was also the Trotskyist position, and therefore also James's.[73]

Stafford Cripps, a Labour MP and leader of the soon-to-be-defunct Socialist League, contributed a foreword to *Africa and World Peace*. Cripps's life and legacy would become increasingly entangled with the colonial struggle through his 'mission' to India in 1942, and through the marriage of his daughter, Peggy, to the Gold Coast anticolonialist Joe Appiah shortly after his death in 1952. He complained that the problem of imperialism 'has never been fully understood within the Labour movement of Great Britain' and praised Padmore for performing 'another great service of enlightenment in this book'.[74] Reginald Reynolds, review-ing the book for the *New Leader*, judged it better than Leonard Barnes's *Skeletons of Empire*. He said that Padmore's 'exposure of the Mandates System and of the treatment of the colonial problem by the Popular Front governments in France and Spain should be read by every Socialist'.[75]

The book was reviewed far more harshly by Padmore's old comrade, Reginald Bridgeman. Bridgeman called *Africa and World Peace* politi-cally 'confusing', because '(i) while recognising the imminence of war, it develops the argument that the League of Nations can never serve the cause of peace, being dominated by imperialist nations; (ii) it ignores the

---

71  Ibid., p. 256.
72  Ibid., p. 5.
73  Ibid., p. 257.
74  Ibid., pp. ix–xi.
75  Reginald Reynolds, 'Skeletons of Empire', *New Leader*, 2 July 1937, p. 5.

principle of collective security, implying that the Soviet Union is a mere spectator of events and unconcerned with the position of the oppressed peoples.' Bridgeman was following Communist Popular Front policy. He asserted that the 'democracies of Europe are determined to support the League of Nations'; Padmore's attack on the League of Nations thus delayed 'the formation of that unity of struggle between the white workers and coloured workers'. For all Padmore's invocation of Lenin and socialist revolution, 'the arguments which he presents in the book are of a nature to divide the workers of the world'.[76]

While *Africa and World Peace* exemplified the Marxist pan-Africanism that dominated the IASB's official statements, Kenyatta's *Facing Mount Kenya*, published the following year, was an expression of the author's revolutionary nationalism. In 1935, Kenyatta began attending Bronisław Malinowski's anthropology seminars at the London School of Economics.[77] Bruce Berman has examined how *Facing Mount Kenya* 'developed out of Malinowski's project for social anthropology (ethnography as politics) and, more importantly, expressed Kenyatta's attempt to resolve the dilemmas of representing the Kikuyu (politics as ethnography)'.[78] In *Facing Mount Kenya*, Kenyatta examined Kikuyu society by combining his insider knowledge with the methods of the Western academy. In this way, Kenyatta calls to mind Daniel Matlin's idea of the African American 'indigenous interpreter' (particularly in Matlin's discussion of Kenneth B. Clark, a psychologist who wrote about the 'urban crisis' and Black uprisings of the 1960s).[79] Assuming the roles of both subject and object, Kenyatta aimed to vindicate Kikuyu culture through the description of a sophisticated society ravaged by settler colonialism.

Like James and Padmore, Kenyatta was introduced to Fredric Warburg by Brockway. After seeing a 'part-written' version of the book, Warburg was impressed by its originality and signed a contract almost immediately.[80] Simon Gikandi has identified a 'turning point' in

---

76  Reginald Bridgeman, 'Africa: A Confused Argument', *Labour Monthly*, September 1937, pp. 577–9.

77  Jeremy Murray-Brown, *Kenyatta* (London, 1972), p. 188.

78  Bruce Berman, 'Ethnography as Politics, Politics as Ethnography: Kenyatta, Malinowski, and the Making of *Facing Mount Kenya*', *Canadian Journal of African Studies* 30 (1996), p. 315.

79  Daniel Matlin, *On the Corner: African American Intellectuals and the Urban Crisis* (Cambridge, MA, 2013), esp. Chapter 1.

80  Fredric Warburg, *An Occupation for Gentlemen* (London, 1959), p. 251.

Photograph of Jomo Kenyatta used as the frontispiece of *Facing Mount Kenya*
Getty Images

Kenyatta's 'self-representation' at the time of the book's publication. Previously, Kenyatta had been a 'would-be colonial gentleman' identifying with 'Englishness'. However, in 1938 he transformed from 'Johnstone' to 'Jomo', and appeared in the frontispiece of *Facing Mount Kenya* 'wearing a colobus monkey skin, the symbol of traditional moral authority, and holding a spear, the insignia of what he considered Africanness'.[81] Gikandi is correct to identify a shift in Kenyatta's self-representation, but it was not so much a 'turning point' as a fork in the road. As discussed in previous chapters, Kenyatta presented himself as a colonial gentleman when writing to *The Times* or being interviewed by *East Africa* – but he wrote and spoke like a revolutionary nationalist when working with the CPGB or IAFE. By the second half of the 1930s, Kenyatta had made the decision to adhere to the latter image more consistently. His change of name and adoption of Kikuyu attire represented a consolidation of this decision.

Kenyatta was assisted in the preparation of the book by Dinah Stock, an English Oxford graduate of Irish parentage, born in 1902.[82] Stock had been an anticolonial activist since the 1920s. Her thinking about imperialism during this later period is illustrated by an article in which she criticised the Popular Front ('co-operation with any capitalist party must mean acquiescing in an imperialist policy') and called colonial labourers 'the real proletariat of Great Britain'.[83] She was introduced to Kenyatta in May 1937 at a meeting in Trafalgar Square. McGregor Ross, upon whose financial generosity Kenyatta had relied in his early years in London, finally broke with Kenyatta in 1935, so the destitute Kenyatta was happy to take a room in Stock's flat in Camden, on the same street as Padmore and Pizer's.[84] Reynolds, who had worked closely with Stock over the previous decade, never doubted Kenyatta's 'political convictions', but had other misgivings about him ('mostly petty things – conceit and snobbery, for example'). Stock had 'a higher opinion of Jomo'.[85] When Kenyatta met Stock, he had only a collection of essays. It was Stock who arranged the essays into publishable form – a task which, according to Makonnen, took her only 'about three weeks'.[86] Unfortunately, Makonnen's is the fullest account of Stock's involvement in the book's production. As I discuss more fully below, however, male activists

---

81 Simon Gikandi, 'Pan-Africanism and Cosmopolitanism: The Case of Jomo Kenyatta', *English Studies in Africa* 43 (2000), pp. 6, 10.

82 For more on Stock's life, see Basil Clarke, *Taking What Comes: A Biography of A. G. Stock (Dinah)* (Chandigarh, 1999).

83 Dinah Stock, 'British Fascism: (i) In the Empire', *Controversy*, July 1938, p. 190.

84 Murray-Brown, *Kenyatta*, p. 182; Clarke, *Taking What Comes*, p. 83.

85 Reginald Reynolds, *My Life and Crimes* (London, 1956), p. 152.

86 Makonnen, *Pan-Africanism from Within*, p. 162.

often trivialised the role played by women in intellectual production. It is possible that her role was more significant.

For Kenyatta, the book fulfilled the IASB mission: to educate both Europeans and Africans. He said that the book was 'for the benefit both of Europeans and of those Africans who have been detached from their tribal life'.[87] As ever, he placed land at the centre of *Facing Mount Kenya*. The most fertile land having been appropriated by White settlers, Kenyatta said that land tenure 'is the key to the people's life; it secures for them that peaceful tillage of the soil which supplies their material needs and enables them to perform their magic and traditional ceremonies in undisturbed serenity, facing Mount Kenya'.[88] This statement also points to the central tension within *Facing Mount Kenya*. Did Kenyatta seek a return to precolonial Kikuyu society? Or, like James and Padmore, did he seek a society that figured as part of a global modernity, now free from imperialist exploitation? This tension remained unresolved. Kenyatta praised the old system of land tenure based on 'private property' (though without 'the exclusive use of the land by the owner, or the extorting of rents') and the old Kikuyu religion, which fostered 'tribal unity'.[89] He detailed how these systems and beliefs were being destroyed by British imperialism. He occasionally hinted at the necessity of a new Kikuyu culture, but the book was mostly a paean to the old ways. Finally, in the conclusion, Kenyatta praised 'some progressive ideas' of Europeans, such as 'the ideals of material prosperity, of medicine, and hygiene, and literacy'.[90] He conceded that European technology could 'offer the African a way of life which was really superior to the one his fathers lived before him', adding that, while Africans did not want 'the gas bomb or the armed police force', they would 'choose what parts of European culture could be beneficially transplanted, and how they could be adapted'.[91]

Warburg called the book 'a dismal flop'. Only 517 copies of the first edition were sold.[92] Nevertheless, Peter Abrahams recalled that, upon

---

87 Jomo Kenyatta, *Facing Mount Kenya: The Tribal Life of the Gikuyu* (London, 1938), p. xvi.

88 Ibid., p. xxi.

89 Ibid., pp. 26, 251.

90 Ibid., p. 317.

91 Ibid., p. 318.

92 Warburg, *Occupation for Gentlemen*, p. 253. The book was reissued after the outbreak of the Mau Mau uprising, and sold many more copies.

his arrival in London in 1940, *Facing Mount Kenya* 'was still a great talking point among those interested in African affairs, and [Kenyatta] himself was something of a lion in certain left-wing socialist circles'.[93] Unsurprisingly, Stock gave the book a glowing review in the *New Leader*. She was struck by Kenyatta's depiction of precolonial Kikuyu life, romantically calling the Kikuyu 'a people who valued freedom, equality and co-operation', and chiding British socialists who thought of 'their anti-Imperialist activities in terms of "doing something for" the Colonial peoples who are presumed to be backward and to need guidance'. *Facing Mount Kenya* was 'a good cure for that mentality'.[94]

H. N. Brailsford's friendly yet deeply condescending review must have done little to alleviate Padmore's distrust of him. Brailsford enquired:

> How often has a man of a primitive race written a book about the customs, rites and institutions of his own people, and done it, moreover, with scientific competence and some literary power? . . . While he is at pains to be accurate in his detailed accounts of the family system of the Gikuyu, their economic life, their rites and magic, he is not afraid to write with strong feeling, and when he does so, he can use our language with power and skill.[95]

Ironically, the most substantial criticism of the book from the British socialist movement came from James. The Marxist Group, in an article probably written by James, had analysed the Kenyan situation in 1937. Like Kenyatta, James argued that, before European colonialism, Kenyans 'had one of the most democratic systems in the world' and were 'a happy people'. But James was unequivocal about the need for African modernity:

> Lenin . . . said that the colonial peoples need not pass through the capitalist stage. The socialist state can assist them to pass from their primitive conditions straight to the socialist form. And he is quite right. For that would benefit both the Colonials and the British workers. However admirable a form of life primitive communism is,

---

93  Peter Abrahams, *The Coyaba Chronicles: Reflections on the Black Experience in the Twentieth Century* (Kingston, 2000), pp. 36–7.

94  Dinah Stock, 'An African Describes His Own People', *New Leader*, 1 July 1938, p. 7.

95  H. N. Brailsford, 'An African on African Life', *New Statesman and Nation*, 17 September 1938, p. 420.

thoughtful Africans realise to-day that in the modern world, this has no place. The African must adopt Western technique in production.[96]

James was therefore ambivalent in his review of *Facing Mount Kenya*. He welcomed the publication of the book, but expressed some reservation:

Are [Africans] to go back to the old life, merely selecting what they approve of in European civilisation? This seems to be Mr Kenyatta's view. That religion and that life, vilely slandered as they have been and admirable as they are, rested on a certain method of industry. When the land is won the African will have to modernise his method of production, and his religion will inevitably follow.[97]

James was making this argument as a materialist: the Kikuyu religion and other cultural forms would evaporate as Africa industrialised; new social relations would emerge as the means of production were transformed. James appreciated Kenyatta's vindication of African society against European slanders, but balked at the suggestion of a return to Kikuyu 'magic and traditional ceremonies'.

James's own major work in this period was his masterful history of the Haitian Revolution, *The Black Jacobins*. As Laurent Dubois has observed, James had a long history of using the story of the revolution and its leader, Toussaint Louverture, to challenge European racism.[98] With funding from his friend from Nelson, Harry Spencer, James researched the revolution in Paris. He continued to refine Toussaint's story, most notably in his play, *Toussaint Louverture*, and in his other 1938 book, *A History of Negro Revolt*. The latter book was published in the left-wing *Fact* series edited by Raymond Postgate. James surveyed the history of Black revolutions as a means of exploring contemporary potentials for Black liberation.[99]

There is a voluminous interpretive literature on *The Black Jacobins*. It has been understood variously as an intervention about the place of

---

96 'Kenya', *Fight*, January 1937, pp. 12–13.

97 C. L. R. James, 'The Voice of Africa', *International African Opinion*, August 1938, p. 3.

98 Laurent Dubois, 'Foreword', in C. L. R. James, *Toussaint Louverture: The Story of the Only Successful Slave Revolt in History*, ed. Christian Høgsbjerg (Durham, NC, 2013 [1934]), p. vii.

99 James, *History of Negro Revolt*.

armed struggle in the anticolonial movement, a reformulation of Marxist ideas of time or the revolutionary subject, and a meditation on the
relationship between individual agency and historical forces.[100] It is
beyond the scope of this book to intervene in all of these debates. But it
should be noted that, as discussed above, *The Black Jacobins* was informed
by the various crises of the 1930s and by the IASB's theory of interdependent revolutions. James himself later remembered that this theory
'was most unambiguously stated in . . . *The Black Jacobins*, which not
only influenced but was very much influenced by the work of The
Bureau.'[101] He aimed the book not only 'against the imperialists', but also
against Communists who 'continually wrote and spoke in terms of
"giving" freedom to Africans'.[102] He ended the book with a call for a
global revolution to achieve international socialism. He theorised that
the process of revolution would teach the European working class to
accept African revolutionaries as their allies: 'The white workers in
Europe, as indifferent to-day as the French before August 1792, will
recognise their allies in time as did the Paris workers in the hour of
danger.'[103]

The book was well received in James's circles. He kept a clipping of
Brailsford's review, which said James had 'accomplished a difficult task
with spirit and skill'.[104] Pizer reviewed the book for both *International
African Opinion* and *Controversy*. She approved of James's analysis that
it was only through the combination of 'the pressure of the Paris masses'
and 'the tenacity and revolutionary instinct of the Negroes' that the
revolution was successful. Developing James's argument, Pizer looked to
the 1848 revolutions, the impetus that the Bolshevik Revolution had
given to revolutionary movements across Europe, and the influence of
the 1936 French general strike on African and Caribbean workers, to
argue that revolutions were 'as much the consequence of example as the

100 For discussions of *Black Jacobins*, see Anthony Bogues, *Black Heretics, Black
Prophets: Radical Political Intellectuals* (New York, 2003), Chapter 3; Charles Forsdick
and Christian Høgsbjerg, eds, *The Black Jacobins Reader* (Durham, NC, 2017); Christian
Høgsbjerg, *C. L. R. James in Imperial Britain* (Durham, NC, 2014), Chapter 5; David
Scott, *Conscripts of Modernity: The Tragedy of Colonial Enlightenment* (Durham, NC,
2004).
101 James, 'Notes on the Life of George Padmore', p. 40.
102 James, *Nkrumah and the Ghana Revolution*, p. 68.
103 James, *Black Jacobins*, p. 315.
104 H. N. Brailsford, 'Black Spartacus', *Reynolds News*, 25 September 1938.

economic and political conditions'.[105] Arthur Ballard, James's Trotskyist comrade and newly resubscribed ILP member, similarly saw in *The Black Jacobins* a model for contemporary revolution.[106] Both Pizer and Ballard reviewed the book for ILP publications, and in these reviews criticised the Popular Front distinction between 'democratic' and fascist imperialist powers. They urged metropolitan and colonial workers to defeat their own imperialist bourgeoisie before waging a war for 'democracy'. It is therefore worth examining in detail how the IASB and the ILP, after the turbulence over Ethiopia, came to be so closely politically aligned.

## The IASB and the ILP

As Gidon Cohen has argued, 'By 1938 the ILP could plausibly, if not completely accurately, claim to have a consensus agreement on its basic philosophy, which would have appeared an extremely unlikely characterisation of the divided and factionalised Party of the early 1930s.'[107] This new political coherence is true of the ILP's anti-imperialism. The wide-ranging views of the 1920s, which often had paternalism at their core, were replaced by analyses of imperialism that were at least broadly Leninist, and recognised the agency of colonial peoples. Moreover, the ILP's increasingly materialist rather than moralistic analysis meant that anticolonialism was no longer treated as a peripheral issue that could be separated from critiques of domestic capitalism.

Padmore's praise of ILP anti-imperialism in February 1938 was thus not an isolated incident. As noted above, publishing in ILP outlets was central to IASB strategy. Padmore wrote articles for the ILP's journal, *Controversy*, on practically a monthly basis during the first half of 1938. Topics ranged from the Caribbean labour rebellions to South African intrigue in the protectorates of Basutoland, Bechuanaland and Swaziland. These articles consistently identified capitalist-imperialism as the

---

105  Dorothy Pizer, 'How Blacks Fought for Freedom', *International African Opinion*, October 1938, pp. 11–12; Dorothy Pizer, 'A Lesson in Revolution', *Controversy*, January 1939, pp. 318–20.

106  Arthur Ballard, 'In the Empire', *New Leader*, 9 December 1938, p. 6.

107  Gidon Cohen, *The Failure of a Dream: The Independent Labour Party from Disaffiliation to World War II* (London, 2007), p. 211.

source of colonial peoples' woes, and featured appeals to assistance from the British labour and socialist movements. Even Kenyatta, less convinced than James or Padmore about the importance of European socialism for the African revolution, contributed an article about land rights in Kenya to *Left* (the rebranded *Controversy*) in November 1939.[108] Articles by IASB members appeared in the *New Leader* from the organisation's inception in 1937, and with increasing regularity from 1938 onwards. The newspaper even published an 'Empire Special' on 29 April 1938, featuring contributions from Kenyatta and Padmore. Brockway contributed a comparison between fascism and imperialism, concluding: 'Fascism is Capitalist dictatorship in developed countries. Imperialism is Capitalist dictatorship in underdeveloped countries.'[109]

Carol Polsgrove has argued that the IASB, in publishing through the *New Leader*, 'could speak to an audience already created rather than having to create their own audience from scratch'. She notes that the newspaper's socialist readers were 'a most appropriate audience'.[110] This begs the question of whether the IASB's relationship with the ILP was a marriage of convenience or a more fundamental alliance. Makonnen, while voicing respect for Brockway and James Maxton, later recalled: 'I felt that George Padmore was really seeing too much of the ILP office . . . To me this was almost as treasonable as working for the British Communist Party.' Makonnen 'wanted to be a purist, in the revolutionary sense, and in the sense of racial self sufficiency'. He felt that Padmore writing for the *New Leader* damaged this ambition.[111]

Padmore apparently assured Makonnen that 'he was doing it because it was good publicity'.[112] But this does not square with the IASB's, and especially Padmore's, immersion within the ILP. It is likely that Padmore said this to fend off Makonnen's accusations, or that Makonnen himself fabricated the statement in order to promote a narrative of pan-Africanist independence. Not only was the IASB's 'Manifesto Against War'

---

108  Jomo Kenyatta, 'Democracy in Kenya', *Left*, November 1939, pp. 297–9.

109  Fenner Brockway, 'Has Hitler Anything to Teach Our Ruling Class?', *New Leader*, 29 April 1938, p. iv.

110  Carol Polsgrove, 'George Padmore's Use of Periodicals to Build a Movement', in Fitzroy Baptiste and Rupert Lewis, eds, *George Padmore: Pan-African Revolutionary* (Kingston, 2009), p. 99.

111  Makonnen, *Pan-Africanism from Within*, pp. 179, 182.

112  Ibid., p. 179.

published in the *New Leader* in September 1938, but the following week Padmore, in his capacity as chair of the IASB, was one of the signatories to another manifesto against war published in the *New Leader* (signed by the likes of Brockway, Maxton, Alfred Salter, Campbell Stephen, J. F. Horrabin, Harold Moody, Vera Brittain, Havelock Ellis, Laurence Housman, C. E. M. Joad, Ethel Mannin and George Orwell). In a similar spirit to the IASB's manifesto, it proclaimed: 'If war comes, it will be our duty to resist.'[113] The IASB did not simply use the *New Leader* as a platform, but also as a place to formulate and express joint policy with the ILP. Polsgrove's observation that the IASB published in the *New Leader* to reach a larger audience is correct, but does not go far enough. The IASB viewed the ILP as the only British party that placed imperialism at the centre of its analysis, and, following the Bureau's belief in revolutionary interdependence, as a crucial nodal point in the global struggle against capitalist-imperialism. If the breakdown of imperialism in the metropole was crucial to the overthrow of colonial rule, then making alliances with the most revolutionary party in Britain was an essential tactic.

Moreover, there were broader links between the IASB and ILP than simply publishing. Padmore spoke at the ILP's 1937 summer school in Letchworth. The *New Leader* report described him as 'a figure of a man, with a vigorous and genial personality, and the students listened to him with great interest'. Padmore set out his proposed war policy for socialists: turn imperialist war into civil war in the event of war between two capitalist groups if the Soviet Union is neutral or in the opposite camp; overthrow the British government, and then go to the assistance of the Soviet Union if it is an ally; and implement workers' sanctions in the event that an imperialist government attacks a colonial people.[114] He returned the following year, and was joined by Kenyatta.[115] Earlier in the year, Kenyatta had given greetings to the ILP annual conference in Norwich on behalf of the Kikuyu Central Association.[116] In November

---

113 'If War Comes, We Shall Still Resist', *New Leader*, 30 September 1938, p. 4; 'A Manifesto from the Colonial Workers', *New Leader*, 23 September 1938, p. 4.

114 'Socialist Issues Discussed at the ILP Summer School', *New Leader*, 13 August 1937, p. 3.

115 'ILP Summer School for Comradeship and Keen Discussion', *New Leader*, 15 July 1938.

116 'British, American, Italian and Colonial Workers Greet Conference Opening', *New Leader*, 22 April 1938 (conference supplement), p. ii.

1938, Chris Jones addressed a meeting at Glasgow City Hall alongside Bob Edwards 'to celebrate the 21st anniversary of the Russian Revolution'.[117] As Christian Høgsbjerg has observed, 'For Braithwaite [Jones's original name] to be invited to address such a rally alongside a national figure such as Edwards is testament to the high standing and regard in which he was held'.[118]

The most significant rallying point for the IASB in this period, other than the looming world war, was the Caribbean labour rebellions. Sweeping the arc of the islands from the oilfields of Trinidad to the sugar estates of Jamaica, the disturbances reached their peak with a series of violently repressed revolts in 1937 and 1938. Schwarz has observed that the events encouraged new '(if shaky)' alliances between activists in London and emerging labour leaders in the Caribbean.[119] Høgsbjerg and Daniel Whittall have both convincingly refuted Stephen Howe's argument that many Caribbean figures in Britain, including the IASB, 'responded to the risings in surprisingly muted fashion'. The series of uprisings animated both the IASB and the more moderate League of Coloured Peoples (LCP).[120]

What has gone unremarked, however, is the collaboration of the ILP and IASB in responding to the rebellions. When the Trinidadian labour leader Uriah Butler was sentenced to two years' imprisonment, Maxton defended Butler in the House of Commons. The transcript of the speech was approvingly printed in the IASB's *African Sentinel*.[121] The uprisings prompted a series of sympathetic articles in the *New Leader* from the likes of Brockway, Ballard and John Aplin. Complementing the IASB's appeal to the TUC to aid striking workers, Aplin argued that it was 'up

---

117	John McNair, 'News from Somewhere', *New Leader*, 18 November 1938, p. 7.

118	Christian Høgsbjerg, *Mariner, Renegade and Castaway: Chris Braithwaite: Seamen's Organiser, Socialist and Militant Pan-Africanist* (London, 2014), p. 57.

119	Bill Schwarz, 'Introduction: Crossing the Seas', in Schwarz, *West Indian Intellectuals in Britain*, pp. 6–7.

120	Christian Høgsbjerg, ' "A Thorn in the Side of Great Britain": C. L. R. James and the Caribbean Labour Rebellions of the 1930s', *Small Axe* 15 (2011), p. 33; Stephen Howe, *Anticolonialism in British Politics: The Left and the End of Empire, 1918–1964* (Oxford, 1993), p. 103; Daniel Whittall, 'Creolising London: Black West Indian Activism and the Politics of Race and Empire in Britain, 1931–1948', doctoral thesis, Royal Holloway, University of London, 2012, p. 309.

121	James Maxton, 'Three Cheers for Uriah Butler', *African Sentinel*, March–April 1938, p. 9.

to the rank and file . . . to make the Government acutely aware of the fact that British Trade Unionists regard Negro Trade Unionists as brothers and comrades'.[122] In June 1938, the ILP's F. A. Ridley spoke on a platform in Trafalgar Square with Kenyatta, James, Jones and Padmore about conditions in the Caribbean. He noted: 'Much talk was made today of the hardships suffered by the minorities in fascist countries, but these minorities were being treated very well in comparison to the negroes in the British Empire.'[123] Ridley's speech, equating fascism and colonialism, illustrates both the ideological confluence and the practical relationship reached by the ILP and IASB in the late 1930s.

The IASB and ILP also collaborated on an anti-imperialist 'counter-exhibition' to the Empire Exhibition held in Bellahouston Park in Glasgow. Ballard was the lead organiser. He secured space in Kingston Public Hall, two miles from the main exhibition, for two weeks in August.[124] Sarah Britton observes that the ILP's Workers' Exhibition should not be seen 'as merely a crank voice from the political fringe', especially due to the ILP's strength in Glasgow.[125] The party stated in the week before its exhibition opened that 'the visitors to Kingston Public Hall will learn far more truth about the Empire than in all the impressive buildings of the official exhibition'.[126] The Workers' Exhibition was formally opened by Ethel Mannin and James Carmichael, and messages were received from Maxton, Brockway and Jawaharlal Nehru.[127]

The IASB declared that the anti-imperialist exhibition was a significant development in British socialism:

This is indeed a great step forward in Socialist history; it marks a sharp departure from theory to practice. British organisations who hitherto used the colonial question as a mere decoration in the framework of their political platform will see the seriousness of the question which they have not understood or have handled lightly: that while the

122 John Aplin, 'Those Dirty N******', *New Leader*, 14 January 1938, p. 2; IASB Executive Committee, 'To the Delegates of the Trades Union Congress', p. 2.

123 TNA, MEPO 38/91 (IASB), 26 June 1938.

124 For more on the exhibition and counter-exhibition, see Sarah Britton, '"Come and See the Empire by the All Red Route!": Anti-Imperialism and Exhibitions in Inter-war Britain', *History Workshop Journal* 69 (2010).

125 Ibid., p. 82.

126 'The "Other" Exhibition', *New Leader*, 12 August 1938, p. 5.

127 'Success of Anti-Imperialist Exhibition', *New Leader*, 19 August 1938, p. 5.

> colonial workers are in bondage, the British workers labour but in vain
> to free themselves from the burdening yoke of Imperialism.[128]

The ILP was, according to the IASB, the first British socialist party to give a central place to imperialism in its analysis and practice. It was therefore the pioneer whom other socialists should emulate. The reasons why the IASB stressed the novelty of this development are best exemplified through a comparison of two congresses held by the ILP's international group, the International Bureau for Revolutionary Socialist Unity, held in 1936 and 1938.

In October and November 1936, IBRSU members gathered in Brussels for the Revolutionary Socialist Congress. A spirit of internationalism pervaded the event. A resolution on war, fascism and imperialism condemned the League of Nations, treated fascism as a reactionary form of capitalism, and declared that the European working class must do more to win the confidence of colonial peoples.[129] But this was an overwhelmingly European affair. The only movements from outside Europe to be represented were from the United States, Canada and Palestine (a Zionist organisation).[130] The Spanish Civil War dominated the discussion. The Partido Obrero de Unificación Marxista (POUM) – affiliated to the IBRSU – was a belligerent in the Civil War. It was represented at the congress by Julián Gorkin, who throughout a long speech made only the following statement about the war's significance for imperialism: '[T]he resistance of the Moors in North Africa against General Franco is increasing. This rebel General was forced to shoot 24 Moorish notabilities who protested against the further recruiting of Moors for the Fascist campaign in Spain. Our brothers in Morocco are beginning to realise that Morocco can only be saved if Spain is saved by the workers.'[131] Gorkin failed to interrogate North Africans' earlier disillusionment in the Republican government, which had led to Franco's ability to recruit African troops in the first place. Furthermore, he implied that the anticolonial struggle was dependent on the Spanish workers' struggle, but not the inverse.

---

128 'Anti-Imperialist Exhibition in Glasgow', *International African Opinion*, July 1938, p. 16.

129 *Report of Revolutionary Socialist Congress, 1936* (Barcelona, 1936), pp. 27–32.

130 Ibid., pp. 2–3.

131 Ibid., p. 13.

Much had changed by the time of the next Revolutionary Socialist Congress, held in Paris in February 1938. The European parties were joined by Padmore as a delegate of the African Workers' Party. Observers were sent by the Ligue de Défense de la Race Nègre (LDRN), Indo-Chinese Colonial Union, Madagascar National Liberation Society, Pondicherry Native Trade Unions and the Étoile Nord-Africaine (these groups were 'for organisational reasons unable to send full delegates').[132] The delegates were overwhelmingly European and the observers over-whelmingly African and Asian – but this was a congress that was much more global in reach and perspective. Speaking of the 1938 conference, the ILP itself said that the 'main significance of the Conference was the alliance developed between three sections of the International Move-ment: (a) the Bureau Parties, (b) the International Communist Opposition, and (c) the Workers' organisations in the Colonial coun-tries'.[133] This cooperation eventually led to the formation of an 'Enlarged Bureau', which included the IASB, the Indo-Chinese Workers' and Peas-ants' Party, and the Palestine Federation of Socialist Communes.[134] The Enlarged Bureau planned to hold an International Anti-Imperialist Conference, ultimately abandoned because of the Second World War.[135]

The IASB's understanding of the equivalence between imperialism and fascism also began to find frequent expression among ILP members immediately after their return from Paris. Coinciding with Padmore's increased immersion in ILP networks, this was surely no accident, and can be ascribed to Padmore's influence within the party. Travelling and lodging together at congresses fostered both personal and political links; Padmore told the ILP delegate, John McNair, that the congress had been 'splendid'.[136] Padmore, of all the IASB members, was particularly close to the ILP. After the IASB moved into the ILP offices during the second half of 1938, the intelligence services described him as being 'virtually in charge of [ILP] negro activity'.[137]

---

132 *Resolutions Adopted at the Revolutionary Socialist Congress, 1938*, p. 2.

133 ILP, *Annual Report of the NAC, 1938* (London, 1938), p. 8.

134 ILP, *Annual Report of the NAC, 1939* (London, 1939), p. 5.

135 Fenner Brockway, 'Workers' Movement in Other Countries', *New Leader*, 2 September 1938, p. 5.

136 John McNair, 'Towards Revolutionary Socialist Unity', *New Leader*, 4 March 1938, p. 4.

137 TNA, CO 323/1690/5 (IASB), March 1939.

There was a major political confluence between the IASB and ILP, and the ILP offered much material and political support to the smaller organisation, despite its own limited resources. However, there is a question as to how thoroughly this new, militant anti-imperialism enveloped the ILP. James, who left the party in December 1936, remembered that while the ILP, unlike other British left-wing parties, was 'interested in the colonial question, [the] party as a whole left it to Fenner Brockway to actively pursue the issue'.[138] But James's account affirms that most members of the ILP supported the party's anti-imperialism at least in theory, even if not all of them pursued it as energetically as Brockway.

James was in fact being somewhat harsh on other members of the party, such as Edwards, McNair, and especially Ballard, the organiser of the anti-imperialist exhibition in Glasgow (though, given that Ballard was also a member of James's Trotskyist group, James might not have had Ballard in mind when he made this remark). In 1938, the number of *New Leader* articles about imperialism, and particularly about Africa and the Caribbean, proliferated – many of them written by Ballard. Ballard also stocked *International African Opinion* in his Socialist Bookshop and promoted the journal in the *New Leader*.[139] C. A. Smith, as editor of *Controversy*, similarly recommended the first issue of *International African Opinion*, and included Padmore's *Africa and World Peace* in a list of books for a study guide on the British Empire.[140] ILP members spoke at IASB rallies in Trafalgar Square; it was Brockway who introduced James, Kenyatta and Padmore to Warburg; and the ILP allowed the IASB to use its offices. This was neither a marriage of convenience nor an abstract ideological affinity, but a deep institutional relationship. The ILP, guided by its anti-imperialism and a respect for the IASB's activism and ideas, provided support to a group of Black radicals who were not even formal members of the party. In turn, the ILP's political philosophy was shaped by the IASB's pan-Africanism.

---

138  James, 'Autobiography, 1932–38', pp. 49–50.

139  Arthur Ballard, 'West Indian Workers Are Uniting while British Fascism Spreads to Guiana', *New Leader*, 8 July 1938, p. 4; Arthur Ballard, 'Round the Empire', *New Leader*, 10 March 1939, p. 6.

140  'In Brief', *Controversy*, August 1938; 'Study Guide No. 5: The British Empire', *Controversy*, December 1938.

## Ethel Mannin and Reginald Reynolds

IASB members were especially close to Ethel Mannin and Reginald Reynolds. The couple were ILP members but were not part of the leadership. Mannin was a novelist born in 1900. She joined the ILP in 1934, but remained sceptical of party affiliations. In 1939 she wrote that she 'was never a hundred per cent Marxist, being too much of an individualist, and an anarchist by nature'.[141] Reynolds was five years younger than Mannin. He came from a Quaker background. As a sixteen-year-old, he had been converted to socialism, pacifism and vegetarianism by the history master, Stanley King Beer, at his school in Saffron Walden.[142] Like Brockway, combining nonconformism with socialism, vegetarianism and pacifism (though, like Brockway, he abandoned the latter during the 1930s), Reynolds belongs to a strand of British political thought also strikingly concerned with colonialism. He became general secretary of the No More War Movement in 1933, before realising that he and his colleagues 'had ceased to be pacifists'.[143] He left the ILP after the 1939 annual conference, at which he unsuccessfully attempted to pass a vote of censure against John McGovern for his support of Zionism.[144]

Mannin and Reynolds were fiercely committed to internationalism and anti-imperialism. Mannin had written bitingly satirical anti-imperialist articles for the *New Leader* since the early 1930s. In one article, she lampooned colonial governors' attitudes towards colonial peoples, observing the irony that, while children sang patriotic songs on Empire Day, 'the fathers of thousands of these children will be standing hopelessly at the street-corners all over the country, hungry, jobless, despairing'.[145] Reynolds was drawn to anti-imperialism for moral reasons, springing from his Quaker-informed socialism. As a young man he asked himself: 'By what moral right did one man or a group of men impose laws on others, when their title was merely that they were stronger, luckier, or more cunning (or that their ancestors had been so)

---

141  Ethel Mannin, *Privileged Spectator* (London, 1939), p. 78.

142  Reynolds, *My Life and Crimes*, pp. 40–1.

143  Ibid., p. 139.

144  Ibid., p. 166.

145  Ethel Mannin, 'Your Child and Empire Day: Tell Him What It Means', *New Leader*, 19 May 1933, p. 2.

than other mortals?'[146] His activism for Indian anticolonialism led to his writing *The White Sahibs in India* (1937), to which Nehru contributed a foreword.[147]

It was this anti-imperialism that led to a close relationship with the IASB. Reynolds remembers that, through Padmore, he was 'rapidly drawn into a circle of coloured people in London'.[148] Mannin likewise remembered becoming involved with the IASB in 1937, inviting members to meetings of her Colonial Liberties Group in Chalk Farm. She chaired the meetings at which 'George Padmore or some other vigorous coloured anti-imperialist would lecture'.[149] Bunche recorded a meeting at which Wallace-Johnson was on the platform. Following the meeting, the group went to a café, 'apparently at Ethel Mannin's expense'.[150] While buying coffee for the group was itself a small gesture, this event is also illustrative of the ways in which sympathetic White socialists made financial contributions to the IASB and its members, who were often short of money. Bunche and Padmore also visited Mannin's home in Wimbledon on a few occasions. Reynolds was wearing a POUM badge during one visit, on 16 May 1937. This was shortly after the Catalonia May Days, in which Spanish Republicans, including Communists, violently repressed anarchists and the ILP's comrades in the POUM. According to Bunche, he was 'very' anti-Communist and anti-Labour. Reynolds remarked that 'a class analysis of [French prime minister Léon] Blum's African policy would be revealing and damaging to the Popular Front'.[151] All of this reveals a practical and ideological affinity with the IASB. Even Makonnen, the IASB member most hostile to collaboration with White socialists, remembered, when discussing what he considered to be Brockway's tepid response to the Mau Mau uprising in Kenya during the 1950s: 'This is what made it so refreshing to come across an Ethel Mannin whose immediate reaction to the Mau Mau killings might be: "To hell with those settlers. Let the blood flow. Give 'em more!" One needed this kind of hard core, the uncompromising element – people who saw the priorities like Sylvia Pankhurst and would shed no tears'.[152]

---

146  Reynolds, *My Life and Crimes*, p. 56.
147  Reginald Reynolds, *The White Sahibs in India* (London, 1937).
148  Reynolds, *My Life and Crimes*, p. 116.
149  Mannin, *Privileged Spectator*, p. 150.
150  Bunche, 1937 Annual Diary, 28 April.
151  Ibid., 16 May.
152  Makonnen, *Pan-Africanism from Within*, p. 181.

The Black radical to whom Mannin and Reynolds were particularly close was Chris Jones, the IASB's organising secretary. Reynolds remembered: 'At public meetings Chris was dynamite. At his best in the open air, where his tremendous voice scorned the use of a microphone, he would startle a crowd as much by his sudden vocal inflexions as by his blazing revolutionary wrath.'[153] Mannin's *Comrade O Comrade* (1947), a novel based on the British socialist movement of the 1930s, contains a character based on Jones, who had died in 1944. In her author's note, Mannin wrote that 'the socialist and anti-imperialist struggle lost a valiant fighter by his death, and many of us, myself included, a good comrade and friend'. She insisted that 'he would not merely not have minded my short caricatures of him in this book but, on the contrary, feel flattered'.[154] In the novel, Mary Thane (a fictionalised representation of Mannin) goes to a political meeting at which a 'very black Negro [Jones] harangu[ed] the crowd'. Despite the meeting being about the Spanish Civil War, Jones 'went on for a solid hour' putting 'the anti-Imperialist case'.[155]

However, through Reynolds's, and especially Mannin's, reminiscences of Black radicals there runs an exoticising and essentialising thread. Howe observes that James, during his time in Britain, 'often found himself treated as an exotic curiosity'. Mannin, Reynolds and Warburg, 'in their frequently quoted but brief reminiscences of James, treated him in a rather similar if more urbanely expressed style'.[156] Indeed, in her portrayal of James in *Comrade O Comrade*, Mannin made reference to his 'dark rich beautiful voice' and 'rich dark voice [which] flowed like music' during his two-page cameo.[157] Mannin's own essentialising of the difference between Black and White people was spelled out explicitly in *Privileged Spectator* (1939):

Who that ever saw her dance will ever forget the lovely little Florence Mills' lithe brown streak of a body, and her warm eager voice challenging 'Come and catch me while I'm active'? No white woman could ever

---

153  Reynolds, *My Life and Crimes*, p. 118.

154  Ethel Mannin, *Comrade O Comrade: Or, Low-Down on the Left* (London, 1947), p. 5.

155  Ibid., pp. 117–18.

156  Stephen Howe, 'C. L. R. James: Visions of History, Visions of Britain', in Schwarz, *West Indian Intellectuals in Britain*, p. 161.

157  Mannin, *Comrade O Comrade*, pp. 134–5.

put so much expressiveness and fire into those words and the gestures that accompanied them, no matter how 'uninhibited' she might be; the most uninhibited white is restrained compared with a black once they've 'got goin'.' The trouble with us whites is that we never really do get going; it is not in our blood to do so; abandon is a matter of instinct. The white spirit is a comparatively anæmic affair, like our pale skins and our sexuality; at best we are but a pale imitation of black vitality.[158]

Mannin no doubt saw this passage as illustrating her appreciation of Black people, and adding to her antiracist credentials. But her portrayals of 'black vitality' were similar to racist tropes used to justify White supremacy. Mannin and Reynolds both repeatedly referred to Jones's darkness in their reminiscences. Mannin dwelled on the physical differences between herself and Jones, describing how Jones 'clasp[ed] [Thane/Mannin's] hand in his own big black one'.[159] Despite Reynolds's memory of Jones as being 'of medium height', Mannin in *Comrade O Comrade* constantly referred to Jones as 'big' and 'large', her portrayal of him likely shaped by ideas about Black physicality. Both Mannin and Reynolds also perhaps exaggerated Jones's affection for them, in a manner that made him seem the junior partner in their friendships. Mannin noted his 'unbounded admiration for [Thane/Mannin]', while Reynolds recalled his 'deep loyalty and affection for those white people whom he really trusted personally and politically'.[160] This is not to say that Jones did not enjoy a genuine friendship with the couple. However, the picture that emerges from Mannin's and Reynolds's observations is one of a jovial, emotional and earnest anti-imperialist, who admired his better-read and generous White friends.

But there was no doubting the political affinity between the IASB and Mannin and Reynolds, as illustrated by *Why Were They Proud? A Study of Empire* (1938). The book was published by the Pacifist Research Bureau, and Reynolds served as one of the main contributors. Although the book was couched within the logic of pacifism, Reynolds and the authors

---

158  Mannin, *Privileged Spectator*, p. 176. Thane/Mannin also describes Indians as 'nice to look at'. Mannin, *Comrade O Comrade*, p. 136.

159  Mannin, *Comrade O Comrade*, p. 140.

160  Ibid., p. 117; Reynolds, *My Life and Crimes*, p. 118.

remarked that 'pacifist thought too frequently approaches the problem of peace with a disregard for what is clearly the centre of the problem'.[161] Instead, real peace must be based on the overthrow of capitalism and imperialism. The book was greatly influenced by the IASB. The IASB member William Harrison read the proofs; works by Padmore, Kenyatta and Ward were approvingly cited throughout; and *International African Opinion* was listed in the recommended reading. Moreover, the vast majority of the authors' political positions were entirely consistent with those of the IASB. The authors' pacifism (however unorthodox) led to the book placing emphasis on aspects of anti-imperialism, such as Gandhi's non-violent tactics, that did not find much attention in IASB agitation; but the book as a whole illustrated an immense political consonance.

Harrison gave the book a glowing review in *International African Opinion*, declaring: 'It shows clearly and forcefully that imperialism is the motivating factor behind war, and that it is therefore incompatible with peace.' Harrison praised the book for going beyond the usual analysis of pacifism to give 'an historical, social, economic, and political account of imperialism as a phenomenon of capitalist society, showing by dispassionate analysis that the ideals of pacifism . . . can be obtained only through the liberation of the subject peoples now ruled and exploited by imperialist nations'.[162] Much as Padmore praised the ILP for being the first British socialist party to focus chiefly on imperialism, Harrison celebrated the growing mood of militant anti-imperialism, in which the IASB, like the ILP and the group of pacifists around Reynolds, played a central role.

## The IASB, Women and Gender

If it is necessary to examine the racial politics of the IASB's White friends, it is equally necessary to examine the gender and sexual politics of the IASB. As Marc Matera observes, 'Male anticolonialists in London equated black liberation with the rehabilitation and assertion of an

---

161 Pacifist Research Bureau, *Why Were They Proud? A Study of Empire* (London, 1938), p. 13.

162 William Harrison, 'Negro Life and Letters', *International African Opinion*, October 1938, p. 13.

"autonomous, self-determining black revolutionary manhood," displacing women from the political realm.'[163] It should be noted that the IASB maintained a formal commitment to women's equality, as evidenced by the regular 'Women's Page' in *African Sentinel*. But while the IASB advocated women's equality and had no doubt encountered Marxist arguments for women's liberation, it is difficult to see much beyond the most superficial influence of feminist ideas in their writings and activism. This meant that, intentionally or otherwise, societal gender relations were often reinforced in the organisation.

The Black and colonial population of Britain in the 1930s was disproportionately male, but the maleness of the IASB remains striking. Amy Ashwood Garvey, although at the centre of the IAFE, was peripheral to the IASB. As we have seen, Ashwood Garvey played a crucial role in creating political spaces for the group (see Chapter 2). Although she was less involved in the quotidian activities of the IASB, her Florence Mills Social Club in Soho continued to provide an important refuge for activists. Makonnen recalled: 'you could go there after you'd been slugging it out for two or three hours at Hyde Park or some other meeting, and get a lovely meal, dance and enjoy yourself'.[164] The IASB also worked with Constance Horton, a young Sierra Leonean student. Horton was born into an elite family of Krios (descendants of previously enslaved people who settled in Sierra Leone), and had been radicalised by her experience of Jim Crow laws when touring the US South in 1936. After a brief stay in London to complete her studies, during which she met Kenyatta, Padmore and Wallace-Johnson, Horton (now using her married name of Cummings-John) returned to Sierra Leone in October 1937, where she continued her political work with Wallace-Johnson. In 1966, she became mayor of the capital, Freetown.[165]

---

163  Marc Matera, *Black London: The Imperial Metropolis and Decolonization in the Twentieth Century* (Oakland, CA, 2015), p. 142.

164  Makonnen, *Pan-Africanism from Within*, p. 130. See also Minkah Makalani, 'An International African Opinion: Amy Ashwood Garvey and C. L. R. James in Black Radical London', in Davarian L. Baldwin and Minkah Makalani, eds, *Escape from New York: The New Negro Renaissance Beyond Harlem* (Minneapolis, 2013).

165  Constance Agatha Cummings-John, *Memoirs of a Krio Leader*, ed. LaRay Denzer (Ibadan, 1995). During her political self-exile in Britain later in life, Cummings-John joined the Labour Party, campaigned on behalf of London's Black residents, and became involved with the Campaign for Nuclear Disarmament.

Women were perhaps prevented from adopting a more active leadership position in the IASB due to a gendered marginalisation. At an IASB meeting in September 1937, several male members gave political reports while the audience was 'refreshed by the service of tea, prepared by Mrs Amy Ashwood Garvey', who did not give a report.[166] A generous reading could point to Ashwood Garvey's profession as a restaurateur as justification for this division of labour. Still, James recalled of Padmore and Pizer's household:

> The Padmore hospitality was famous. The constant stream of visitors stayed to lunch or to tea or to dinner, sometimes to all three. Dorothy, a fine cook, bore this burden (George washed up, the discussion for the time being moving into the kitchen). Dorothy was constantly on the move between the kitchen and the excitement in the living room. A woman of capacity, a Londoner of unusual sophistication, she had ambitions of her own both in literature and business. She suppressed them in the interests of African emancipation, more concretely helping George.[167]

This was patriarchy in one of its most familiar forms, and this gendered division of labour was completely unremarkable in 1930s Britain. Pizer's intelligence was respected, and Padmore at least washed up, even though Pizer took responsibility for all the cooking. But it is especially illuminating that James linked Pizer's sacrifices for the sake of African emancipation to her personal support of Padmore; many men in the IASB made personal sacrifices for their political cause – but for Pizer, as a woman, this was linked to support for her male partner. It seems that no male IASB members consciously applied feminist politics to their personal lives. James's lover, Louise Cripps, writing about their relationship later in life, believed that James saw her 'in the role of a faithful Krupskaya to his role of Lenin'.[168] She observed that, although 'he made the correct statements of belief on the equality of the sexes on the platform, he evidently found it difficult to follow personally'. He 'felt the man

---

166 'Our Activities: Stemming the Tide', *African Sentinel*, October–November 1937, p. 10.

167 James, 'Notes on the Life of George Padmore', pp. 54–5.

168 Louise Cripps, *C. L. R. James: Memories and Commentaries* (New York, 1997), p. 19.

needed to be the dominant partner' (Cripps acknowledged that this extended to James's relationships with both men and women; James always 'wanted to be the leader').[169]

Relationships, both political and romantic, between IASB members and White women were commonplace. The IASB depended on White women to type their work, prepare stencils for mimeographs, or fund their activism, much as Cunard had aided Padmore with the preparation of *How Britain Rules Africa*. Similarly, Cripps helped to proofread James's novel, *Minty Alley*, and went to the British Museum to help with the research for *The Black Jacobins*.[170] James later remembered of Pizer that she was instantly sympathetic to the IASB's politics, had a Marxist background, and was well read. She helped Padmore with his books, translated them into French and German, and for years worked as a secretary 'so that the household might have a steady income'.[171] Makonnen postulated that, for White women, 'One way of rejecting the oppression of men was to associate with blacks.'[172] He noted that 'Jewish girls' were particularly sympathetic to the cause.[173] However, his description of women like Dinah Stock as 'the typical English type of devoted girl' reduces these women's political determination to a personal attachment.[174]

Pizer's relationship with Padmore, like James's relationship with Cripps, was an example of a phenomenon in the relationships between Black men and White women in which the boundaries between political and romantic relationships were blurred. Bunche believed Padmore's 'choice of a woman' to be incongruent with his racial politics, mistaking Padmore's materialist analysis of racism and imperialism for a racial essentialism.[175] Furthermore, as a working-class Jew, Pizer had personal experiences of oppression and racism. She later recalled growing up 'in London's East End, amid poverty and sickness and racial animosities'.[176]

---

169  Ibid., p. 145.

170  Ibid., p. 19.

171  James, 'Notes on the Life of George Padmore', p. 54; James, 'George Padmore', p. 260.

172  Makonnen, *Pan-Africanism from Within*, p. 147.

173  Ibid., p. 71.

174  Ibid., p. 146.

175  Bunche, 1937 Annual Diary, 18 April.

176  Harry Ransom Center, The University of Texas at Austin, Nancy Cunard collection, Pizer to Cunard, 28 April 1961.

Bunche recorded Padmore saying to him: 'Englishmen don't want Negroes to fool with their women – even the radicals.'[177] However, Makonnen noted that he and Padmore, unlike some other Black radicals, did not believe that it was a 'revolutionary act' to sleep with White women.[178] That Padmore had a twenty-year monogamous relationship with Pizer suggests that their relationship was not based on a fantasy of anticolonial sexual revenge. Even so, sexual encounters between IASB members and White women could adopt a racialised character. One evening Cripps and James went to see a production of *Othello*, after which they slept together for the first time. In bed, James called her 'Desdemona'. Cripps afterwards lay awake happily thinking about the fact that she now 'had a dark lover'.[179]

Stock's relationship with Kenyatta seems to have been a friendship rather than a romantic or sexual partnership. Their relationship is particularly interesting given Kenyatta's supposed distrust of almost all White men. White women were deemed less invested in racism and imperialism than their male counterparts, and therefore more likely to be genuine allies. As well as providing Kenyatta with accommodation, Stock helped him with the completion of *Facing Mount Kenya*. Kenyatta, however, when penning the acknowledgements for the book, neglected to thank Stock for her role.[180] White women, while willing and committed participants in the IASB's work, were intellectually marginalised in the group.

Polsgrove observes that '[v]iewing the Pizer–Padmore relationship from the vantage point of a later day, it would be tempting to see Padmore as exploiting Pizer's talent and interest in writing for his own purposes'. But she argues that Padmore also 'open[ed] a door to her', giving her 'the opportunity to create books, albeit as a junior partner'.[181] Of course, these are not mutually exclusive observations, and Pizer seems to have been granted more intellectual acknowledgement than other women associated with the group. Activists like Pizer and Stock, brilliant writers in

---

177  Bunche, 1937 Annual Diary, 18 April.

178  Makonnen, *Pan-Africanism from Within*, p. 147.

179  Cripps, *C. L. R. James*, p. 57.

180  Conversely, in *Africa and World Peace* Padmore thanked Pizer for gathering material, typing the manuscript and performing 'other thankless literary chores in connection with this work'. Padmore, *Africa and World Peace*, p. 9.

181  Polsgrove, *Ending British Rule in Africa*, p. 84.

their own right, dedicated much of their political energy to aiding men, sometimes without being publicly acknowledged. This had lasting effects on literary careers. Pizer wrote to Richard Wright, an African American author, one month after Padmore's death in 1959 to ask him to write a foreword to the new edition of Padmore's 1956 book, *Pan-Africanism or Communism?* Pizer summarised the arguments that she believed Padmore would have made, before concluding: 'If you feel you could put these thoughts . . . into the right words, perhaps you might then be prepared to do a preface for the book. Your name would lend it prestige. My own has no selling value.'[182] This was a melancholic epilogue to a story of one woman's sacrifices in the cause of African liberation.

## The IASB and the CPGB

While this chapter has so far discussed the IASB's relationships that were generally comradely, there remained an overall enmity between Black radicals and the CPGB, whose congress of May 1937 confirmed its commitment to the Popular Front strategy. General secretary Harry Pollitt, in his opening statement, called on the British working class to make alliances with colonial peoples, and demanded 'freedom of speech, press, meeting and organisation' in the colonies.[183] However, he stopped short of calling for self-determination or independence. Pollitt again acknowledged the 'insufficient attention' that the CPGB had given to colonial work, the party seemingly not having heeded the exact same warning he had given at every congress over the past decade.[184] The CPGB, now seeking to make antifascist alliances with liberal elements in imperialist countries, was not disposed to threaten those alliances through enthusiastic support for anticolonial struggles.

As we have seen, when Padmore surveyed British socialism in February 1938, he was vitriolic in his denunciation of the CPGB. According to Padmore, the party, following the foreign policy interests of the Soviet Union, had decided that 'the colonial peoples living under the yoke of

---

182  Wright papers, box 103 folder 1521, Pizer to Richard Wright, 20 October 1959.

183  CPGB, *It Can Be Done: Report of the Fourteenth Congress of the Communist Party of Great Britain* (London, 1937), p. 36.

184  Ibid., p. 199.

British, French, and American Imperialisms must forgo their struggle for self-determination and line up in defence of "democracy," something they have never known'.[185] Padmore, along with James, Jones and Makonnen, protested against the Popular Front in print and at meetings. Makonnen recalled that Pollitt 'wanted a communist empire'. He noted that the IASB warned its comrades away from Communist associations, as '[t]he real point was that if we were interested in communism we would apply it without having British or Russian commissars telling us how to make communism work'.[186]

But the IASB did offer occasional praise for individual Communists. The *African Sentinel* approvingly reported Willie Gallacher asking the colonial secretary, William Ormsby-Gore, for 'the reasons for which Arab houses in Palestine were blown up'.[187] In fact, some CPGB members, including Gallacher, retained a principled anti-imperialism during the Popular Front era. It is debateable to what extent this is true of the group around the Colonial Information Bureau (CIB), including Ben Bradley, Peter Blackman and Reginald Bridgeman, which replaced the League Against Imperialism (LAI) in May 1937.[188] This group had fully embraced the radical anti-imperialism of the Third Period. Bradley had even been imprisoned in India as a result of the Meerut Conspiracy Case, illustrating his commitment to building left-wing movements in the colonies.[189] With the transition from the League Against Imperialism to the CIB, however, Jonathan Derrick notes that Bradley's circular announcing the formation of the new organisation 'did not mention colonial independence as an aim to support. But neither did it exclude strong condemnations of colonialism.'[190] This

---

185  Padmore, 'Hands off the Colonies', p. 2.

186  Makonnen, *Pan-Africanism from Within*, p. 159. Makonnen qualified his remarks by saying that his comments about Pollitt were 'with due respect to him now he's dead'. One wonders what he might have said had Pollitt still been alive.

187  'March of Events', *African Sentinel*, November–December 1937, p. 11.

188  Bridgeman was never a formal member of the CPGB, but remained loyal to the party line.

189  For Meerut, see Noreen Branson, *History of the Communist Party of Great Britain, 1927–1941* (London, 1985), pp. 59–61; Gopal, *Insurgent Empire*, Chapter 6; Susan D. Pennybacker, *From Scottsboro to Munich: Race and Political Culture in 1930s Britain* (Princeton, 2009), Chapter 4.

190  Jonathan Derrick, *Africa's 'Agitators': Militant Anti-Colonialism in Africa and the West, 1918–1939* (New York, 2008), p. 377.

softening of Bradley and Bridgeman's anti-imperialism had become apparent as early as 1936. Both published articles in the CPGB's journal *Discussion*, neither of which proposed imminent colonial self-determination.[191] As Marika Sherwood has summarised Bradley's article, 'in order to avoid war, colonial independence had to be postponed; campaigns were to focus on Fabian-style measures for improvement of social and economic conditions'.[192]

The CIB launched a monthly journal, the *Colonial Information Bulletin*, under Bradley's editorship. It was primarily an educational tool, informing the reader of oppression and resistance across the British Empire. It only occasionally drew larger theoretical conclusions (and then, of course, only in line with Popular Front policy). The *Bulletin* demonstrated that, for at least a section of the CPGB, anti-imperialism was at the heart of their socialist politics. But while Communist activists like Bradley and Bridgeman continued to detail colonial oppression in uncompromising detail, they did not prescribe the radical solutions to imperialism that they once had. Moreover, amid debates between the IASB and the CPGB, they readily supported Popular Front thinking. Nevertheless, the LAI/CIB group retained institutional and personal links with British Black radicals, despite attempts by certain members of the IASB, particularly James, to downplay these connections. James argued that Arnold Ward, for instance, 'had strong Communist leanings, but he followed George'.[193] However, Ward remained in CPGB circles, moving the resolution on Ethiopia at the LAI's final conference in February 1937.[194]

Of course, Communist support for the IASB was always conditional. In June 1937, Wallace-Johnson wrote to Bridgeman soliciting assistance with the IASB's publications, mistakenly believing Bridgeman to be the secretary of the CIB. Bradley (the actual secretary) then directed Wallace-Johnson to the resolutions of the CPGB's Fourteenth Congress for guidance on the correct approach to anti-imperialism. He added:

---

191  Ben Bradley, 'How to Develop a Broad Anti-Imperialist Movement', *Discussion*, April 1936, pp. 26–7; Reginald Bridgeman, 'Subject Nations', *Discussion*, September 1936.

192  Marika Sherwood, 'The Comintern, the CPGB, Colonies and Black Britons, 1920–1938', *Science & Society* 60 (1996), p. 149.

193  James, 'Notes on the Life of George Padmore', p. 37.

194  Hull History Centre, Papers of Reginald Francis Orlando Bridgeman, DBN/25/1, LAI Sixth Annual Conference, 27 and 28 February 1937.

> If we are able to obtain any information which we think it would be useful to publish in your Bulletin, we will be pleased to forward it to you. Further, if you have any material in connection with the struggle in the African and West Indian colonies, we will be pleased to receive it and publish it in our Bulletin.[195]

The intelligence services believed that Wallace-Johnson 'was not encouraged' by the CIB, but maintained contact with them.[196] Indeed, at the IASB's first quarterly meeting, held at the Taj Mahal restaurant near Cambridge Circus, James's presentation in support of striking Trinidadian workers was followed by a speech from Bridgeman. Bridgeman 'emphasised . . . Mr James' appeal for co-operation between British and Colonial workers'.[197] The IASB in fact regularly shared platforms with Communist anticolonialists during the organisation's first year. They held a mass meeting in Trafalgar Square about the Caribbean labour rebellions on 9 August 1937, at which both Ward and Bridgeman spoke.[198] The intelligence services even noted that 'both Padmore and Bridgeman in their speeches took a common line in identifying the interests of white and black workers'.[199]

In March 1937, Padmore chaired a jointly organised Pan-African Federation and LCP meeting about the Addis Ababa massacre – in which fascist militias had murdered thousands of Ethiopians – at Memorial Hall in Farringdon. Willie Gallacher was one of the speakers. This was a politically broader meeting than the IASB's meeting in Trafalgar Square, featuring speeches from the Labour MPs Ellen Wilkinson and Stafford Cripps – but it was illustrative of the IASB's willingness to make at least temporary alliances with British Communists.[200] Leslie James has argued that Padmore 'was open to working with those who did not share his opinion in order to attain the larger goal. He thus spoke alongside

---

195  TNA, CO 323/1610/2 (IASB), Ben Bradley to I. T. A. Wallace-Johnson, 28 June 1937.

196  TNA, CO 323/1610/2 (IASB), Wallace Johnson and the International African Service Bureau.

197  'Our Activities: Stemming the Tide', *African Sentinel*, October–November 1937, p. 10.

198  'Strikes in West Indies', *Africa and the World*, 14 August 1937, p. 7.

199  TNA, CO 323/1610/2 (IASB), Wallace Johnson and the International African Service Bureau.

200  Bunche, 1937 Annual Diary, 24 March.

CPGB stalwarts at Empire Day rallies and affiliated his own organizational activities with several different political parties on the British
left'.[201] But it was with just one particularly committed anti-imperialist
grouping that the IASB retained these semi-cordial relations. The party
as an institution remained open to rampant criticism.

Tensions remained between the IASB and even the most committed
anti-imperialist Communists. Bunche met Bridgeman on several occasions during his time in London in 1937. At one meeting, Bridgeman
criticised Padmore's *Africa and World Peace*. This was partly because the
book ignored the significance of North Africa, but also because of its
condemnation of the LAI.[202] Later in the month, Bradley visited Bunche's
house. During the conversation, Bradley said that Padmore was 'an
obstacle' to his and Bridgeman's work, and criticised Padmore's 'incon-
sistencies'.[203] Bradley provided a critique of Trotskyism to the CPGB's
1938 Fifteenth Congress. While James was the only Trotskyist in the
IASB, the CPGB often tarred the entirety of the ILP and IASB as 'Trotskyists'. To the allegation that the CPGB had 'abandoned the colonial
peoples', Bradley responded: 'we have not abandoned the colonial
peoples, but in the present situation the main task is to unite all forces
against the fascist war-makers in defence of democracy and peace. To
fight against the fascist war-makers is to fight in the interests of the
colonial peoples.'[204]

By 1938, Bradley was actively briefing against the IASB. In September
of that year, Belfast Communists urgently requested information from
CPGB headquarters about James, who was soon to be speaking for the
Irish Socialist Party in the city. Bradley confirmed the suspicions of his
comrades that James had 'recently published a very anti-Soviet book',
adding (incorrectly) that James was on the international commission for
the defence of Trotsky.[205] The following month, a woman called CPGB
headquarters looking for Kenyatta, whom she had known as an LAI
member. Bradley said he 'had not seen Kenyatta for a long time and did
not know his address'.[206] This comment highlights either the absence of

---


201  James, *George Padmore*, p. 33.
202  Bunche, 1937 Annual Diary, 7 July.
203  Ibid., 24 July.
204  LHASC, CP/CENT/CONG/4/8, Transcribed 1938 congress report.
205  TNA, KV 2/1824 (James), 15 September 1938.
206  TNA, KV 2/1787 (Kenyatta), 13 October 1938.

a relationship by late 1938 or, more likely, given the fact that CPGB and IASB members shared platforms in 1937, Bradley's attempt, for political reasons, to prevent the woman from contacting Kenyatta.

The IASB received hostility not only from White Communists, but also from Peter Blackman. Blackman was born in Barbados in 1912, and came to Britain around 1930 to study theology. After working as a missionary in West Africa, he returned to Britain, becoming involved with the CPGB's colonial department from 1937.[207] In June 1938, a Labour branch was seeking a speaker on Jamaica. James and Padmore had been suggested. Blackman called Paddy McColgan of the Workers' Bookshop to say 'he didn't think it was a good idea to have those two'.[208] In September 1938, Harold Moody of the moderate LCP called Blackman to complain that the IASB had released a statement about the Caribbean rebellions without consulting either the LCP or the Negro Welfare Association. Blackman 'said it was proof that they were not prepared to come in on anything'.[209] Bradley, Bridgeman and Blackman, as the Communists who had been closest to the IASB and therefore most knowledgeable about it, found themselves in a constant struggle to alert both other Communists and the wider British left to what they saw as the 'Trotskyist' and anti-Communist tendencies of the IASB. They offered cautious support to the IASB in 1937, encouraged by the involvement of Wallace-Johnson and Ward. But by 1938, when Padmore's dominance of the group had become apparent and tensions over the Popular Front continued to grow, these relationships became increasingly strained.

## The IASB and the Labour Party

The IASB was also extremely critical of the Labour Party: a 'reformist' and 'opportunist' organisation.[210] The Bureau nonetheless fostered links with sympathetic MPs, and also agitated in the grassroots of the party. As discussed in Chapter 1, James's time in Nelson attuned him to the

---

207  TNA, KV 2/1838 (Peter Blackman), 'Peter Blackman', undated (1938).
208  TNA, KV 2/1824 (James), 1 June 1938.
209  TNA, KV 2/1838 (Blackman), 14 September 1938.
210  Padmore, 'Hands off the Colonies', p. 2.

British working class's political and emotional attachment to the Labour Party. Bunche noted in his 1937 diary seeing Kenyatta and Wallace-Johnson selling copies of the IASB journal at a Labour Party demonstration, appealing to the party's important working-class base.[211] James also remembered that 'leftist Labour Parties and unions' would write to the IASB to ask for speakers.[212] Nevertheless, the IASB had a low opinion of most prominent Labour figures. A flashpoint was the association of Arthur Pugh, a prominent trade unionist, with the report of the 1937 Trinidad Commission. The IASB condemned Pugh for his association with calls 'for government-controlled unions in Trinidad'.[213]

The IASB maintained cordial relations with a handful of anti-imperialists in the party, predominantly left-wing MPs who were often IASB patrons. As we have seen, the March 1937 meeting in Farringdon featured speeches from Ellen Wilkinson and Stafford Cripps. Cripps, who wrote the foreword to *Africa and World Peace*, spoke about the Addis Ababa massacre, saying that Italy 'could be no more blamed than could Britain'.[214] *Africa and the World* regularly contained reports of speeches made or questions asked in the House of Commons by sympathetic MPs (including Arthur Creech Jones, Frank Lee and Reginald Sorensen) at the Bureau's request. In *African Sentinel*, the IASB reprinted an article by Creech Jones in which he urged the creation of a royal commission to investigate labour legislation in the British West Indies.[215]

The IASB was at pains to emphasise that these patrons were not representative of the Labour Party as a whole. It observed that Cripps 'was telling the masses in Jamaica that they must build up their political organisation along with their economic unions and demand self-government'. But in the same breath it criticised Labour figures Leslie Haden-Guest, Morgan Jones and Arthur Pugh.[216] Moreover, these relationships did not imply anything more than a narrow, issue-by-issue political alignment. In a 1937 speech about the Gold Coast, reprinted in

---

211  Bunche, 1937 Annual Diary, 11 July.

212  James, 'Notes on the Life of George Padmore', p. 36.

213  'Democracy Not for Export', *International African Opinion*, February–March 1939, p. 13.

214  TNA, KV 2/668 (Stafford Cripps), 24 March 1937.

215  Arthur Creech Jones, 'Labour Problems in the Colonies', *African Sentinel*, November–December 1937, pp. 2, 15.

216  'Democracy Not for Export', p. 13.

*Africa and the World*, Sorensen, after decrying the exploitation of empire, urged 'the encouragement of the principle of co-operation as well as the supervision of the native capitalists'.[217] Sorensen, unlike the IASB, saw the empire as fundamentally redeemable. For this reason, most Labour MPs, even those sympathetic to damning criticisms of the British Empire, did not share the ILP's broader political affinity with the IASB. Nevertheless, the IASB celebrated when, at the Labour Party's 1937 annual conference, three of its patrons (Wilkinson, Philip Noel-Baker and D. N. Pritt) were elected to Labour's National Executive Committee.[218] Their patronage of the IASB points to the ways in which pan-Africanism had an impact on the political mainstream.

## James's Trotskyism and the IASB

Trotskyism shaped James's relationships with the wider British left, creating tensions with the CPGB and ILP not shared with other IASB members. After leaving the ILP in December 1936, James's Marxist Group spent much of 1937 criticising the Unity Campaign grouping of the CPGB, ILP and Socialist League. The ILP, by entering a reformist front with the CPGB, had gone to 'the extreme limit of muddle and confusion'.[219] This feeling intensified as a result of the Spanish Civil War, with the Stalinist repression of the POUM in May 1937 (which ultimately split the Unity Campaign). The Marxist Group accused the ILP of 'centrism' (confusion over the question of reform or revolution), which they argued had 'betrayed the struggle in Spain'.[220]

The Marxist Group merged with Harry Wicks's Marxist League in February 1938 to form the Revolutionary Socialist League (RSL).[221] *Fight* (later renamed *Workers' Fight*) was relaunched as the organ of the RSL. In the October 1938 issue, James delivered a parting shot at the ILP

---

217  Reginald Sorensen, 'The Gold Coast Today', *Africa and the World*, 27 July 1937, p. 3.

218  'There is Hope!', *African Sentinel*, November–December 1937, p. 6.

219  'The Meaning of the New "Left Bloc"', *Fight*, January 1937, p. 2.

220  'POUM, the ILP & Spain', *Fight*, July 1937, p. 10.

221  'Discussions with Trotsky' (1939), in James, *At the Rendezvous of Victory*, p. 52. For more on the merger, see Harry Wicks, *Keeping My Head: The Memoirs of a British Bolshevik* (London, 1992), Chapter 10.

before his move to the United States. He criticised the ILP leadership for
its negotiations to re-enter the Labour Party, its overtures to the Comintern after disaffiliation in 1932, the position it had taken on Ethiopia, its
'disastrous' Unity Campaign, and its delayed protest against the Moscow
Trials.[222] While James's Trotskyist criticisms of the Popular Front CPGB
found expression among other IASB members, he stood alone in most
of these criticisms of the ILP. Importantly, other than on the Ethiopian
question, these criticisms were not directly related to colonial issues.
Despite these criticisms, James regularly worked with the ILP on anti-
imperialist campaigns. However, after leaving the party he did not throw
himself into ILP activity in the same manner as Padmore.

Although James was the only Trotskyist in the IASB, he claimed there
was no friction with the rest of the group. James later said that he was
'very confused' when people opposed 'Marxism' to the 'nationalist or
racialist struggle' because: 'The Trotskyists read and sold the African
paper and the African nationalists attended each other's meetings and
there were nationalists who read and sold the Trotskyist paper . . . there
was no problem because we had the same aim in general: freedom by the
revolution.'[223]

Kent Worcester notes that, for James, Trotsky's idea of permanent
revolution 'arranged world-historic forces in such a way as to allow for
the complete and secure abolition of colonialism and imperialism'.[224]
Indeed, James published articles in *Fight* extolling his ideas of pan-
Africanist and colonial liberation. He recruited colonial subjects to the
Trotskyist movement, including Ajit Roy, an Indian student with whom
James briefly lived during the late 1930s.[225] A supplement of *Fight*,
written by Robert Williams, provided an annotated bibliography of
Trotskyist literature. Padmore, as the author of *Africa and World Peace*,
was one of only a handful of non-Trotskyists to appear in the review.
Williams commented that Padmore demonstrated 'the futility of collec-
tive security and war for democracy'.[226] This illustrates that Black

222  C. L. R. James, 'Whither the ILP?', *Workers' Fight*, October 1938, p. 2.

223  C. L. R. James, 'Towards the Seventh: The Pan-African Congress – Past, Present
and Future' (1976), in James, *At the Rendezvous of Victory*, p. 242.

224  Kent Worcester, *C. L. R. James: A Political Biography* (Albany, NY, 1996), p. 41.

225  TNA, KV 2/1824 (James), 12 September 1938.

226  Robert Williams, 'The Literature of the Fourth International', *Fight*, November
1937 (special supplement), p. 3.

radicalism had an influence on British Trotskyism that went beyond James's involvement in the movement. This was further demonstrated by an article in *Workers' Fight* three months after James's departure for the United States, in which colonial and fascist methods of racial domination were compared.[227]

Paul Buhle notes that a 'remarkable quality' of James's political activism was 'how little the normal conflicts interfered with cooperation on Pan-African issues', and that James made 'valuable alliances involving non-Marxist anti-colonialists, such as Makonnen, without apparent rancour or prejudice'.[228] Indeed, while even the Marxist Padmore later declared James's Trotskyism to be 'nonsense', this disagreement did not inhibit his political relationship and personal friendship with James during the 1930s.[229] While James's Trotskyism shaped his criticisms of Kenyatta's *Facing Mount Kenya*, these political disagreements were contained and did not lead to significant acrimony.

James was frustrated that some of his comrades did not appreciate Marxism. But he was content with Padmore's intellectual and political leadership of the group, as well as the fact that the leading members opposed the Popular Front and agreed on the need for the African revolution (if not the European one). He therefore did not see any significant opposition between his Trotskyism and the IASB's pan-Africanism. As James himself put it, 'though I looked askance at the practical separation of the colonial movement from the struggle for the socialist revolution in Europe, I was able to work with them without friction'.[230]

In fact, the most significant criticism of James's Trotskyism from within the IASB milieu came from Reynolds. James was parodied in *Comrade O Comrade* as an 'eminent Trotskyist' who had once come to tea at the Mannin/Thane house. James, flanked by two other Trotskyists 'hypnotised' by him, dominates the conversation, apparently barely noticing Thane's presence. The host manages to utter 'exactly twelve words' during the Trotskyists' hour-long visit.[231] Reynolds attested to the

---

227 'Colonies', *Workers' Fight*, January 1939, p. 2.

228 Paul Buhle, *C. L. R. James: The Artist as Revolutionary* (London, 1988), p. 56.

229 Wright papers, box 103 folder 1522, Padmore to Richard Wright, 19 October 1955.

230 James, *Nkrumah and the Ghana Revolution*, p. 64.

231 Mannin, *Comrade O Comrade*, pp. 133–5.

accuracy of this story. He claimed that, while Mannin only managed to say twelve words to their guests, Reynolds 'knew C. L. R. James and a little about his Sacred Cow; so I gatecrashed the argument'.[232] Importantly, Reynolds's criticism of James's Trotskyism was predicated not on the movement's implications for Soviet or European socialism, but on its apparent lack of relevance to the colonial struggle. Reynolds regarded James as 'a man of brilliant intellect and an excellent writer', but said that he 'turned his back on the problems of his own people . . . to follow the barren cult of Trotskyism'.[233] James responded that '*The Black Jacobins* was not conceived within narrow confines . . . And at the time I was editing Padmore's book and paper and being an active member of his committee. I spoke at all the meetings that they had, so I don't see how Reynolds can say that.'[234]

Reynolds's statement that James was not a committed anti-imperialist was clearly incorrect. His sentiment was not shared by James's fellow IASB members. But it is sensible to infer from Bunche's diary that James was not immersed in the same political and social networks as other IASB members. Bunche, despite regularly meeting other members of the Bureau, often several times a week, seems to have met James only twice during a six-month stay in Britain.[235] Similarly, an August 1937 Special Branch report stated that 'James had been present at meetings of the International Service Bureau although he had not been as active as some'.[236] James was clearly extremely important to the IASB intellectually, but his frequent absence from meetings presumably contributed to Reynolds's criticism. This incident demonstrates that, while James believed there to be no tension between his Trotskyism and his pan-Africanism, seeing them as constituent parts of the same struggle, this feeling was not shared by everyone in the IASB's network.

---

232  Reynolds, *My Life and Crimes*, p. 117.
233  Ibid., pp. 116–17.
234  C. L. R. James papers, box 12 folder 8, Alan J. Mackenzie, 'Marxism and Black Nationalism: A Discussion with C. L. R. James' (c. 1975), p. 7.
235  Bunche, 1937 Annual Diary.
236  TNA, KV 2/1824 (James), 31 August 1937.

## The 1938 Conference on Peace and Empire

The Conference on Peace and Empire was held at Friends House on Euston Road on 15 and 16 July 1938. It was organised by the India League in collaboration with the London Federation of Peace Councils. The conference was presided over by Jawaharlal Nehru, who was touring Europe in 1938 to promote the cause of Indian nationalism, while the keynote speech was delivered by Stafford Cripps. There were 587 delegates representing 254 organisations, as well as 380 observers. British socialist parties were well represented. There were seventy-seven CPGB delegates, sixty-three Labour Party delegates and thirty-four ILP delegates. A sole Liberal Party delegate also attended. Fifteen colonial organisations were represented by thirty-nine delegates, including two from the India League, four from the IASB and four from the NWA.[237]

Nicholas Owen contextualises Nehru's 1938 visit to Britain by analysing the attempts of British advocates of the Popular Front, including Cripps (who in supporting the Popular Front damaged his relationship with the IASB), to win Nehru's support for this cause. Owen observes that the ILP argued that the Popular Front 'bought security for the imperialist powers at the expense of the colonised'; the support of Nehru, a famous anticolonial leader, was therefore 'an invaluable prize' in rebutting this charge.[238] The Conference on Peace and Empire presents the most illuminating case study of left-wing British anticolonialism on the eve of the Second World War. The fundamental tension at the conference was between one grouping around the CPGB, the India League and the left wing of the Labour Party, who viewed antifascism as the most pressing political concern, and another grouping around the ILP and IASB, who viewed fascism as the logical outcome of imperialist rivalry and refused to make distinctions between rival imperialisms. The conference therefore highlighted the fissures within left-wing opinion on the topics of fascism, imperialism, capitalism and war, and the relationships between these phenomena. Furthermore, it illustrated how the

---

237 Papers of Reginald Bridgeman, DBN/27/3, 'Conference on Peace and Empire: Report of the Credentials Committee', pp. 1–3.

238 Nicholas Owen, 'The Cripps Mission of 1942: A Reinterpretation', *Journal of Imperial and Commonwealth History* 30 (2002), p. 64.

alliance around the IASB and ILP had by the end of the 1930s become the most militant anti-imperialist force in Britain.

The political goals of the India League in organising the Conference on Peace and Empire should be understood in relation to the CPGB's 1938 statement, 'Peace and the Colonial Question'. The statement argued against colonial concessions to the fascist powers, and insisted there could be 'no "just" or "harmonious" division of colonies between the Imperialist Powers'.[239] However, the CPGB sought an antifascist alliance with liberals and social democrats. Therefore, while stating that the 'Peace Movement should regard the colonial peoples and their national liberation movements as allies in the struggle for peace', it did not call for anticolonial revolution.[240] Instead, it argued that the British labour and peace movements should agree on a 'minimum Charter of Rights of Colonial Peoples'.[241] The statement was instantly criticised by the ILP in the *New Leader*: 'One of the worst features of the Popular Front Policy advocated by the Communist Party is the betrayal of the colonial workers which it involves.'[242] The ILP's criticism illustrates how anti-imperialism was a driver of both alliances and divisions within the British left during the 1930s.

The India League, under whose auspices the conference was held, had been led since the late 1920s by V. K. Krishna Menon, who would later become a key figure shaping India's foreign policy under Nehru. Owen notes that Menon attempted to forge a position on India independent of the CPGB. However, with the collapse of the left-wing Unity Campaign, as well as the Labour Party's tightening discipline, 'he found himself orbiting the Communist Party'.[243] Privately, Menon expressed his concerns that the CPGB 'had not taken up a strong enough line with regard to the colonial question'.[244] Due to his dependence on the CPGB, however, the ideas contained in 'Peace and the Colonial Question'

239 'Peace and the Colonial Question', *Report of the Central Committee to the 15th Party Congress* (London, 1938), p. 138.

240 Ibid., p. 140.

241 Ibid., p. 143.

242 'Communists and Colonial Workers', *New Leader*, 3 June 1938, p. 4.

243 Nicholas Owen, *The British Left and India: Metropolitan Anti-Imperialism, 1885–1947* (Oxford, 2007), pp. 242–3.

244 Tom Buchanan, '"The Dark Millions in the Colonies are Unavenged": Anti-Fascism and Anti-Imperialism in the 1930s', *Contemporary European History* 25 (2016), p. 648.

permeated the general resolution proposed at the Conference on Peace and Empire.

Nehru opened the conference by saying that, in combating fascism, 'you inevitably combat imperialism'; he rejected any distinction between the two.[245] The conference's dividing lines became apparent as soon as it began, with a debate about the correct interpretation of 'collective security'. Nehru stated that his idea of collective security was 'not to retain a *status quo* which is based on injustice'; rather, its 'essential corollary is the removal of imperialism and fascism'.[246] In its report, the ILP attempted to conscript Nehru to its position, noting that 'Nehru denounced Imperialism as an evil as great as Fascism, demanded full independence for subject peoples, and said that, whilst India would welcome a system of real collective security, that did not mean the collective security of the present League of Nations'.[247] This debate continued during the discussion of the general resolution the following day. Reynolds argued that, while the Indian National Congress's February 1938 session in Haripura had advocated collective security, it had done so in a different sense from the conference resolution. Ben Bradley retorted that the resolution 'correctly interpreted' the Congress line.[248]

Nehru was followed on the Friday evening by Cripps. The ILP contrasted Nehru's call for 'real collective security' with Cripps's caution that 'there were parts of the British Empire which were not fit for independence and which should be put under international control'.[249] The Executive Committee of the IASB subsequently attacked Cripps in a statement published in *International African Opinion*. Like the ILP, the IASB criticised Cripps's plans for 'trusteeship' for Africa: 'It is clear that Sir Stafford Cripps has the typical vice of many European socialists, even revolutionaries. He conceives Africans as essentially passive recipients of freedom given to them by Europeans.'[250] This clearly implied criticism of Cripps's allies in the CPGB, and made a claim for the revolutionary agency of African peoples.

---

245  Jawaharlal Nehru, 'Peace and Empire', in *Selected Works of Jawaharlal Nehru: Volume 9* (New Delhi, 1976), p. 62.

246  Ibid., p. 65.

247  'ILP or Communist Policy for Colonial Workers?', *New Leader*, 22 July 1938, p. 5.

248  'Peace and Empire Conference', *Colonial Information Bulletin*, 1 August 1938, p. 4.

249  'ILP or Communist Policy for Colonial Workers?', p. 5.

250  IASB Executive Committee, 'Sir Stafford Cripps and "Trusteeship"', *International African Opinion*, September 1938, p. 3.

Anglophone Black radicals were joined at the conference by a Francophone comrade, Emile Faure. Faure was a Senegalese pan-Africanist who was president of the Ligue de Défense de la Race Nègre and secretary of the pan-colonial Rassemblement Coloniale in France. The LDRN had previously been aligned with the Comintern, but, like Padmore, had broken from the movement. Faure was sympathetic to Padmore's brand of pan-Africanism, and by 1940 had become a member of the IASB's Executive Committee.[251] Faure addressed the conference on the second day. He accused the French Popular Front government of exacerbating colonial oppression, citing the re-establishment of forced labour in West Africa, as well as the imprisonment of journalists in Indochina and of his comrade in the Rassemblement Coloniale, Messali Hadj. He continued: 'Parties supposed to be on the Left have been willing agents of this vicious repression', and warned colonial peoples against 'the specious "anti-Fascist" slogans adopted by these bodies in an attempt to cloak their own Imperialist-Fascist designs'.[252] The ILP report of the conference praised Faure's speech for giving 'details of the oppressive measures of the Popular Front Government and accus[ing] the Communists of being the worst enemies of colonial peoples'.[253] Conversely, Bridgeman responded by arguing that 'the Popular Front had saved France, and therefore saved England'.[254]

The report published in the *Colonial Information Bulletin* omitted a summary of Faure's speech – but it approvingly detailed the response of Julius Jacobs, a Communist representative of the London Trades Council. Jacobs said that Faure 'had apparently omitted to notice that there was a class struggle in France, that the Popular Front had improved the conditions of the masses and that the type of attack made upon it that afternoon could only bring grist to the mill of the supporters of Fascism'.[255] This prompted Reynolds to launch a blistering attack on Jacobs and the CIB in the pages of the ILP's discussion journal, *Controversy*. Reynolds

---

251  TNA, MEPO 38/91 (IASB), 'International African Service Bureau Manifesto', 29 January 1940.

252  Lelia Seleau, 'The French Colonies Under the Popular Front', *International African Opinion*, August 1938, p. 5.

253  'ILP or Communist Policy for Colonial Workers?', p. 5.

254  Reginald Reynolds, 'Under Which King Bezonian?', *Controversy*, September 1938, p. 236.

255  'Peace and Empire Conference', p. 5.

began by criticising the Comintern for closing the LAI the previous year, when Moscow decided that 'perhaps after all French Imperialism was rather a Good Thing'.[256] He countered Bridgeman's argument that the Popular Front had 'saved' France by claiming that French democracy merely 'gave certain limited rights to 40,000,000 people in France, including the right to exploit, oppress, persecute, massacre and do exactly as they pleased with some 60,000,000 outside France'.[257] He told Jacobs that, if Faure had failed to notice the class struggle in France, it was because 'the Communists and their allies had so successfully liquidated [it] in the interests of French imperialism'.[258]

The conference's general resolution was discussed during the final session, held on Saturday afternoon. It was introduced by Leonard Barnes.[259] The resolution went further than 'Peace and the Colonial Question', declaring that 'the national freedom and independence of all colonial countries and subject peoples are indispensable to world peace'. But it did throw its weight behind the Popular Front and collective security. It called for the 'united action of all progressive and peaceful forces', and couched the importance of national independence within the language of the 'strengthening of the democratic and progressive movements everywhere' and of 'halt[ing] Fascist aggression'.[260] The ILP tabled a series of amendments to delete the references to collective security, to include an explicit statement of support for the struggles of colonial peoples against imperialism, and to 'correct the emphasis of the resolution' so that independence was demanded as a 'death-blow to Imperialism rather than as a means of securing assistance for European "democracy"'.[261] This set of amendments was defeated by 141 votes to 23.[262] Reynolds and C. A. Smith therefore spoke for the ILP against the resolution, while CPGB members Bradley and Robin Page Arnot spoke in favour.[263]

Makonnen and Jones represented the IASB. Makonnen attempted to alert delegates to the contradictions of the general resolution: 'How

---

256  Reynolds, 'Under Which King Bezonian?', p. 236.
257  Ibid., p. 237.
258  Ibid., p. 238.
259  'Peace and Empire Conference', p. 3.
260  Ibid., pp. 3–4.
261  'ILP or Communist Policy for Colonial Workers?', p. 5.
262  Papers of Reginald Bridgeman, DBN/27/3, Amendments to Resolution.
263  'Peace and Empire Conference', pp. 4–5.

can you have peace with empire? What you really want is peace of mind to continue to loot your empire. In fact we want war not peace, because only war will settle the contradictions latent in this empire.'[264] Jones's intervention came when Reynolds was heckled during his speech. Reynolds later recalled that Communist delegates realised the inappropriateness of heckling Faure, a Black man, speaking about colonialism, but were conversely unrestrained when Reynolds himself spoke. When Reynolds was met with shouts of 'lies' and 'liar', Jones, 'like an avenging black angel', shouted: 'It's the truth. It's the truth that yuh can't stand!' Reynolds claimed that the Communists, again confronted by a Black opponent of the Popular Front, relapsed into temporary silence.[265]

Despite this protest, the general resolution was passed – according to the CIB, by 'an overwhelming majority'; the ILP claimed it was by a ratio of three-to-one, and that this level of support for its position was 'significant'.[266] At a meeting of the ILP's National Administrative Council two weeks later, Fenner Brockway remarked that the ILP was 'well represented' at the conference, and that its case 'received adequate expression'.[267] This suggests it was, at least, genuinely content with its showing. Similarly, Reynolds remembered: 'we were out-numbered by the well-drilled Communist contingents; but there was still a marginal floating vote and I have never seen a Communist-staged conference so closely challenged'.[268] It is a testament to the strength of the ILP-IASB's arguments and organisation that they were able to cause such a stir at a Communist-controlled conference.

The ILP report commented that a 'feature of the conference was the support given to the ILP point of view by most of the delegates from the colonial workers' organisations' – most notably the IASB, but also by the Ceylon and Arab Palestinian delegations.[269] The language of colonial support for the ILP position incorrectly implied a hierarchical relationship between resisters against the politics of the Popular Front. However,

---

264  Makonnen, *Pan-Africanism from Within*, p. 157.

265  Reynolds, *My Life and Crimes*, p. 120.

266  'Peace and Empire Conference', p. 5; 'ILP or Communist Policy for Colonial Workers?', p. 5.

267  BLPES, ILP/3/26, Meeting of NAC, 30 and 31 July and 1 August 1938.

268  Reynolds, *My Life and Crimes*, p. 119.

269  'ILP or Communist Policy for Colonial Workers?', p. 5.

this premium placed on the opinions of colonial, and particularly African and Caribbean, peoples was significant, and something of a novelty in the history of British anticolonialism. Of course, as the ILP report tacitly acknowledged, its position did not have a monopoly on colonial opinion. Blackman and Menon supported the general resolution, the latter concluding the discussion with 'a strong appeal that the resolution should be passed with enthusiasm'.[270]

The CPGB was eager to contest the amount of colonial support received by the ILP. Pollitt, reporting to the party's congress in September 1938, condemned 'Trotskyists' for their 'well-organised attempt to wreck the Peace and Empire Conference'. Given the apparent absence of Trotskyists from the conference, seemingly including even James, it appears that Pollitt was referring to the ILP and IASB as Trotskyists. But Pollitt did not explicitly mention the IASB. Instead, he portrayed the conference's tensions as being between 'disruptionist', presumably White, Trotskyist forces, on the one hand, and the mainstream of a conference 'presided over by Nehru', on the other.[271] This was a misleading statement, ignoring the fact that Black and colonial activists were an important part of this 'disruption'. It lends credence to Owen's argument that Nehru's support was an important asset for the CPGB in deflecting anti-imperialist criticism of the Popular Front.

The Conference on Peace and Empire illustrates the tensions within British anticolonialism during the late 1930s, and the IASB's position within this debate. By 1938, its relationship with the CPGB and the Comintern had been irreparably damaged. While it maintained links with anti-imperialist Communists like Bradley and Bridgeman, the Popular Front had significantly strained even these relationships. In contrast, the IASB and ILP were increasingly aligned. Kenyatta and Makonnen had misgivings about working with White socialists, and James maintained Trotskyist criticisms of the party; but the ILP's anti-imperialism had hardened since the muddle over Ethiopia. Over the course of the 1930s, the ILP had gone through a process of what Gopal has called 'unlearning paternalism', and developed instead a militant

---

270  'Peace and Empire Conference', p. 5.
271  CPGB, *For Peace and Plenty! Report of the Fifteenth Congress of the Communist Party of Great Britain* (London, 1938), pp. 69–70.

                                    

anti-imperialism that recognised the agency of colonial peoples.[272] Black radical influence played no small part in that transformation. Jones and Padmore were party members in all but name (and perhaps would have joined the ILP had they not been stung by the Comintern). Other Black radicals, despite their misgivings, collaborated with the ILP at events like the Conference on Peace and Empire. If the CPGB's watchword in the second half of the 1930s was 'against fascism and war', then the IASB's and ILP's was, in effect, *against capitalism and imperialism, and thus against fascism and war*. The fundamental theoretical disagreements about the relationships between these four phenomena led to a cleavage within the British socialist movement that would endure throughout the Second World War.

---

272  Gopal, *Insurgent Empire*, p. 18.

# 4

# War and Dispersal, 1939–1943

The Second World War induced a downturn in the activities of the International African Service Bureau (IASB). Members of the group refused to enlist in the war effort and feared repercussions. Most of them dispersed from London.[1] C. L. R. James was the first to leave, in October 1938, beginning a fifteen-year sojourn in the United States. Amy Ashwood Garvey spent the war in New York and Jamaica, Ras Makonnen in Manchester, and Jomo Kenyatta in Sussex. George Padmore increasingly came to embody the IASB, working from the offices of the Independent Labour Party (ILP). Chris Jones also remained in London, and the IASB was joined by the newly arrived South African writer, Peter Abrahams.

This chapter begins by tracing the dispersal of the IASB's members, briefly discussing their lives and political activities away from London. It then moves to a discussion of the IASB members who maintained the Bureau's activities during the war. It analyses Padmore and Jones's increasing immersion within the ILP and the significant currency that Black radical ideas enjoyed within the party. The IASB's relationships with Communist and Labour party members are also detailed – a story in which institutional antagonisms were punctuated by a handful of warm personal relationships. While the IASB was mostly treading water during the war years, its activities informed its prodigious activism at

---

1 T. Ras Makonnen, *Pan-Africanism from Within*, ed. Kenneth King (London, 1973), pp. 132–3.

the war's conclusion. The daily lives of its members disrupted, geographically isolated, and facing a paper ration, it consolidated alliances and retained hostilities, positioning it for another flurry of activity as the war ended. While the CPGB and other forces on the left shifted their positions according to developments in the war, the IASB and the ILP maintained a strict anti-imperialist stance.


## Dispersal

James left Britain for the United States on 8 October 1938 to deliver a series of lectures and recover from an illness. He planned to return to Britain soon, and the IASB described him as a 'good-will ambassador in America'.[2] In the event, he stayed for fifteen years, before returning to Britain in 1953 because of McCarthyite repression. James threw himself into the American Trotskyist movement, adopting the pseudonym J. R. Johnson. He formed the Johnson–Forest tendency with Raya Dunayevskaya and Grace Lee Boggs, precipitating his formal break with the Trotskyist movement after the Second World War. While James eventually broke from Trotskyism, his meeting with Trotsky in Mexico in April 1939 in fact reaffirmed his belief in the compatibility of Trotskyism and pan-Africanism. He said that Trotsky was 'the keenest of the keen on the [Negro] question'.[3]

James's Trotskyism continued to drive a wedge between him and the ILP. At the 1939 meetings, James and Trotsky agreed on a policy of 'compromis[ing] the ILP with tremendous and pitiless attacks on Maxton'. James admitted he had been wrong in thinking that the ILP would descend into Stalinism, but still sought the destruction of the party.[4] Notably, however, neither James nor Trotsky criticised the ILP's anti-imperialist work. The ILP, while unaware of James's machinations (though aware of his very public criticisms), continued to speak highly of James throughout the Second World War. C. A. Smith, in an article

2  TNA, KV 2/1824 (James), 19 October 1938; 'Good-will Ambassador in America', *International African Opinion*, February–March 1939, p. 16.

3  Schomburg Center, C. L. R. James letters, box 1 folder 3, James to Connie Henderson, May 1939.

4  'Discussions with Trotsky', in C. L. R. James, *At the Rendezvous of Victory* (London, 1984), pp. 53–9.

criticising the Trotskyist rank-and-file's 'zeal, courage, cocksureness, arid dogmatism and intolerance', cited James as one of the 'outstanding minds' that had been attracted to Trotskyism.[5]

Ashwood Garvey was the next to go, leaving for New York in December 1938. She spent most of the period from 1939 to 1944 in Jamaica, before returning to New York. Tony Martin identifies in this period a development in her political thought towards both class politics and feminism. The first of these Martin ascribes to the influence of socialists like James and Padmore, while the latter is demonstrated by her contribution to the 1945 Fifth Pan-African Congress in Manchester. Ashwood Garvey highlighted the plight of Black women in the Caribbean, remarking: 'Very much has been written and spoken of the Negro, but for some reason very little has been said about the black woman.'[6]

According to Special Branch reports, Makonnen was 'anxious to leave for America' in October 1939, but was unable to leave Britain because of a lack of money.[7] Instead, Makonnen left London for Manchester by the end of the year, living with the Guianese physician Peter Milliard. Milliard had lived in Manchester for fifteen years, and was involved in Black welfare groups in the city.[8] In Manchester, Makonnen created a small empire of clubs and restaurants, and continued to practise what Kenneth King calls 'practical pan-Africanism'.[9] He co-founded the African Co-operative League with his Sierra Leonean colleague, Reverend Jones; petitioned local politicians about the mistreatment of Somali restaurant owners; funded the legal fees of Black people; and set up a publishing house so that Black writers would not have to have their work assessed by White publishers.[10] The networks and infrastructure he created in Manchester would later be crucial to the organisation of the Fifth Pan-African Congress.

Kenyatta also left London at the beginning of the war, living and working on a farm in Storrington in Sussex. He wrote to the Kikuyu

---

5 C. A. Smith, 'Trotsky and Trotskyism', *Left*, October 1940, p. 298.

6 Tony Martin, *Amy Ashwood Garvey: Pan-Africanist, Feminist, and Mrs Marcus Garvey No. 1: Or, A Tale of Two Amies* (Dover, MA, 2007), pp. 149–70; George Padmore, *Colonial and . . . Coloured Unity: A Programme of Action: History of the Pan-African Congress* (1947), reprinted in Hakim Adi and Marika Sherwood, eds, *The 1945 Manchester Pan-African Congress Revisited* (London, 1995), p. 98.

7 TNA, KV 2/1838 (Blackman), 2 October 1939.

8 Padmore, *Colonial and . . . Coloured Unity*, p. 77.

9 Kenneth King, 'Introduction', in Makonnen, *Pan-Africanism from Within*, p. xv.

10 Makonnen, *Pan-Africanism from Within*, Chapter 9.

Central Association that he 'left London because of the war and of all the upset connected with it'.[11] Highover, the farm on which Kenyatta lived for the first year of the war, belonged to a friend of Dinah Stock. Stock briefly joined Kenyatta there, before taking a teaching job in Bingley in late 1939.[12] As an agricultural worker, Kenyatta avoided conscription. He met Edna Grace Clarke in 1940, and married her in May 1942. She gave birth to Kenyatta's son, Peter, the same year.[13] Kenyatta gained a certificate for lecturing to troops in February 1942, and even tried to join the Home Guard, but was not allowed. Jeremy Murray-Brown comments: 'No doubt officials drew the line at issuing him with a gun.'[14]

Kenyatta took part in little political activity during the war.[15] By the end of 1944, however, he had thrown himself back into political activism. He even re-established connections with the Communist Party, speaking at an open district meeting in Manchester on 17 December. He presented a resolution calling for the abolition of the flogging of African troops, which was passed unanimously.[16] This seems to have been a one-off engagement, and was an open rather than closed meeting; yet it demonstrates that, at the war's end, Kenyatta was still not completely opposed to creating political alliances with Communists.

In 1944 Kenyatta published the pamphlet, *Kenya: The Land of Conflict*, through the Panaf Service, Makonnen's publishing house. The pamphlet was a typical Kenyatta history of and manifesto for Kenya, condensed to the point of losing the sophistication of *Facing Mount Kenya*. Precolonial Kenya was described in idyllic terms. Kenyatta emphasised his differences with the IASB's Marxists by asserting that European colonisation had been prophesied by a Kikuyu seer.[17] He concluded the pamphlet by calling for 'a non-Imperialist social order' in which Africans could operate as equals with Europeans.[18]

---

11  TNA, KV 2/1787 (Kenyatta), Kenyatta to Secretary of the KCA, 4 January 1940.

12  Basil Clarke, *Taking What Comes: A Biography of A. G. Stock (Dinah)* (Chandigarh, 1999), p. 84.

13  For more on Kenyatta's time in Sussex, see Jeremy Murray-Brown, *Kenyatta* (London, 1972), Chapter 18.

14  Ibid., p. 211; TNA, KV 2/1788 (Kenyatta), 9 January 1945.

15  W. O. Maloba, *Kenyatta and Britain: An Account of Political Transformation, 1929–1963* (Cham, Switzerland, 2018), Chapter 4.

16  TNA, KV 2/1788 (Kenyatta), 23 December 1944.

17  Jomo Kenyatta, *Kenya: The Land of Conflict* (London, c. 1944), p. 7.

18  Ibid., p. 23.

## The IASB During the War

Padmore remained in London for the duration of the war. He considered leaving for Ireland, Norway, Haiti or the United States, but for financial and political reasons decided against these moves.[19] Leslie James has made the case for Padmore's 'transformation' during the Second World War, as he began to cultivate a 'more liberal, "respectable" network'. She argues that this was the result of Padmore's 'analysis of the shifting political climate' and involved more than 'a temporal "playing nice" with a man like [Harold] Moody'.[20] James rightly identifies greater hints of political moderation in Padmore's thought and writing, notably in his only book published during the war, *The White Man's Duty* (1943). However, James's argument that by the end of the war 'the prominence of Marxist language in his writing became much less prevalent than it had been with regard to his attack on fascism and imperialism in the 1930s and early 1940s' overstates the case (though James qualifies this by acknowledging that Padmore was still a Marxist).[21] In fact, Padmore's articles for the ILP and his book *How Russia Transformed Her Colonial Empire* (1946) illustrate a near constant Leninist analysis of imperialism. If Padmore's relationship with Moody was more than a 'temporal "playing nice"', we may ask why Moody's League of Coloured Peoples disassociated itself from the 1945 Pan-African Congress. During the war Padmore was isolated from his previous radical pan-Africanist networks. Paper rations and censorship limited the ideas he could express in writing. All of this precipitated alliances with more moderate figures. But the most significant moment in turning Padmore away from his older strategies of anti-imperialism (see Chapter 5 and the Epilogue) was not the Second World War, but rather the postwar moment, when it became apparent that the war would not be accompanied by European revolution.

The IASB's wartime activities began with a series of anti-imperialist statements and manifestos. Although these were ascribed to multiple members of the group, they were most likely written by Padmore in

19 TNA, KV 2/1838 (Blackman), 2 October 1939; Carol Polsgrove, *Ending British Rule in Africa: Writers in a Common Cause* (Manchester, 2009), pp. 44–5.

20 Leslie James, *George Padmore and Decolonization from Below: Pan-Africanism, the Cold War, and the End of Empire* (Basingstoke, 2015), pp. 48–9, 63.

21 Ibid., p. 63.

George Padmore
Public domain

London. However, the IASB found it increasingly difficult to express its ideas. Despite James's bold plans to finance *International African Opinion* from the American Trotskyist movement, the final issue appeared in the summer of 1939.[22] Padmore became increasingly dependent on sending his 'dispatches' to magazines around the world, encouraging editors to forward these dispatches to other periodicals. He asked for a 'nominal fee' of five shillings for these articles, which was often not forthcoming.[23]

The IASB continued to find a British outlet in the *New Leader*, as the ILP was happy to promote the Bureau's brand of pan-Africanist socialism. A November 1939 manifesto signed by the IASB's Executive Committee (including I. T. A. Wallace-Johnson, apparently remotely readmitted from Sierra Leone) was issued with the support of the West African Youth League, the Kikuyu Central Association, the Trade Union Congress of Sierra Leone, the West Indian National Federation and the

---

22 'Discussions with Trotsky', p. 44.

23  Peter Abrahams, *The Coyaba Chronicles: Reflections on the Black Experience in the Twentieth Century* (Kingston, 2000), p. 38.

Abyssinian Freedom League. This illustrated the transnational links that the group had fostered during the 1930s. The manifesto argued that Black people had got 'Nothing' out of the First World War: 'If the British and French Imperialists really want to convince the coloured races . . . that they are really concerned about ridding the world of "evil things" (Mr Chamberlain's phrase), now is an excellent opportunity for them to start by putting their own empires in order.' It concluded with a call for the replacement of 'Capitalist-Imperialism' with 'a World Socialist Federation of Equal Nations and Peoples'.[24] The IASB's statement on May Day 1940, signed by Padmore, Kenyatta, Jones and Wallace-Johnson, sent 'fraternal greetings of International Solidarity to the British Workers'. It informed its British working-class audience that 'Europe is to-day paying the price for the injustices committed in the past to the so-called backward races of the world. It is time, therefore, that white workers realise that so long as they permit their rulers to enslave others, they cannot themselves be free.'[25]

In October 1940, Jones and Padmore were joined in London by Peter Abrahams – a twenty-one-year-old 'Coloured' South African writer. He became one of Padmore's closest comrades. Abrahams later remembered entering 'a great bustling metropolitan city at war', where he was struck by the 'hard dilemma' of the colonial subject: not wanting Britain to lose the war, but also 'not want[ing] the empire to emerge unchanged from it'.[26] Abrahams met Padmore before the end of 1940, when Padmore was recovering from an operation on his palate after developing 'some throat ailment which had robbed him of speech'.[27] The illness and subsequent recovery from surgery greatly limited Padmore's activism during 1940 and 1941, as he was unable to undertake any public speaking. The ILP's new general secretary, John McNair, provided regular updates on Padmore's health for *New Leader* readers. Notably, McNair often mentioned in these updates that many branches had requested Padmore as a speaker, and recalled his own meetings with Padmore and Jones. This highlights both Padmore's popularity within the party and Black radicals' personal relationships with ILP leaders like McNair.

24  'African Workers Ask "What Can the Blacks Know of Democracy?" ', *New Leader*, 24 November 1939, p. 3.
25  'Black Workers Challenge Whites', *New Leader*, 2 May 1940, p. 8.
26  Abrahams, *Coyaba Chronicles*, p. 27.
27  Ibid., p. 37.

In October 1943, after his recovery, Padmore received notices from the Ministry of Labour. Unlike Kenyatta, working on a farm in Sussex, Padmore refused any employment that aided the war effort. He replied to the ministry that 'as a Negro and a colonial subject suffering all the disabilities of the "lesser breed without the law," I am determined not to help to maintain British Imperialism, which denies the economic, political and social equality which the Englishman enjoys'. He said he was prepared to face punishment for this refusal. The *New Leader* reported the story and congratulated Padmore on his 'stand'.[28] The authorities did not pursue the matter, perhaps because, as James Hooker has speculated, 'Padmore was the one black the authorities were determined not to martyr'.[29]

With the IASB increasingly organised around Padmore's activities, his flat on Cranleigh Street continued to be an important hub of pan-Africanist organising and socialising. In 1943 the intelligence services reported that Padmore and Dorothy Pizer's typewriter was 'used so frequently as to cause occasional complaints from neighbours'.[30] Pizer played a crucial role in Padmore's writing, often typing and editing his manuscripts. However, Abrahams, in his novel *A Wreath for Udomo* (1956), savaged Padmore and Pizer's relationship. By the 1950s, Abrahams had become disillusioned with the direction of pan-Africanism. His novel offered a critical history and gloomy forecast for the movement. Padmore, fictionalised as Thomas Lanwood, is portrayed, in Marc Matera's words, as 'a tragic figure of impotent black masculinity' whose relationship with Pizer conceals 'a more profound attachment to Britishness'.[31] Pizer ('Mary Feld' in the novel) is depicted as a domineering woman who has no respect for Padmore/Lanwood.[32]

This perhaps says as much about Abrahams's race and gender politics as it does about Padmore and Pizer's relationship. If male anticolonialists were concerned with reclaiming a Black revolutionary manhood (see Chapter 3), Abrahams may have seen Pizer as compromising Padmore's

---

28 'Colonials Refuse to be Conscripted', *New Leader*, 26 February 1944, p. 2.

29 James R. Hooker, *Black Revolutionary: George Padmore's Path from Communism to Pan-Africanism* (London, 1967), p. 59.

30 TNA, KV 2/3833 (Dorothy Padmore [Pizer]), 25 June 1943.

31 Marc Matera, *Black London: The Imperial Metropolis and Decolonization in the Twentieth Century* (Oakland, 2015), p. 233.

32 Peter Abrahams, *A Wreath for Udomo* (London, 1965 [1956]), pp. 44–8.

pan-Africanist credentials. But Abrahams further problematised British pan-Africanist gender relations. A White female character in the novel, Lois Barlow, challenges Michael Udomo (who most closely resembles Kwame Nkrumah) for thinking her 'the primitive backward woman'.[33] Abrahams portrays Black men's attraction to White women as inherently racialised. Udomo enters a relationship with Barlow, but cheats on her with another White woman in the group after being excited by her 'mass of corn-coloured hair'.[34] To Abrahams it seemed that both sorts of relationships were problematic. Udomo's trysts caused an unnecessary distraction for the group, and hurt innocent White women. Simultaneously, Padmore/Lanwood's twenty-year relationship with Pizer/Feld left him resembling 'a white man with a black skin'.[35]

Abrahams's ideas were informed by his own romantic experiences in London. His landlady, Dorothy Pennington, was a CPGB member. He drunkenly slept with her shortly after arriving in London, and they married two weeks later. He remembered that Padmore 'approved of the marriage', as Pennington was 'a good comrade'. Padmore often visited the couple at their flat in Belsize Park, where 'sometimes he and Dorothy talked about me almost as though I was not there'. He believed that Padmore had wanted this to happen, seeing it as a means of 'control'.[36] The couple separated shortly after the war, and Abrahams resented what he saw as Padmore's attempts to pressure him into the sort of personal-political relationship that Padmore and Pizer had.

Indeed, two White women, Pizer and Nancy Cunard, played a crucial role in Padmore's only book published during the war, *The White Man's Duty*. The Atlantic Charter, signed by US president Franklin D. Roosevelt and British prime minister Winston Churchill in August 1941, proclaimed the postwar objectives of the Allies. Its third clause contained an ambiguous commitment to self-determination. A few days after the charter was signed, the Labour deputy prime minister, Clement Attlee, spoke at a meeting of the West African Students' Union. When asked if the third clause would apply to colonial peoples, Attlee answered that this was indeed what was meant by the declaration. But Churchill contradicted

---

33  Ibid., p. 15.
34  Ibid., p. 20.
35  Ibid., p. 193.
36  Abrahams, *Coyaba Chronicles*, pp. 40–1.

Attlee in the House of Commons on 9 September, saying that the third clause concerned the restoration of sovereignty to the occupied nations of Europe.[37] The Atlantic Charter did, however, create space for anti-imperialists to challenge the British government on its own terms.[38]

By this time, it was clear that European imperialism was in crisis. Fascism had exposed the ugliness of the racial ideologies that underpinned imperialism, the Allied powers depended on their colonies to sustain the war effort, and Japan's victories in Asia had dented notions of White superiority. In this context of moribund colonialism, Padmore increasingly began to feel that colonial peoples were in a position from which to negotiate with the British ruling class. *White Man's Duty* took the form of a series of conversations with Cunard conducted in the spring of 1942. These conversations, which were typed up by Pizer, consisted mostly of Cunard asking questions about the colonies, with Padmore responding. Cunard, contra Abrahams, believed that Padmore and Pizer were 'a superb team'.[39] The premise of the book was that Cunard and Padmore would take 'at their word' the statesmen who had made promises of democracy.[40] Padmore dogged the Allied powers about their undelivered promises. He argued that the 'ideal solution of postwar reconstruction is the *application of Clause 3 of the Atlantic Charter to all peoples*'.[41]

Padmore went beyond calling for liberal self-determination, insisting: 'we would like to see the collaboration and co-operation of all the lands which now comprise the British Empire put on a Federal basis, evolving towards a Socialist Commonwealth'.[42] Still, in *White Man's Duty*, Padmore rarely went beyond social democracy. There were no discussions of Marx, Lenin or the Soviet Union. Moreover, Padmore's concrete proposals were strictly reformist. As has been observed by Jenny

---

37 George Padmore, 'No Atlantic Charter for Colonies', *New Leader*, 24 January 1942.

38 Mark Reeves, '"Free and Equal Partners in Your Commonwealth": The Atlantic Charter and Anticolonial Delegations to London, 1941–3', *Twentieth Century British History* 29 (2018).

39 Harry Ransom Center, The University of Texas at Austin, Nancy Cunard collection, Cunard to Pizer, November 1959.

40 Nancy Cunard and George Padmore, *The White Man's Duty: An Analysis of the Colonial Question in the Light of the Atlantic Charter* (London, 1943), p. 9.

41 Ibid., p. 19. Emphasis in original.

42 Ibid, p. 19.

Greenshields, Cunard and Padmore's proposals were for a top-down model of transformation – more decolonisation than liberation.[43] *White Man's Duty* contained almost no discussion of the necessity of socialism in the metropole or of the role of the British and colonial proletariats in achieving the transformations sought by Padmore. It is the text that adds most weight to Leslie James's argument that Padmore's Marxism became markedly less pronounced during the war.

We can speculate as to why *White Man's Duty* was more moderate than the rest of Padmore's output. Perhaps he had to moderate his views in order to get the book published, particularly at a time when paper was rationed. After all, the first draft of Padmore's more revolutionary book, *How Russia Transformed Her Colonial Empire*, was rejected by publishers in 1942.[44] Leslie James has argued that Padmore tailored his output for specific audiences; Padmore, writing during the Second World War and unlikely to achieve a wide circulation, addressed his arguments to British elites more than in other works.[45] He was less hamstrung by these factors when writing for publications like the *New Leader*. Perhaps Padmore simply wished to use *White Man's Duty* as a rhetorical exercise to expose the hypocrisy of British liberals. Regardless of the reason, his other writings during the Second World War, including his work with the ILP, displayed a continuation of his interwar militancy.

## The ILP and the Socialist Peace Offensive

The Second World War had a huge impact on the ILP's ability to coordinate its activities. The ILP's offices, along with Arthur Ballard's Socialist Bookshop, were destroyed in an air raid in May 1941.[46] Despite these setbacks, and contrary to the general declinist narrative of the historiography, the CPGB in May 1943 noted 'a certain revival of the ILP'.[47] This

---

43 Jenny Greenshields, 'Nancy Cunard: Collector, Cosmopolitan', doctoral thesis, University of Sussex, 2016, p. 180.

44 Polsgrove, *Ending British Rule in Africa*, pp. 63–4.

45 James, *George Padmore*.

46 John McNair, 'Head Office Destroyed: But the Party and the Paper Carry On', *New Leader*, 14 June 1941, p. 8.

47 LHASC, CP/CENT/ORG/12/1, Report on Trotskyite Activities, May 1943.

was a result of its having become perhaps the most significant national opposition, however small, to Churchill's war ministry.

During 1939 the ILP considered reaffiliation to the Labour Party. It abandoned these plans after the outbreak of war, when Labour announced that it would not contest by-elections against the government.[48] The ILP, conversely, contested elections against pro-war coalition candidates for the duration of the war. Having concluded some time earlier that the coming war would be one of imperialist rivalry, the ILP remained opposed to it. Regarding the British Empire, the ILP advocated 'The immediate withdrawal of all repressive administration in the colonial territories, so that liberty of speech, press and organisation shall be allowed. The recognition of the right of all colonial peoples to independence and to determine for themselves whether they shall participate in the war.'[49]

A 1940 pamphlet written by Fenner Brockway and McNair claimed that socialism, as well as preventing future wars, could also defeat Nazism and win the current war. They dubbed this approach 'a Socialist Peace Offensive'.[50] As Brockway later remembered, 'The idea of a socialist revolution to inherit the war was not fanciful. Had not the First World War ended with the Soviet revolution?'[51] A socialist Britain would declare racial and national equality, transfer the ownership of natural resources to colonial peoples, and free political prisoners in the colonies. This would 'immediately make clear to the peoples within the Empire that Britain sincerely desired to break with the old régime'.[52] Padmore aligned himself with these ideas. He argued that the Spanish Republican government's failure 'to renounce its sovereignty over its colonies' had contributed to its defeat in the civil war.[53]

The Socialist Peace Offensive, deeply interweaving the domestic with the colonial, became the basis of ILP propaganda during the war. Brockway and McNair concluded their pamphlet by stating: 'The workers of

---

48  ILP, *Annual Report of the NAC, 1940* (London, 1940), p. 9.

49  Ibid., p. 23.

50  Fenner Brockway and John McNair, *Socialism Can Defeat Nazism* (London, 1940), p. 10.

51  Fenner Brockway, *Outside the Right* (London, 1963), p. 18.

52  Brockway and McNair, *Socialism Can Defeat Nazism*, p. 7.

53  George Padmore, 'To Defeat Nazism We Must Free Colonials', *New Leader*, 25 July 1940, p. 5.

Britain would defend a Socialist Britain so long as the Nazi attack continued. The colonial workers would defend their new-won liberties.'[54] This was not a pacifistic antiwar position, but instead a call to arms in the name of socialism. Moreover, their position was that it might not even be necessary to fight the war, as socialist revolution in Britain and other countries would potentially inspire revolution against Nazism in Germany and German-occupied territories.[55] Crucially, the authors stressed: 'we must not get in the mood of thinking that the Empire problem is only India'; they made a point of citing 'Palestine, Kenya, West Africa, South Africa, the West Indies.'[56]

The larger presence of Africa and the Caribbean in the ILP's anti-colonial thinking was likely a result of their alliance with the IASB. In 1939, the IASB was promoted to full membership of the International Bureau, now renamed the International Marxist Centre.[57] In December 1939, the ILP, the IASB and other affiliated organisations of the Centre signed a statement advocating that colonial peoples use the war to win their independence. They also branded the Second and Third Internationals 'bankrupt accomplices of the Imperialist bandits', and called for the formation of a 'Socialist United States of Europe.'[58]

At the beginning of 1939, the ILP and the IASB were the driving forces behind the formation of the British Centre Against Imperialism (BCAI). As a result of the outbreak of war, the BCAI was never able to undertake any substantial political activism. But it highlighted the ways in which the IASB-ILP coalition was attempting to fulfil the promise of the League Against Imperialism without an attachment to organised Communism. The organisation was launched at a conference at Friends House on Euston Road on 21 January 1939.[59] Brockway presided over the conference, while Kenyatta gave a speech detailing conditions in Kenya. Padmore's influence was also apparent. His favourite Marxist aphorism – 'Labour with a white skin cannot emancipate itself while Labour with a black skin is branded' – was written on a banner behind the platform.

---

54  Brockway and McNair, *Socialism Can Defeat Nazism*, p. 11.

55  Ibid., pp. 10–11.

56  Ibid., p. 6.

57  ILP, *Annual Report of the NAC, 1940*, p. 6.

58  'British and German Socialists Join with Comrades of Twelve Countries in Lead against War', *New Leader*, 22 December 1939, p. 1.

59  Arthur Ballard, 'In the Empire', *New Leader*, 9 December 1938, p. 6.

The politics of the Popular Front were marginalised at the conference. The *New Leader* reported that the 'only controversy was raised by a Left Book Club [a Communist-aligned organisation] delegate, who wanted the conference to concentrate on defeating Neville Chamberlain and defending "democracy"'. Reginald Reynolds responded, in an effort to proscribe Communist involvement, that the condition for BCAI membership should be whether one was 'for or against Imperialist war'.[60]

Ballard was secretary of the group, and often promoted its activities in the *New Leader*. It was through him that one of the group's early manifestos was produced. He sent his draft to Reynolds asking for notes; it was forwarded to Jones, to Ceylonese socialist S. M. Perera, and finally to Kenyatta, to be returned to Ballard himself within a fortnight. The BCAI's committee would decide on the manifesto at a meeting held the following week.[61] The centre hoped to present its manifesto to the colonial secretary, Malcolm MacDonald, on Empire Day, but was ultimately only able to see his private secretary. A group of colonial activists (including Padmore and Kenyatta) and ILP representatives submitted the document, which called for 'complete independence for the colonial peoples'. The delegation later addressed a mass meeting in Hyde Park, at which Brockway 'called for the unity of the British working class with the struggle of the colonial masses for complete independence from British Imperialism'.[62] The BCAI also protested the imprisonment of labour leaders in Sierra Leone at public meetings and in circulars sent to British labour organisations.[63] However, the group lapsed into almost complete inactivity during the war, hindered by the IASB's dispersal as well as by war conditions.

Activists like Kenyatta, who had been heavily involved in the formation of the BCAI, were thus now almost completely outside the networks of British socialism. One IASB member who did remain involved with ILP politics, however, was Jones. He was a regular speaker at branch meetings and summer schools, and contributed to the *New Leader*. Writing in June 1939, he expressed the antiwar sentiment that permeated

---

60  'Important Decisions at Colonial Conference', *New Leader*, 27 January 1939, p. 4.

61  TNA, KV 2/1787 (Kenyatta), 17 March 1939.

62  ' "Empire Day" Deputation to Colonial Secretary', *New Leader*, 2 June 1939, p. 5.

63  'The African World', *International African Opinion*, May–June 1939, pp. 6–7; TNA, MEPO 38/91 (IASB), IASB and BCAI, circular letter to Labour and trade union organisations, July 1939.

the IASB and the ILP, noting that 'colonial workers have not forgotten the last World War', after which promises of greater freedom had been broken. He looked to the imprisonment of Barbadian trade unionist Ulric Grant and 'the shameful betrayal of Abyssinia by the so-called League of Nations' to conclude that he had 'no faith in Capitalist governments, regardless of whether they call themselves democratic or Fascist'.[64] Jones addressed meetings close to home, in Wood Green and Romford, but also travelled as far as Bristol and Gateshead to speak to ILP branches. At the Romford meeting, he appealed to the need for solidarity between metropolitan and colonial workers, citing the example of the crew of the HMS *Exeter*, who had refused to repress striking West Indian workers. The *New Leader* consistently reported warm receptions of Jones's speeches; he was 'a great turn on any platform', able to make his audiences both laugh and cry.[65]

At the 1941 summer school in Bangor (at which Padmore was unable to speak due to his illness), Jones praised Padmore as 'the greatest political leader of the Negroes in any part of the world'. Jones – like Padmore, unambiguously a Marxist – spoke about labour discrimination in Rhodesia and read out Padmore's declaration to the school: 'The problem of the oppressed subject workers is to free themselves from the domination of British Capitalism. It will then be possible for white workers and coloured workers to associate in genuine fraternity and to move forward to the building of the Socialist Commonwealth.' The *New Leader* reported that the students left the session 'with a burning sense of the injustices suffered by the colonial workers'.[66]

As well as this clear political affinity between Jones and the ILP, his personal friendship with Mannin and Reynolds developed during the war. Jones had a White working-class wife with whom he had six children. He had previously limited his relationship with Mannin and Reynolds to the political. According to Reynolds, 'It had never occurred to him, till we asked him about them, that we might be interested in his children.' After this, Jones visited with his family on Sundays, providing Mannin and Reynolds 'with some of the happiest

64  Chris Jones, 'Why the Colonial Workers Oppose Conscription', *New Leader*, 9 June 1939, p. 4.

65  Fenner Brockway, 'Extracts from a Socialist Diary', *New Leader*, 8 March 1940, p. 2. See the *New Leader* for further reports of Jones's speeches.

66  'Two Negro Leaders', *New Leader*, 23 August 1941, p. 6.

memories of the war years'. Mannin even became godmother to one of Jones's sons.[67]

Wallace-Johnson's imprisonment in Sierra Leone became a *cause célèbre* in ILP circles. He was imprisoned under defence regulations in September 1939, at the outbreak of the war. Padmore brought the issue to the attention of *New Leader* readers, railing against the colonial 'Fuehrers'.[68] The *New Leader* protested Wallace-Johnson's imprisonment, and Susan Prain, an ILP member, raised the issue at the 1941 TUC congress. She observed that George Hall, as Labour's under-secretary of state for the colonies, was complicit in this repression. She argued that the TUC 'should have insisted that the release of the persecuted men be a condition of Labour's entering the Government'.[69]

Wallace-Johnson was released in 1942, but 'deported to an isolated town and not allowed out after dark'. He managed to send an article to the *New Leader* in which he set out 'immediate demands' for West Africa. Invoking the Atlantic Charter, Wallace-Johnson called for the announcement of plans for 'the rapid expression of native institutions and culture', universal adult suffrage, and reforms to allow greater 'native' representation on the various councils.[70] He remained in correspondence with Brockway, and was in regular receipt of the *New Leader*.[71] In 1945, the ILP welcomed Wallace-Johnson to Britain for the World Trade Union Conference. They celebrated the fact that his 'release from internment in Sierra Leone had been largely due to the intervention of the ILP'.[72] The ILP no doubt exaggerated their role in Wallace-Johnson's release, but could rightly claim to be important allies in the struggle.

Despite Jones's popularity as a speaker and the ILP's solidarity with Wallace-Johnson, Padmore was the IASB member to attain greatest prominence in the wartime ILP. In December 1942, Padmore reviewed Brockway's autobiography, *Inside the Left*, for the *New Leader*. But, rather

---

67  Reginald Reynolds, *My Life and Crimes* (London, 1956), p. 120. Padmore was the godfather.

68  George Padmore, 'Police Swoop on Workers' Leaders in Colonies', *New Leader*, 20 October 1939, p. 2.

69  Walter Padley, 'Walter Padley Reviews the TUC', *New Leader*, 13 September 1941, p. 3.

70  I. T. A. Wallace-Johnson, 'What We Africans Demand', *New Leader*, 31 October 1942, p. 4.

71  TNA, KV 2/1920 (Brockway), 16 February 1943.

72  ILP, *Annual Report of the NAC, 1945* (London, 1945), p. 6.

than a simple review, Padmore offered a critical history of the ILP. Looking back on the ILP's pacifist objection to the First World War, Padmore criticised the party's reformism and 'political backwardness', but noted its 'obstinate internationalism'. He argued that the party had taken a 'revolutionary turn' with disaffiliation from the Labour Party in 1932, but lamented that, despite its turn to revolutionary socialism, it was still 'unable to assume the task of the vanguard party of the working-class'. This was because its 'organisational structure' was not 'in keeping with its revolutionary programme'. Although Padmore remained vague about the necessary structural changes, he feared that without them the ILP would 'find itself unable to exploit the favourable objective situation towards which we are inevitably moving'.[73] Nevertheless, Padmore's praise for the ILP's revolutionary programme and the importance to which he attached reforming its structures illustrates his commitment to the necessity of the European revolution and his belief that the ILP was best placed to lead it.

It is therefore unsurprising that Padmore, especially given his isolation from his pan-Africanist networks, became increasingly immersed in ILP activity. Like Jones, he travelled the country speaking at meetings and summer schools, except when prevented by his illness. Many branch secretaries wrote to McNair to express their appreciation for Padmore's work.[74] During the promotion of the 1941 summer school, at which Padmore was ultimately unable to speak, he was listed as one of the main attractions, mentioned in the same breath as Maxton and Brockway.[75] He also frequently contributed articles to the *New Leader* and the ILP's discussion journal *Left* (an especially important outlet during his illness).

Having joined the editorial board of *Left* in 1941, Padmore became its co-editor, alongside Jon Evans. Discussions about Padmore and Evans assuming the editorship began in early 1942. The outgoing editor, C. A. Smith, announced his departure in May, welcoming 'the well-known Negro leader' as one of his replacements.[76] However, by the end of 1943 there were stirrings on the National Administrative Council that the

---

73  George Padmore, 'The ILP in the Past and Now', *New Leader*, 12 December 1942, p. 7.

74  ILP, *Annual Report of the NAC, 1940*, p. 3.

75  John McNair, 'Our Summer School', *New Leader*, 28 June 1941, p. 7.

76  BLPES, ILP/3/30, Meeting of NAC, 7 and 8 February 1942; C. A. Smith, 'Change of Editor', *Left*, May 1942.

editorship was unsatisfactory. F. A. Ridley moved a motion at the November meeting 'that the existing system of the two Editors be changed and that the Journal be edited by a comrade appointed by the NAC and that it be run as a theoretical organ generally expressing the point of view of the Party'. Maxton and Brockway opposed the change, but Ridley's motion passed by eight votes to five.[77] As the war was coming to an end and postwar plans were being drawn up, the ILP was eager that its discussion journal, which had previously been open to all socialist views, should now predominantly express party policy. While remaining open to contributions from the new Common Wealth Party and the left wing of the Labour Party, *Left* placed greater restrictions on who could contribute. A majority of the NAC clearly viewed Padmore, never a party member, as an inappropriate person for this task.[78]

While this episode highlights friction in Padmore's relationship with the ILP, he continued to work enthusiastically with the party, and never publicly expressed any bitterness about his removal; Padmore's position in the party was generally celebrated by his comrades. The *New Leader* often included a sketched portrait of Padmore to accompany his articles, perhaps due to his prominence as a figure. Articles by ILP leaders like Maxton were also accompanied by such portraits. The portraits of Padmore may also have been to emphasise the fact of his Blackness, and his authenticity and authority when speaking about imperialism with which it was associated. Indeed, articles by Wallace-Johnson, a less prominent figure than Padmore in British socialist circles, were also accompanied by portraits. Padmore's involvement with the ILP was a major coup for the party because he was a crucial nodal point in transnational anti-imperialist networks, because he was a virtuosic journalist and activist, and because the mere fact of his Blackness added authority to the ILP's anti-imperialism. According to interviews conducted by James Hooker with Ridley and Walter Padley, the ILP even attempted on several occasions – unsuccessfully – to persuade Padmore to stand for parliament.[79]

77  BLPES, ILP/3/31, Meeting of NAC, 6 and 7 November 1943.

78  Interviewed in 1986, Ridley remembered Padmore as somewhat 'pro-Communist' and 'more nationalist than he was socialist', which helps to explain his logic in having Padmore removed. C. L. R. James papers, box 28 interior box 4, James remembered by F. A. Ridley, 13 August 1986.

79  Hooker, *Black Revolutionary*, p. 46.

Padmore's authority also became important for White ILP anti-imperialist writers. Oliver Brown, in *War for Freedom or Finance?* (1941), argued that the British war effort was motivated by imperialism rather than a desire for freedom. He quoted from Padmore's *Africa and World Peace* – 'There is as much fascist terrorism in India and Africa as would make Hitler and Mussolini blush' – and cited this as 'An African's View' in order to strengthen his own condemnation of British colonialism.[80] For his part, Padmore wrote to McNair asking to be sent more copies of the pamphlet and expressing hope of a wide circulation.[81] His request for further copies indicates that he was probably distributing the pamphlet in his pan-Africanist networks. McNair himself, challenging imperialism in 1942, caustically remarked that the 'apologists of Imperialism gravely inform us that they went into the dark places of the earth to take *our* culture and *our* civilisation to *save* such benighted individuals as our coloured friends like Nehru and George Padmore!'[82] Padmore's intellect was so well-known in ILP circles that the ludicrous idea that he needed civilising could be used to condemn imperialism.

In fact, Padmore carried such authority that his ideas were even used by ILP members to buttress arguments that he did not himself support. During the summer of 1941, *Left* editor C. A. Smith began to criticise 'the myopic "revolutionary," who "can see no difference" between the present German system and the present British social and political systems'.[83] He declared his support for the British war effort and signalled his break from ILP policy, which would culminate in his joining the Common Wealth Party in 1942. This initiated a lengthy debate in the pages of *Left*, with Ridley and Bob Edwards defending ILP policy. Edwards countered that Smith, like a Stalinist, divided the world into 'good' and 'bad' capitalist states. Using distinctly Padmorian language, Edwards argued that the '400 million colonial peoples of the British Empire can paint just as gory a picture of British rule *now* . . . as C. A. Smith does of Nazi rule in occupied Europe'.[84]

---

80  Oliver Brown, *War for Freedom or Finance* (London, 1941), p. 10.

81  John McNair, 'Summer School Despite the War', *New Leader*, 24 May 1941, p. 6.

82  John McNair, *Make Britain Socialist Now!* (London, 1942), pp. 5–6. Emphasis in original.

83  C. A. Smith, 'A Critique of Political Futility', *Left*, August 1941, p. 171.

84  Bob Edwards, 'The Third Camp', *Left*, September 1941, pp. 200–1. Emphasis in original.

Padmore did not intervene in the debate, though he undoubtedly would have sided with Edwards and Ridley. But Smith mined articles by Padmore in order to defend his position. Arguing against the idea (advanced by Ridley) that the war was solely an imperialist war, Smith quoted Padmore as having written in the previous month's *Left* that China was 'fighting a progressive war of national liberation'.[85] In his final contribution to the debate, Smith framed much of his argument around Padmore's dissection of the war into three arenas: '(a) The inter-imperialist conflict between Anglo-American and Axis capitalists; (b) The defence of the Soviet Union; (c) The Sino-Japanese conflict, in which we have a semi-colonial country defending itself against imperialist aggression.' Smith argued that both he and Padmore saw (b) and (c) as progressive. He then detailed all the ways in which he agreed with Padmore and Ridley did not – a conclusion that nonetheless apparently led him to support a war effort condemned by Padmore.[86] Nevertheless, Padmore carried such weight that Smith was eager to conscript him to his position.

Indeed, the IASB's two major theoretical pillars – the interdependence of the European and colonial revolutions and the equivalence between fascism and colonial rule – found regular expression in ILP circles during the war. The 1940 statement of policy declared: 'The struggles of the subject peoples of the Empire and of the revolutionary workers in Britain will inevitably react on each other because they share in common the objective of the overthrow of British Imperialism.'[87] The ILP eschewed its earlier language of 'giving' freedom to colonial peoples. It instead used the language of revolutions 'react[ing] on each other', in vocabulary that might have come straight from *The Black Jacobins* in describing the French and Haitian revolutions.

But some elements of paternalism remained. Brockway himself remarked in *The Way Out* (1942): 'We have a special responsibility towards the subject peoples in the Empire. No capitalist-imperialist government will liberate them. *Only a Socialist Britain will do so*'.[88] He argued elsewhere in the pamphlet that the anti-imperialist lead would

---

85  C. A. Smith, 'Is This Solely an Imperialist War? No', *Left*, October 1941, p. 228.

86  C. A. Smith, 'Fight Hitler Now', *Left*, January 1942, pp. 10–11.

87  ILP, *The Socialist Challenge: ILP Policy on Poverty, Nazism, Imperialism, War and Peace* (London, 1940), pp. 11–12.

88  Fenner Brockway, *The Way Out* (London, 1942), p. 17. Emphasis in original.

come from the colonies, suggesting that this was merely a clumsily worded passage – but the implication was that colonial peoples would be incapable of winning national liberation without socialism in Britain. No such reciprocal relationship was suggested, indicating that the interdependence of revolutions was asymmetrical. Indeed, in a 1940 article, Brockway had written of colonial workers that the 'only conditions under which they could be expected to act would be through the stimulus of a European or British revolution'.[89]

While it would therefore be a mistake to ascribe to Padmore intellectual dominance in the wartime ILP, he was nevertheless an immensely important figure. Though there remained a degree of equivocation on the interdependence of revolutions, and Padmore was deemed an unsuitable editor of *Left* in 1943, he became a byword for African radicalism. He was a lauded speaker and writer, and his Black radical ideas found frequent expression in ILP meetings and publications.

## The Communist Party's Twists and Turns

Following the 1938 Conference on Peace and Empire, debates between the IASB and the CPGB about the Popular Front and anti-imperialism continued until the outbreak of war. Daniel Whittall notes that 'Padmore's tense relationship with Communism was also played out at other public gatherings, such as the 1939 Conference on African Peoples, Democracy and World Peace'.[90] The conference, organised primarily by CPGB member Peter Blackman, was held in July 1939 at Memorial Hall. Blackman worked closely with Harold Moody in organising the conference, and promoted it in the League of Coloured Peoples' periodical, *The Keys*. In their promotion, Blackman and Moody focused on issues like welfare, poverty and health, invoking the liberal principles of 'freedom and liberty'. The language was moderate rather than revolutionary.[91] This

---

89  Fenner Brockway, 'The War: A Socialist Perspective', *Left*, July 1940, p. 200.

90  Daniel Whittall, 'Creolising London: Black West Indian Activism and the Politics of Race and Empire in Britain, 1931–1948', doctoral thesis, Royal Holloway, University of London, 2012, p. 241.

91  Peter Blackman, 'The British Parliament and the British Empire', *The Keys*, July–September 1939, pp. 3–4; Harold Moody, 'President's Message', *The Keys*, July–September 1939, pp. 4–5.

moderation was reflected at the conference. The main resolution, introduced by Stafford Cripps, was shaped by Popular Front concerns; there
was no mention of either capitalism or socialism, but repeated references
were made to 'fascism' and 'democracy'. The implication was that self-
determining colonies would be a useful bulwark against fascism. The
conference therefore called for universal adult suffrage and representative institutions; universal education; freedom of speech, the press and
organisation; political and labour rights; and the 'immediate abrogation
of all existing repressive legislation'.[92]

There was also Communist erasure of IASB involvement. The *Colonial
Information Bulletin* reported that the main resolution was 'passed unanimously'.[93] Neither that report nor the *Daily Worker*'s mentioned any IASB
involvement in the conference; but Kenyatta moved an emergency resolution, which was defeated, on behalf of the IASB.[94] The *New Leader* even
reported that Padmore, Kenyatta, Jones, Makonnen and William Harrison
had been among the conference's principal organisers. However, Communists had 'packed' the hall in order to disrupt a conference that had been
organised 'by a number of Negro organisations'. The report claimed that
Padmore's suggestion that 'white friends' be admitted only as fraternal
members of the standing orders committee 'had almost the full support of
the Negro delegates present' but was 'voted down by the supporters of the
Communist platform'. By the ILP's reckoning, it was only the insistence
of the IASB delegates that forced the conference to accept the principle of
self-determination.[95] The report seems to contain several fabrications and
embellishments (there is no other evidence that IASB members were
principal organisers; Black activists like Blackman and the Gold Coast
activist, Desmond Buckle, sided with CPGB members over the IASB; and
support for self-determination seems to have been in the original draft of
the resolution), but the *New Leader* report played an important role in
recording the IASB's presence at the conference.

In fact, the outbreak of war in September 1939 was accompanied by a
dramatic revision of CPGB policy. On 23 August 1939, a week before the

---

92  'African Peoples, Democracy and World Peace', *Colonial Information Bulletin*, 15
July 1939, p. 2; 'Coloured Peoples Claim Democracy', *Daily Worker*, 10 July 1939, p. 8.
93  'African Peoples, Democracy and World Peace', p. 1.
94  TNA, KV 2/1787 (Kenyatta), 11 July 1939.
95  'Conference on African Races: Self-Determination Demanded', *New Leader*, 14
July 1939, p. 8.

war began, the Soviet Union signed the Molotov–Ribbentrop Pact with Germany, plotting the carving up of Poland. On 2 September 1939, the day after the German invasion of Poland, the Central Committee published a manifesto calling for a war on two fronts: the first against fascism, the second against the Chamberlain government. The Colonial Information Bureau was aligned with this policy during September 1939. Its statement of 1 September celebrated the Molotov–Ribbentrop Pact as 'a great victory for the peace policy of the Soviet Union'. It also argued that 'the immediate danger to the struggle of the colonial peoples for democratic rights and national independence comes from Fascism'.[96]

On 14 September, however, Moscow declared that the war was an inter-imperialist conflict in which the working class should not take sides. At the Central Committee meeting of 24–25 September, R. P. Dutt called for the CPGB to adopt the Soviet position, while Harry Pollitt defended the original Popular Front policy. As the meeting unfolded, David Springhall, a leading Communist, arrived from Moscow, where he had spoken with the head of the Comintern, Georgi Dimitrov, who had explained to Springhall that the war was an imperialist one. After Springhall's intervention, the meeting adjourned. The Central Committee reconvened on 2 October, and adopted Moscow's position. Pollitt, J. R. Campbell and Willie Gallacher were the only dissenters. Dutt replaced Pollitt as general secretary, and a new manifesto was published on 7 October 1939. The British and French governments were denounced as reactionary imperialists whose war efforts workers should resist.[97] In *We Fight for Life* (1940), Dutt declared: 'Two world blocks of robber Powers are fighting one another in this war for world domination.' As IASB members had long been doing, Dutt mocked British colonialist claims to 'democracy', and said that the Axis powers were 'equally' – but not more – 'piratical'.[98] Launching the new journal, *Inside the Empire*

---

96  'Colonial Peoples and the Pact', *Colonial Information Bulletin*, 1 September 1939, p. 1.

97  For more on the CPGB at the outbreak of war, see Noreen Branson, *History of the Communist Party of Great Britain, 1927–1941* (London, 1985), Chapter 19; Hugo Dewar, *Communist Politics in Britain: The CPGB from its Origins to the Second World War* (London, 1976), Chapter 10; Keith Laybourn and Dylan Murphy, *Under the Red Flag: A History of Communism in Britain, c. 1849–1991* (Stroud, 1999), Chapter 3; Kevin Morgan, *Against Fascism and War: Ruptures and Continuities in British Communist Politics, 1935–41* (Manchester, 1989), Chapter 5; Andrew Thorpe, *The British Communist Party and Moscow, 1920–43* (Manchester, 2000), Chapter 10.

98  R. P. Dutt, *We Fight for Life* (London, 1940), pp. 7–8.

(which replaced the *Colonial Information Bulletin*), in February 1940, Dutt declared: 'Between the British working class and the colonial peoples there is complete unity of interest. The common enemy is British imperialism.'[99]

One might, therefore, have expected a rapprochement between the IASB and the CPGB. Indeed, in February 1941, Kenyatta worked with the National Council for Civil Liberties (NCCL), alongside Buckle, to campaign for civil liberties in the colonies. Buckle reiterated the NCCL demands in *Labour Monthly*, including a protest against Wallace-Johnson's imprisonment.[100] Communist-aligned activists, particularly Ben Bradley, Reginald Bridgeman and Krishna Menon, played a significant role in shaping NCCL positions on colonial issues, so the involvement of Buckle and Kenyatta illustrates the continued possibilities, however limited, for solidarity between Communists and Black radicals.[101]

As Tom Buchanan has observed, however, 'the CPGB did not suddenly return to its anti-imperialist activism of the early 1930s.'[102] Blackman in fact distanced himself from CPGB activities around the time of the outbreak of war, though he remained in the party. He believed the CPGB treated colonial activity 'as a side-line', and later described party members 'as both racist and anti-semitic' – apparently never having been invited to the home of any White comrade.[103] In addition to lack of conviction proving an obstacle (much as it had done during the Third Period), there were also concerns about the permanence of the CPGB's rediscovered anti-imperialism. The *New Leader* expressed these concerns in January 1940, insisting the 'CPGB cannot be regarded as a reliable anti-war organisation. If the policy of Soviet Russia should change, the CPGB policy will change with it.'[104]

---

99  R. P. Dutt, 'The Empire and the War', *Inside the Empire*, February 1940, p. 2.

100  Desmond Buckle, 'Civil Liberty in the Empire', *Labour Monthly*, February 1941, pp. 83–6; TNA, KV 2/1788 (Kenyatta), 10 April 1941. For more on Buckle, see Hakim Adi, 'Forgotten Comrade? Desmond Buckle: An African Communist in Britain', *Science & Society* 70 (2006).

101  Chris Moores, *Civil Liberties and Human Rights in Twentieth-Century Britain* (Cambridge, 2017), pp. 63–7.

102  Tom Buchanan, '"The Dark Millions in the Colonies are Unavenged": Anti-Fascism and Anti-Imperialism in the 1930s', *Contemporary European History* 25 (2016), p. 663.

103  TNA, KV 2/1838 (Blackman), 28 June 1941; Marika Sherwood, 'The Comintern, the CPGB, Colonies and Black Britons, 1920–1938', *Science & Society* 60 (1996), p. 148.

104  'Labour Opposition to War', *New Leader*, 5 January 1940, p. 4.

The ILP was in due course proved correct. On 22 June 1941, Germany invaded the Soviet Union, breaking the Molotov–Ribbentrop Pact and prompting the Soviet Union to join the Allied forces. Communists around the world rallied to the defence of the Soviet Union. The CPGB now supported the Allied war effort, and Pollitt was reinstated as general secretary.[105] On 8 July 1941, Pollitt declared that the CPGB had 'changed its political line to meet the new position and tasks imposed upon it'. The 'war for the defeat of Hitler is now the supreme issue before the whole of democratic and progressive mankind'.[106] While calling for some social reform (such as the implementation of the Beveridge Report), the CPGB, with the Soviet Union now under attack, became even more vociferously antifascist than it had been during the Popular Front. It called for a second front (eventually established by the Normandy landings in June 1944) and decried the fifth column (those in Britain sympathetic to fascism). The ILP and 'Trotskyists' (a designation also applied to the IASB) were considered part of this 'fifth column', as they opposed the British war effort.[107] In May 1943, in the interests of the Allied war effort, the Comintern was dissolved, prompting the CPGB to rename itself the Communist Party (CP).[108]

The implications for Communist anti-imperialism were clear. The CPGB's first statement about colonial issues since the German invasion of the Soviet Union, 'The War and the Colonial Peoples', was a reversion to Popular Front analysis. The statement declared that the 'criminal war plans' of the fascists for 'the enslavement of the world' were directed at the peoples of Africa and Asia. Fascist imperialism was deemed qualitatively worse than 'democratic' imperialism. As the Soviet Union stood 'for the freedom and equality of nations', the Nazi attack on it was 'the most direct threat to all the subject and semi-Colonial peoples throughout the world'. While the CPGB called for colonial support of the 'British–Soviet Alliance in this just war', it acknowledged that the 'greatest responsibility' rested with the British people in overcoming the 'obstacles' that prevented colonial cooperation in the war effort; but it also deemed social-democratic reforms sufficient to remove these obstacles.[109]

---

105  Branson, *History of the Communist Party of Great Britain*, p. 332.

106  LHASC, CP/CENT/CIRC/70/5, Pollitt to all branches, 8 July 1941.

107  LHASC, CP/CENT/CIRC/1/3, Political Bureau to all branches, 'After the Three-Power Conference: The Tasks of the Communist Party', 8 November 1943.

108  Branson, *History of the Communist Party of Great Britain*, p. 335.

109  LHASC, CP/CENT/STAT/1/3, 'The War and the Colonial Peoples', 30 August 1941.

During the prelude to the Quit India movement, which began in August 1942, Pollitt wrote to Nehru, unsuccessfully pleading with him to support the war effort. Pollitt advised Nehru he 'would make the position of Congress a thousand times stronger if, while fighting for the complete independence of India and without in any way lowering your fundamental demands, at the same time in the present urgent situation you put to one side the suggestion of non-co-operation'.[110] While opposing radical anticolonialism, Communist policy after 1941 remained critical of British imperialism. When the Indian National Congress launched the Quit India movement ten days later, Pollitt blamed 'the reactionary character of British official policy' for creating the conditions for the movement.[111] Moreover, Pollitt could not be accused of hypocrisy; his language around the British miners' strikes of 1944 mirrored that of his proclamations about India. The CP would 'ceaselessly fight against any strikes or interference with production', but placed 'responsibility for the crisis where it belongs, on the Government and the coal owners'.[112] The CP subordinated the class and colonial struggles to the interests of antifascism, but did not subordinate the interests of colonial peoples to those of the British working class.

British Communists supported Indian independence, but Pollitt's criticisms of the Quit India movement made it clear that anti-imperialist movements were not to be supported unconditionally. There was some private resistance to this. Bridgeman saw a draft statement on the colonial question before the CPGB national conference in May 1942. Concerned, he wrote to Pollitt: 'It seems to be important to avoid giving the impression that a Communist statement on the colonial question is influenced by the compulsion of events, that it is primarily governed by the desire to enlist all colonial peoples in the struggle to smash Fascism'. Instead, Bridgeman suggested, 'the right of the colonial peoples to freedom should be plainly announced as a matter of principle'. He also argued that the resolution should move away from its sole focus on India to discuss the entire colonial empire.[113] Pollitt assured Bridgeman that he would raise this issue in his report to the conference, but Bridgeman was

110  LHASC, CP/IND/POLL/3/11, Pollitt to Nehru, 29 July 1942.
111  CPGB, *Communist Policy* (London, 1943), p. 11.
112  LHASC, CP/CENT/CIRC/63/2, Pollitt, 'Our Weekly Letter', 6 April 1944.
113  Papers of Reginald Bridgeman, DBN/26/2, Bridgeman to Pollitt, 21 May 1942.

frustrated to find Pollitt's promise unfulfilled.[114] The CPGB's Political Bureau eventually released a statement, 'The Negro Peoples and the War', in February 1943. The statement was consistent with the CPGB's India policy, as the party called for the granting of more rights to African and Caribbean peoples in the expectation that they would then join the fight against fascism.[115]

Padmore in fact agreed with the CPGB about the importance of defending the Soviet Union. In an article written in response to the 1941 invasion, he argued that the 'defence of the Soviet Union against Nazi imperialism is the obligation of every worker, colonial and progressive intellectual, regardless of our justifiable contempt for the Communist contortionists in Britain'.[116] But Padmore's argument that colonial peoples should focus on overthrowing imperialism before pivoting to the anti-Nazi struggle was met with a frosty reception by the CPGB. While the party refrained from criticising the IASB during the period of the Molotov–Ribbentrop Pact, it was fierce in its denunciations both before and after. In May 1939, Jimmy Shields branded the IASB, along with the ILP, as 'Trotskyists', writing that the 'chief aim of the Trotskyists in Britain is to sow confusion and disruption with the aim of splitting the labour and progressive forces'. He accused the IASB in particular of 'spreading Trotskyist corruption in relation to the colonial peoples'.[117] The August 1939 Central Committee statement, 'Colonies and Fascism', declared that Trotskyist propaganda 'in the name of repudiating existing imperialist domination, in practice acts as the apologist of fascist aggressive aims in relation to the colonial peoples'.[118]

Between September 1939 and June 1941, the attacks on the IASB subsided, but they resumed after the invasion of the Soviet Union. With the Soviet Union now facing an existential threat, 'vigilance' against fifth-column 'Trotskyists' became paramount. The CPGB started monitoring Makonnen and Padmore more closely. One report inaccurately

---

114  Papers of Reginald Bridgeman, DBN/26/2, Pollitt to Bridgeman, 29 May 1942; Bridgeman to Pollitt, 5 June 1942; CPGB, *The Communist Party on the Way to Win: Decisions of the National Conference of the CPGB, May, 1942* (London, 1942), pp. 24, 47.

115  CPGB, *Communist Policy*, pp. 34–6.

116  George Padmore, 'The Socialist Attitude to the Invasion of the USSR', *Left*, September 1941, pp. 193–9.

117  Jimmy Shields, 'The No Conscription League', *Party Organiser*, May 1939, pp. 7–10.

118  'Colonies and Fascism', *Labour Monthly*, August 1939, p. 473.

described Makonnen as an 'Open trotskyist'. It recommended that his café 'should be located and watched'.[119] The party recorded Padmore's political history dating back to his time in the Comintern (apparently he was expelled for his 'ultra-nationalist, anti-white line'), collected his articles published in the ILP press, and even made notes on his physical appearance ('Coloured – Tall, lanky, Typical Negroid countenance').[120]

The CPGB relied partly on Black activists, such as Abrahams and Blackman, who had better access to Padmore's networks, to aid with this surveillance. A May 1943 report highlights how much more knowledge-able about Padmore's political philosophy and activism these people were. The anonymous author incorrectly identified Padmore as a 'Trot-skyist', but added that Blackman took the view that Padmore was 'not a Trotskyist'. Both Abrahams and Blackman – the former part of the party's networks, though not a member – told the CPGB they had attended meetings of Black people at Padmore's flat in order to 'win some of the Negroes away from Padmore's influence'.[121] This may have been true of Blackman, but almost certainly was not true of Abrahams. It seems likely that Abrahams invented a cover story to prevent the Communist bureaucracy from objecting to the time he had spent with Padmore.

As before, the IASB found little support from the anti-imperialist wing of the CPGB. In April 1939, Bradley wrote to Richard Hart of the *Jamaica Labour Weekly* that British Communists were 'much disturbed' to see an article praising James and Padmore in the newspaper. Bradley advised Hart that James and Padmore had 'done more harm than good to the working class movement generally, and particularly to the Colo-nial Peoples, by the policy they have pursued'. By following a 'racialist line' they had 'opposed the struggle for the united front of all democratic peoples against fascism'.[122] Hart responded to Bradley to thank him for the information. He wrote: 'we are entirely in agreement with you, and shall avoid further mistakes in future'.[123] In an ironic moment, the metro-politan socialist dictated to the colonial socialist the appropriate forms

---

119  LHASC, CP/CENT/ORG/12/1, Vigilance work in the universities, 17 December 1942.

120  LHASC, CP/CENT/ORG/12/3.

121  LHASC, CP/CENT/ORG/12/1, Report on Trotskyite activities.

122  TNA, KV 2/1824 (James), Ben Bradley to Richard Hart, 17 April 1939.

123  TNA, KV 2/1824 (James), Hart to Bradley, 7 May 1939.

of anticolonialism, obstructing pan-Africanist solidarity between the IASB and the nascent Jamaican labour movement.

Despite these tensions, Bradley still centred imperialism in his political activism. Buchanan, while dismissive of the broader party's anti-imperialist credentials, notes: 'A few individuals did continue to press the anti-imperialist cause during the early phase of the war', most notably Bradley, who on Empire Day in 1940 was, alongside Arthur Clegg and Jacob Lerner, arrested and later sentenced to three months' imprisonment for telling a meeting in Walthamstow that only 50 million out of 450 million people in the empire supported the war effort.[124] This was, of course, during the time of the Molotov–Ribbentrop Pact. Buchanan remarks that, after June 1941, Bradley's 'principled stand would seem rather outdated'.[125]

Nevertheless, Bradley's relationship with the IASB after 1941 was not always characterised by friction. In 1943, he sent a warm letter to Cunard in which he discussed *White Man's Duty*. Bradley said he 'like[d] it very much', and that '[m]any of the coloured seamen [were] taking a great interest' in it. He also commented that he 'would have liked to have had a chat with Padmore'.[126] This indicates that Bradley and Padmore were not in regular contact with each other, but also that Bradley respected Padmore's work. Of course, *White Man's Duty* was politically moderate by Padmore's standards. This made the book much more compatible than most of Padmore's output with the position of the post-1941 CPGB. It is hard to imagine Bradley pouring such praise on Padmore's revolutionary articles for the *New Leader*.

Nonetheless, Padmore seems to have forged a genuine friendship with Arthur Clegg, a member of the CPGB's Colonial Committee. Clegg later recalled 'being shown around a Soviet Exhibition in London in 1941 by an enthusiastic Padmore'.[127] But the greatest friendships that IASB members held with Communists were with women. When Abrahams arrived in London, he initially stayed with four Communist women (one British, three White South Africans). Abrahams recalled, 'I was grateful

---

124  Buchanan, '"The Dark Millions"', p. 663; 'Empire Day in England', *Inside the Empire*, July 1940, p. 3.

125  Buchanan, '"The Dark Millions"', p. 663.

126  Nancy Cunard collection, Bradley to Cunard, 8 March 1943.

127  Barbara Bush, *Imperialism, Race and Resistance: Africa and Britain, 1919–1945* (London, 1999), p. 243.

to these women who had taken me in, fed me, found a room for me and promised to help me find a job'.[128] His next landlady (and eventual wife), Dorothy Pennington, was also a CPGB member. Padmore approved of her as a 'good comrade', and enjoyed visiting Pennington.[129] Abrahams believed that Padmore 'always got on better with the women of the Communist Party than with the men'.[130]

Abrahams did not speculate as to why Padmore enjoyed more amicable relationships with Communist women, but it is consistent with the assertions of several IASB members that White women were more sympathetic to pan-Africanism than were White men. Abrahams himself had some unpleasant personal experiences with the CPGB's male-dominated formal structures. He got a job at the *Daily Worker*, but was 'startled' by a racist outburst from the editor Bill Rust ('He had nothing against coloured people, but he did not see why he had to like them').[131] As we have seen, Abrahams had no qualms about misleading the party concerning his relationship with Padmore. He was eventually sacked by the *Daily Worker* when it was discovered that he was not a party member, having refused to join because he felt it 'inevitably meant subordinating detachment and objectivity to the interests of the party'.[132]

Old divisions therefore remained between the IASB and the CPGB during the Second World War. Even though the CPGB reoriented as a result of the Molotov–Ribbentrop Pact, this did not allow previous fractures to heal. Although the CPGB declared for a policy that resembled that of the IASB and the ILP, it was clear that this antiwar position would not survive were the Soviet Union to enter the conflict. Nevertheless, this twenty-one-month period allowed a brief cooling of hostilities. After the invasion of the Soviet Union in June 1941, the old tensions of the Popular Front re-emerged in more heated fashion. The Communists regarded the IASB as a fifth column, and even a target of surveillance. Personal friendships with Communists were forged while an institutional antagonism remained.

---

128  Abrahams, *Coyaba Chronicles*, p. 30.
129  Ibid., p. 41.
130  Ibid., p. 42.
131  Ibid., p. 44.
132  Ibid., pp. 59–60.

## The IASB and the Labour Party

An institutional antagonism was also maintained with the Labour Party, which joined Churchill's government in May 1940 as the junior partner. In October 1943, Padmore argued that 'the Labour Party in practice differ little from the Tories on the fundamental principle of Imperialism'. He conceded that Labour leaders were 'in favour of a more widespread extension of social services, education, and the like' (compared with the 'undisguised exploitation' favoured by their Conservative counterparts), but criticised the party for envisaging 'self-government of some of the colonies at a hazily distant future'.[133] The following year he argued that the trade union leadership had sought to 'wring concessions from the ruling class' rather than struggle for socialism, advocating an 'ultra-imperialism' that would not solve the problems facing Britain and the world.[134]

Padmore was particularly disappointed by Stafford Cripps's involvement in Churchill's government. While Cripps's embrace of the Popular Front had damaged his relationship with members of the IASB, he was still generally regarded as a principled member of the Labour left. In 1940, however, Churchill appointed Cripps ambassador to the Soviet Union, and in 1942 he was sent on his 'mission' to India. Cripps offered Dominion status to India at the conclusion of the war in exchange for Indian support for the British war effort. The breakdown of these negotiations – Cripps's offer was considered insulting by Congress leaders – inspired the Quit India movement. Padmore remarked: 'Sir Stafford Cripps, the hope of certain sections of the Left, has visited India and failed in his mission. The plan put forward by the British Government through the medium of this one-time most intransigent champion of complete independence for India, aims at breaking up the "national front" which has been achieved under the dominance of British rule.'[135]

While Padmore's criticisms of Cripps illustrate a deterioration of relations, his criticisms of Cripps's former Socialist League comrade,

---

133 George Padmore, 'Blue-print of Post-war Anglo-American Imperialism', *Left*, October 1943, pp. 201–2.

134 George Padmore, 'Imperialism: The Basis of the Labour Crisis', *Left*, June 1944, pp. 124–9.

135 George Padmore, 'Socialists Can't Bargain for India's Freedom', *New Leader*, 4 July 1942, p. 3.

H. N. Brailsford, were a continuation of hostilities. Writing in November 1941, Brailsford lamented that India would not support the British war effort. He placed the blame foursquare with the British government for not 'satisfying [India's] self-respect': 'Had we and our fathers allowed her to grow strong and prosperous by industry, instead of condemning her to dire poverty as a backward agricultural dependency, she could have equipped this army herself, with something to spare for Russia's needs.'[136] Padmore retorted: 'what Mr Brailsford fails to appreciate is that this liberty of India to expand industrially would have struck at the very base of the British imperialist structure, for it would have led to India emerging as an additional competitor of British capitalism'.[137] Padmore was responding to what he saw as Brailsford's attempts to promote anticolonialism without also directly challenging metropolitan capitalism.

Padmore also enjoyed a complicated relationship with the Fabian Colonial Bureau (FCB), founded in 1940 to research colonial issues. The FCB followed the Fabians' gradualist perspective. This frustrated the revolutionary Padmore, but, unlike the Labour leadership, the FCB could not be dismissed as unprincipled opportunists – Padmore and the FCB engaged seriously with each other's ideas. Rita Hinden, the FCB's secretary, wrote to Cunard in 1943 that she had enjoyed reading *White Man's Duty*, but wondered if Padmore 'does not rather over-simplify the problems'. She argued that, for the colonies 'to have a reasonable standard of living, they will continue to require capital and other help from abroad in the same way as the backward areas of the USSR have been considerably helped by the industrial areas of Russia'.[138] A review of *White Man's Duty*, most likely written by Hinden, also appeared in the FCB journal, *Empire*. The reviewer was surprised to find such a 'mild' conclusion to the book after its ' "Marxist" exposition on imperialism'. The reviewer criticised Padmore for not suggesting any 'concrete measures' to right the abuses of imperialism; he

---

136  H. N. Brailsford, 'Give India a Chance to Fight for Her Freedom', *Reynolds News*, 9 November 1941, p. 4.

137  George Padmore, 'Not Nazism! Not Imperialism! But Socialism!', *New Leader*, 27 December 1941, p. 5.

138  Nancy Cunard collection, Rita Hinden to Cunard, 20 April 1943. This was something that Padmore would explore in great detail in *How Russia Transformed Her Colonial Empire*, though he had also made the argument prior to Hinden's intervention.

had 'no more . . . to contribute than the "pink idealists" of which he is always so contemptuous'.[139]

For his part, Padmore wrote an equally critical review of Hinden's *Plan for Africa* in 1942. Tying his criticism in with a discussion of *The Colour Bar in East Africa*, by Norman Leys (another Labour Party colonial researcher), Padmore argued: 'Both have ideas for alleviating the disabilities of the African natives, but they want to achieve these humanitarian ends within the framework of the existing social order, which is impossible.' This echoed his criticism of Brailsford. Padmore claimed that parliamentary methods and development funds would not solve Africa's problems. In fact, these had provided 'nothing more than a few Labour Advisers, whose aim is to obstruct the natural development of militant Trade Unionism among the native workers'.[140]

Nevertheless, Black radicals continued to praise select Labour politicians, writers and activists. In *Kenya: The Land of Conflict*, Kenyatta approvingly quoted Leonard Woolf, an adviser to the Labour Party on colonial issues. He used Woolf's work to argue that in Kenya 'the interests of three million Africans have been sacrificed to those of a handful of Europeans'.[141] Padmore continued to praise Labour MPs, such as Reginald Sorensen and Arthur Creech Jones, who hounded the wartime government on colonial oppression and exploitation.[142] However, this was almost always contrasted with the official position of the Labour Party, which was characterised as gradualism at best and opportunism at worst. In July 1941, Padmore reported that Sorensen had pressed the Labour under-secretary of state for the colonies, George Hall, about the internment of the Jamaican socialist W. A. Domingo. Hall 'made the customary evasive replies', and Padmore described him as 'a so-called Socialist'.[143] While Padmore no longer deployed charges of 'social fascism', as he had while working for the Comintern, his opinion of the Labour Party leadership had barely improved in the intervening years.

~

---

139  'Guide to Books', *Empire*, July 1943, pp. 6–7.

140  George Padmore, 'No Solution within Empires', *New Leader*, 9 May 1942, p. 4.

141  Kenyatta, *Kenya*, p. 20.

142  Cunard and Padmore, *White Man's Duty*, p. 24; George Padmore, 'Why Was West Indian Leader Arrested?', *New Leader*, 26 July 1941, p. 3.

143  Padmore, 'Why Was West Indian Leader Arrested?', p. 3.

Throughout the war, the IASB, now represented chiefly by Padmore, continued to refuse to make distinctions between its antifascism and a broader anti-imperialism and anticapitalism. In December 1941, Padmore wrote:

> Nazism and all other manifestations of Fascism must be destroyed. There can be no compromise with this evil thing.
>
> This, however, is no justification for Socialists to apologise for, and even attempt to whitewash, so-called 'democratic' Imperialism which, in its colonial application, is indistinguishable from European Fascism. It is not a question of which is better: Fascism or Imperialism. Both are bad. Both have the same common origin – monopoly capitalism – and can only be eradicated by abolishing the social system which permits the exploitation of man by man, class by class, race by race.[144]

He wrote this piece for the *New Leader*, illustrating the increased political consonance of the IASB and the ILP. Indeed, this was also the ILP's position during the war, as they called for a 'Socialist Peace Offensive' to overthrow British capitalism while also challenging the fascism of the Axis powers. Despite the dispersal of many of the IASB's members, its profile within the ILP grew during the war. Jones and Padmore became increasingly popular speakers and journalists, and Padmore's ideas and personality became especially prominent aspects of ILP propaganda.

The Communist and Labour parties offered no such home for IASB ideas. Despite the Communist realignment between September 1939 and June 1941, there was no reconciliation with the IASB. The CPGB's primary concern was the defence of the Soviet Union. While the IASB deemed the socialist motherland worthy of protection, it would not compromise its anti-imperialism in order to achieve this. Indeed, it considered the abandonment of anti-imperialism counterproductive to this task, as it ignored the root cause of fascism: capitalist-imperialism. The IASB expected less of the Labour Party, considered to have been an expression of the interests of the labour aristocracy since its foundation; but it maintained alliances with sympathetic members like Sorensen and Creech Jones.

The Second World War, and the dispersal of Black radicals from London that accompanied it, limited IASB activity. However, by 1943 it

---

144  Padmore, 'Not Nazism! Not Imperialism! But Socialism!', p. 5.

was becoming increasingly apparent that the Allies would win the war. In the last years of the war, the IASB began to wrestle with the question of what the world should look like at the war's conclusion. As more people of African descent arrived in or returned to Britain and restrictions on activism eased, the IASB was prepared to hit the ground running in its discussions about the postwar order.

# 5

# Planning the Postwar World, 1944–1947

The end of the Second World War offered the prospect of a radically reconfigured world. The global left believed a new postwar order must emerge from the turmoil and destruction of the previous three decades. Even conservatives and liberals, whose complicity in and complacency about imperialist rivalry during the 1930s had frustrated left-wing activists, began to embrace forms of internationalism as embodied by the United Nations, founded in 1945. But socialists believed the UN did not go far enough: without the liquidation of capitalism, the root causes of war would remain unchecked. Pan-Africanists and socialists in Britain had long declared their desire to achieve a world socialist federation. Now, in the immediacy of debates about the nature of the postwar world, they began to draw up more concrete plans for the transformation of the world. The proposed next step took many forms: the formation of the United Socialist States of Europe (USSE) – a movement that gained significant traction in the Independent Labour Party (ILP); the federation of an independent Africa – a policy adopted at the 1945 Fifth Pan-African Congress; the transformation of the British Empire into a socialist commonwealth – as advocated by George Padmore in *How Russia Transformed Her Colonial Empire* (*HRTHCE*). While these proposals offered divergent paths, they all rested on socialism and anti-colonialism. All had as their final objective world federation. Forks in the road would eventually converge.

This chapter begins with a history of the Pan-African Federation (PAF), formed in 1944 with the International African Service Bureau

(IASB) as its leading constituent body. Its major achievement was organising the Fifth Pan-African Congress. The chapter then considers the PAF's relationship with the ILP, the Communist Party (CP) and the newly formed Labour government. It discusses whether the promise of the first Labour majority government affected pan-Africanists' strategy for colonial liberation. As we shall see, the PAF, which had a theoretical understanding of the institutional shortcomings of the Labour Party, was from the start sceptical about the Labour government's implications for its activism. The chapter concludes with a thorough discussion of competing socialist and pan-Africanist visions for the postwar order. It focuses in particular on Padmore's *HRTHCE*, F. A. Ridley's agitation for a USSE, and the ideas of the broader pan-Africanist movement. This will involve an interrogation of the meaning of 'pan-Africanism' for Padmore, who seemingly advocated African federalism at the Pan-African Congress but a socialist 'British' commonwealth in *HRTHCE*. It concludes that pan-Africanism was, for Padmore, a methodology through which colonial liberation, and eventually world socialism, could be achieved. In this sense, it was inseparable from his Marxism.

## The Pan-African Federation and the Fifth Pan-African Congress

Writing in June 1946, Ridley compared the Pan-African Federation and the United Nations, two organisations founded in the preceding years. He concluded that the PAF was 'an institution of much greater historical significance' than the UN.[1] At first glance this seems absurd. But Ridley's assertion provokes the question of which organisation offered the greater promise of colonial liberation and the socialist reconfiguration of the world. Would it be the revolutionary, agitational strategy of the PAF or the liberal constitutionalism of the UN? As Mark Mazower has highlighted in his study of the intellectual origins of the UN, there was much ambiguity in the organisation's founding charters and declarations. While many now see the UN as a force for anticolonialism, Mazower has posed the question of what to make of the segregationist South African premier Jan Smuts's involvement in drafting the UN's

---

1 F. A. Ridley, 'Out of Africa', *New Leader*, 15 June 1946, p. 4.

preamble.[2] The PAF, conversely, offered an alternative, more radical path to a postcolonial world.

Old Black radical networks began to reconvene at the end of the Second World War. Jomo Kenyatta returned to London. While Ras Makonnen remained in Manchester, Special Branch reported that he was 'attempting to revive the negro left wing organisation with which he was concerned in London before the war'.[3] IASB members formed the Pan-African Federation in late 1944. Padmore recalled that it was formed through a merger of pan-Africanist organisations, which, by 'pooling resources and liberating themselves from the eroding influence of doctrinaire Marxism which British Communists . . . were trying to impose upon the African national liberation movements' were able to 'take an independent ideological position on the colonial question'.[4] However, Padmore was exaggerating the discontinuities of this new organisation. The biggest organisations to affiliate, the Kikuyu Central Association and the West African Youth League, were already within the IASB's orbit due to the influence of Kenyatta and I. T. A. Wallace-Johnson, respectively. Other small Black associations in Britain affiliated to the PAF, but they were not joined by the largest Black organisations in Britain, the League of Coloured Peoples (LCP) and the West African Students' Union (WASU). The political dominance of the old IASB therefore went unchallenged. As Makonnen recalled, the most significant reason for forming a new organisation was the desire for a 'more explicitly political' organisation with 'Pan-African' in its name.[5]

Chris Jones did not live to see the new organisation. He died from pneumonia in September 1944, aged fifty-nine. Padmore paid tribute to him in the *New Leader*, describing Jones's death as 'a great loss to the cause of the colonial peoples as well as International Socialism'. He recalled that it was 'always a pleasure to hear Chris, who was of a most gay and youthful temperament, relate his many sailor's yarns, and, in his more serious moments, to listen to him describing the conditions of the

---

2  Mark Mazower, *No Enchanted Palace: The End of Empire and the Ideological Origins of the United Nations* (Princeton, 2009), pp. 19–20.

3  TNA, KV 2/1788 (Kenyatta), 7 May 1945.

4  George Padmore, *Pan-Africanism or Communism? The Coming Struggle for Africa* (London, 1956), pp. 149–50.

5  T. Ras Makonnen, *Pan-Africanism from Within*, ed. Kenneth King (London, 1973), p. 163.

working-class in the various lands it was his good fortune to visit'.[6] Ethel Mannin struck a similar note in her tribute, remarking that 'the socialist and anti-imperialist struggle lost a valiant fighter by his death, and many of us, myself included, a good comrade and friend'.[7]

Jones was survived by six children, for whom his widow was unable to care. A committee was set up to raise funds and find foster parents for Jones's children. Mannin acted as treasurer, Padmore as secretary. They were joined on the committee by Makonnen, Reginald Reynolds and John McNair.[8] The *New Leader* regularly appealed to its readers for funds, and found foster parents for Jones's youngest child (a twenty-month-old son), who was taken into 'the care of some very kind Midlands comrades'.[9] Reynolds recalled that much of the money 'came in small but regular postal orders from poor people who either knew Chris or cared about the things he had stood for'.[10] The linkages between the IASB and the ILP extended beyond grand political programmes and into the more personal solidarities of coping with the financial implications of a premature death.[11]

Although missing Jones, the PAF drew into its orbit the man who would become the most significant figure of postwar pan-Africanism. Kwame Nkrumah, who led the Gold Coast (renamed Ghana) to independence in 1957, was born to a poor family in Nkroful in September 1909. He left to study in the United States in 1935. Nkrumah met C. L. R. James in New York in 1943, later remembering that it was through James that he 'learned how an underground movement worked'.[12] It was at this time that Nkrumah began to study seriously the 'problem of imperialism'. He recalled: 'Karl Marx and Lenin particularly impressed me as I felt sure that their philosophy was capable of solving these problems', but that 'the book that did more than any other to fire my enthusiasm was *Philosophy and Opinions of Marcus Garvey*'.[13]

---

6 George Padmore, 'Chris Jones: Fighter for the Oppressed', *New Leader*, 23 September 1944, p. 7.

7 Ethel Mannin, *Comrade O Comrade: Or, Low-Down on the Left* (London, 1947), p. 5.

8 John McNair, 'The Late Chris Jones', *New Leader*, 2 December 1944, p. 8.

9 John McNair, 'Party Notes and News', *New Leader*, 10 March 1945, p. 6.

10 Reginald Reynolds, *My Life and Crimes* (London, 1956), pp. 120–1.

11 Mannin and Reynolds had by this time left the ILP, but were still part of its networks.

12 Kwame Nkrumah, *The Autobiography of Kwame Nkrumah* (Edinburgh, 1957), p. 44.

13 Ibid., p. 45.

Nkrumah arrived in London from the United States in late May or early June 1945. James wrote to Padmore that Nkrumah was 'not very bright but . . . was determined to throw the imperialists out of Africa'. Padmore then met Nkrumah upon his arrival, and gave him a political education.[14] Nkrumah stayed briefly at the WASU hostel, before taking a room in a house in Tufnell Park, where he planned to complete his doctoral thesis on Akan philosophy at the London School of Economics.[15] However, the political excitement of the day engulfed his time in London. Makonnen later remembered that the PAF quickly identified Nkrumah as a leader.[16]

Pan-Africanist activity in Britain during 1945 was dominated by the planning of the Fifth Pan-African Congress, a successor to W. E. B. Du Bois's congresses held between 1919 and 1927 (and, before that, the 1900 Pan-African Conference organised by Henry Sylvester Williams). However, while earlier meetings had been composed of small numbers of African diasporic elites, the new congress was to feature representation from the labour movement and other colonial associations and societies. Marika Sherwood therefore calls the congress 'the first time that representatives of the anglophone working peoples of the colonies came together to discuss what they wanted from the future'.[17] The congress's organisers, while praising Du Bois's foundational work, contrasted the 1945 congress favourably with its forerunners. Abrahams remembered the Manchester Congress as 'the first truly representative one'; Nkrumah said it was attended by 'practical men and men of action'; and Padmore called it an 'expression of a mass movement'.[18]

---

14  C. L. R. James, *At the Rendezvous of Victory* (London, 1984), p. 173.

15  Nkrumah, *Autobiography*, pp. 49–51.

16  Makonnen, *Pan-Africanism from Within*, p. 154.

17  Marika Sherwood, 'Introduction', in Hakim Adi and Marika Sherwood, eds, *The 1945 Manchester Pan-African Congress Revisited* (London, 1995), p. 9. The disproportionately Anglophone reach of the Congress was partly practical, but also ideological. Makonnen believed that educated Black French colonials were more assimilated into the imperial system. He remembered that uneasy relations between peoples colonised by Britain and France 'was to be one of the toughest obstacles once independence had come to West Africa'. Makonnen, *Pan-Africanism from Within*, p. 166.

18  Peter Abrahams, *The Coyaba Chronicles: Reflections on the Black Experience in the Twentieth Century* (Kingston, 2000), p. 46; Nkrumah, *Autobiography*, p. 53; Padmore, *Pan-Africanism or Communism?*, p. 161.

Plans for the congress were put in place after the February 1945 World Trade Union Conference. The conference met in London as a preliminary step towards reviving the International Federation of Trade Unions – the 'Amsterdam International' that had been derided by Padmore in his Comintern days. The colonial workers' case was represented by Wallace-Johnson, J. S. Annan of the Gold Coast, John Asfour of Palestine, T. A. Bankole of Nigeria, Hubert Critchlow of British Guiana, Ken Hill of Jamaica, and S. K. Pramanik of India, among others. The colonial delegates argued that, as well as defeating fascism, the labour movement must overthrow the systems of capitalism and imperialism. More immediately, they called for the extension of the third clause of the Atlantic Charter to include colonial peoples. The colonial delegations suggested amendments to the conference's Declaration on the Attitude to the Peace Settlement to make it explicit that imperialist rivalry was the main cause of war, and to attach more urgency to colonial self-determination. These amendments were defeated, however.[19]

Padmore was frustrated by the conference decisions; but he celebrated the fact that that, 'for the first time in the history of international labour, coloured Colonial workers – the most oppressed and exploited section of the world proletariat – were given the opportunity of voicing their grievances and of expressing their hopes and aspirations'.[20] In fact, it was the ILP that reacted with most fury to the conference decisions. The *New Leader* denounced 'collaborationist' trade unionism, portraying Wallace-Johnson as the hero of the conference. The article concluded that the conference would 'stand as a symbol of the way in which the most powerful Trade Union movements diverted their efforts from the real path of progress'. Yet it also saw 'features that kindle a hope that when the war is ended and the workers' movements of all countries have reorganised themselves, the collaborationists and opportunists will find it difficult to maintain their hold'.[21]

After the conference, Padmore suggested holding a Pan-African Congress later in the year. He gained the support of Makonnen, Kenyatta,

---

19 George Padmore, *The Voice of Coloured Labour* (Manchester, 1945), Chapter 6.
20 Ibid., p. 3.
21 'They Were Challenged at World Trade Union Congress: Labour's "Big Three"', *New Leader*, 17 February 1945, p. 1.

Wallace-Johnson and Peter Milliard.[22] As C. L. R. James later observed, it was the political organisation and activism of the previous decade that had placed the PAF in a position to be able to convene the congress.[23] On 24 February 1945, there was a meeting in Manchester of representatives of the IASB, the Negro Welfare Association and the Negro Association of Manchester. They agreed that the congress should be held in Paris in September, and Padmore was appointed secretary of the organising committee.[24]

Hakim Adi has described the congress as 'a successfully staged coup by George Padmore'. He notes that several organisations were planning Pan-African meetings at this time, and that Padmore's recognition of the Du Boisian tradition was something of an afterthought to grant the congress legitimacy.[25] Peter Abrahams described Padmore as the 'master planner'. One of Makonnen's restaurants in Manchester served as head office, while Abrahams took responsibility for publicity, and Padmore's 'network of contacts throughout the Commonwealth and empire was alerted . . . in a steady stream'.[26] Makonnen served as treasurer, and 'was responsible for raising most of the funds to defray the expenses'.[27] Nkrumah remembered working 'day and night' in Padmore's flat. The table in Padmore's kitchen was 'completely covered by papers', Padmore 'typing at his small typewriter so fast that the papers were churned out as though they were being rolled off a printing press'.[28]

Despite the absence of the LCP and WASU from the PAF, the congress was not a sectarian affair. The PAF worked with the LCP and WASU to organise the congress, and even published joint manifestos with those groups. While WASU had become more radical as the war progressed,

22  George Padmore, *Colonial and . . . Coloured Unity: A Programme of Action: History of the Pan-African Congress* (1947), reprinted in Adi and Sherwood, *1945 Manchester Pan-African Congress Revisited*, pp. 60–1.

23  C. L. R. James, 'George Padmore: Black Marxist Revolutionary – A Memoir' (1976), in C. L. R. James, *At the Rendezvous of Victory* (London, 1984), p. 260.

24  Henry Moon to W. E. B. Du Bois, 9 April 1945, in W. E. B. Du Bois, *The Correspondence of W. E. B. Du Bois: Volume III: Selections, 1944–63*, ed. Herbert Aptheker (Amherst, MA, 1978), pp. 57–9.

25  Hakim Adi, 'George Padmore and the 1945 Manchester Pan-African Congress', in Fitzroy Baptiste and Rupert Lewis, eds, *George Padmore: Pan-African Revolutionary* (Kingston, 2009), p. 66.

26  Abrahams, *Coyaba Chronicles*, pp. 45–6.

27  Padmore, *Pan-Africanism or Communism?*, p. 146.

28  Nkrumah, *Autobiography*, p. 52.

the LCP was anxious to maintain its respectable, moderate reputation.[29] Its 1944 Charter for Coloured Peoples made the case for the legal equality of Black people throughout colonial empires. It further declared that dependent territories should be developed 'in the interest of the peoples of the regions concerned', but did not tender a systematic anti-imperialist argument.[30]

However, there were permeable boundaries between the IASB/PAF and the LCP (Abrahams, for example, was a member of both). The IASB even signed the 1945 LCP manifesto, 'Africa in the Post-war World'. Michael Carritt, secretary of the Communist Colonial Information Bureau, responded positively to the manifesto. It was addressed to the April 1945 San Francisco conference (which led to the formation of the UN). While it did not call for African independence, it demanded greater representation for the colonies. Carritt called it 'an excellent document' and one the CIB could 'wholeheartedly support'.[31] The constitutionalism of the document, and the LCP's appeal to diplomacy between the Soviet Union, the United States and Britain was highly palatable to the Communists. While the IASB simply signed the manifesto, and seemingly played no role in drafting it, there is something incongruous about seeing Padmore's name published alongside the manifesto in the CP's *Labour Monthly*.[32]

Padmore's support for 'Africa in the Post-war World' ostensibly adds further weight to Leslie James's argument that Padmore underwent a political realignment during the latter stages of the war. In fact, his relationship with Harold Moody and the LCP was never more than a precarious coalition. Moody initially supported the PAF's call for a Pan-African Congress, but did not want to tie it to the labour movement. He believed the problem to be 'humanitarian and not political or economic'.[33] In the event, the LCP was not represented at the congress; any account of Padmore's increasing number of 'respectable' alliances (of

29  Adi notes that 'the leftwards shift in the politics of WASU' was facilitated by the absence of WASU founder Ladipo Solanke, a moderating influence who spent the period between 1944 and 1948 in West Africa. Hakim Adi, *West Africans in Britain, 1900–1960: Nationalism, Pan-Africanism and Communism* (London, 1998), p. 121.

30  LHASC, ID/CORR/LCP, Charter for Coloured Peoples.

31  Schomburg Center, St Clair Drake papers, box 64 folder 5, Michael Carritt to LCP, 13 April 1945.

32  'Africa in the Post-war World', *Labour Monthly*, May 1945, pp. 154–6.

33  Moon to Du Bois, 9 April 1945, in *Correspondence of W. E. B. Du Bois*, p. 58.

which there can be no doubt) must note their fragility, as Padmore's continued Marxism remained incompatible with more moderate strains of anticolonialism.

The preparation for the congress was further punctuated that summer by the Subject Peoples' Conference and the Nigerian general strike. The PAF sponsored the Subject Peoples' Conference, held in Holborn Hall on 10 June 1945, which attracted forty-five delegates representing colonies from across the British Empire. The Ceylonese activist T. B. Subasinghe and WASU general secretary H. O. Davies were the conference's driving forces.[34] The resulting manifesto was published in the ILP's journal, *Left*. Like most political texts of the day, the manifesto located itself in the 'historic moment' of fascism's defeat and the need for reorganisation of the world. It contended that the imperialisms of other Western powers had inspired the methods of Nazi rule, and argued for 'the liquidation of imperialism in all its manifestations' – though it stopped short of explicitly advocating socialism.[35] The alliances forged at events like the Subject Peoples' Conference demonstrate that the PAF was not pursuing a narrow pan-Africanism concerned only with African liberation. Rather, it pursued an expansive pan-Africanism that recognised European imperialism as a global system, requiring a global anti-imperialist movement to defeat it. The group's pan-Africanism was thus a vehicle contributing towards an even broader project of liberation.

Eleven days after the conference, a general strike broke out in Nigeria. The colonial government refused to raise wages in line with the cost of living, prompting up to 200,000 railway, port and communication workers to strike. The journalist and activist Nnamdi Azikiwe's newspapers were banned, and, as Adi and Barbara Bush have observed, the strike developed a political and anticolonial character.[36] The PAF and WASU convened meetings in London, Manchester and Liverpool to raise money for the strikers and to call on the British TUC to intervene in the

---

34  LHASC, JD/CORR/COL, H. O. Davies and T. B. Subasinghe to the secretary of the Labour Party, 28 May 1945; Subasinghe to the secretary of the Labour Party, 16 June 1945.

35  'The Colonies and the Peace', *Left*, June 1945, pp. 417–19.

36  Adi, *West Africans in Britain*, p. 124; Barbara Bush, *Imperialism, Race and Resistance: Africa and Britain, 1919-1945* (London, 1999), p. 123.

dispute.[37] The *New Leader* assisted with the publicity, and granted platforms to the likes of H. O. Davies and Padmore.[38]

For logistical reasons, the Pan-African Congress was moved to London, and eventually Manchester. Manchester was chosen because Makonnen's restaurants and clubs provided the infrastructure necessary to accommodate the delegates. Makonnen later recalled: 'I sometimes saw myself like Engels whose father had made a lot of money in Manchester and was able to support Marx in his great undertaking.'[39] The congress opened on 15 October 1945 in Chorlton-on-Medlock Town Hall. Amy Ashwood Garvey chaired the first session, and Du Bois chaired the remainder of the congress. There were eighty-seven delegates and around 200 observers.[40]

The congress made the case for socialism. 'The Challenge to the Colonial Powers' declared: 'We condemn the monopoly of capital and the rule of private wealth and industry for private profit alone. We welcome economic democracy as the only real democracy.'[41] The 'Declaration to the Colonial Workers, Farmers and Intellectuals' called on colonial peoples to use '[their] weapons – the Strike and the Boycott'. Colonial workers 'must be in the front of the battle against Imperialism'. The declaration concluded with a rallying call adapted from *The Communist Manifesto*: 'Colonial and Subject Peoples of the World – Unite!'[42]

Abrahams declared at the congress that 'the European left, with rare exceptions, has forfeited the right to leadership of the struggle against imperialism'.[43] While Abrahams did not specify the minority about which he was speaking, Padmore a few months later used a similar formulation, in which he included the ILP among the 'few honourable exceptions'.[44] Read in conjunction with Abrahams's statement, this makes clear that the ILP was excused from the congress's criticisms. Indeed, as recounted at the beginning of this book, ILP general secretary

37  Padmore, *Voice of Coloured Labour*, pp. 43–5.

38  See *New Leader*, 14 July, 21 July, and 28 July 1945.

39  Makonnen, *Pan-Africanism from Within*, p. 164.

40  A comprehensive list of delegates can be found in Adi and Sherwood, *1945 Manchester Pan-African Congress Revisited*, pp. 125–61.

41  Padmore, *Colonial and . . . Coloured Unity*, pp. 55–6.

42  Ibid., pp. 56–7.

43  Ibid., p. 60.

44  George Padmore, 'Trusteeship – The New Imperialism', *New Leader*, 2 February 1946, p. 3.

John McNair opened the congress by offering fraternal greetings.[45] McNair told the delegates that they had 'to win the battle for complete political independence' and 'return to their respective countries and inform the colored peoples that British Imperialists will never voluntarily leave Africa and the Colonies'. Allying himself with the PAF's revolutionary pan-Africanism, he said that the colonies would 'never win self-government by trusting the hypocrisy of the British Imperialist class'.[46] The *New Leader* claimed that McNair 'had a great reception'. Given Padmore's celebratory report in the *Chicago Defender*, this seems a reasonable claim. The *New Leader* also reproduced the text of 'The Challenge to the Colonial Powers'.[47] Six months later, the ILP invited a PAF fraternal delegate to open its annual conference.[48]

Dinah Stock was also welcomed to the Pan-African Congress as the delegate from the Freedom Defence Committee of London. She collected signatures for a petition demanding amnesty for political prisoners. Fraternal greetings were also received from the Common Wealth Party, the Socialist Vanguard Group and the Lancashire ILP.[49] Pat Devine, the Communist Lancashire and Cheshire district secretary, also sent greetings. While Devine did not invoke the revolutionary rhetoric of Padmore or McNair, he advised that the basis of the congress's campaigns in Britain should be for the extension of the Atlantic Charter to the colonial peoples. He wished the congress 'the very best success'.[50]

This friendly if moderate greeting is easy to dismiss, especially if, as W. O. Maloba has suggested, the Communist Party sent the message out of a recognition that it could not simply boycott the congress.[51] However, despite Padmore's assertion that the PAF was formed to break the influence of 'British Communists operating through certain Negro fellow travellers', Adi has pointed to the involvement of Desmond Buckle and Ken Hill to argue convincingly that 'there seems to be very little basis for

---

45 Padmore, *Colonial and . . . Coloured Unity*, p. 75.

46 George Padmore, 'Colonials Demand Freedom', *Chicago Defender*, 27 October 1945, p. 1.

47 'Africans to Protest in London', *New Leader*, 3 November 1945, p. 2.

48 BLPES, ILP/3/34, Meeting of NAC, 19 April 1946.

49 Padmore, *Colonial and . . . Coloured Unity*, p. 116.

50 Ibid., pp. 115–16.

51 W. O. Maloba, *Kenyatta and Britain: An Account of Political Transformation, 1929–1963* (Cham, Switzerland, 2018), p. 94.

such an assertion.'[52] It was Buckle who drafted 'Africa in the Post-war World', the LCP manifesto discussed above.[53] Hill, who also allied himself with Wallace-Johnson at the World Trade Union Conference, was a delegate to the Pan-African Congress. Moreover, in March 1946 Padmore reported sympathetically on his labour movement in Jamaica.[54] While its relations with White Communists remained frosty, the PAF worked closely with Black Communists. Padmore's subsequent erasure of their contribution, in his Cold War polemic, *Pan-Africanism or Communism?*, was a misleading account of history.[55]

In a less immediate way, organised Communism also provided an important organisational and ideological basis for the Pan-African Congress. Several historians have noted that Padmore's experience of organising the 1930 Hamburg conference had provided him with the skills necessary to organise the 1945 Manchester congress.[56] The Marxist politics that informed the Manchester congress owed more to Hamburg than they did to Du Bois's interwar congresses. However disillusioned Padmore was with contemporary Communism, the legacies of his Comintern work ran deep within him.

The experience of the Pan-African Congress, with its demonstration of strength and solidarity, provided a moment of euphoria. Abrahams recalled being 'sure, now, that one day, no matter how far in the future, Africa would be free'. However, when the congress ended, 'the mood of tension, of high excitement, gradually evaporated. We returned to our daily routine.'[57] Delegates were particularly frustrated by the lack of British press coverage. The Gold Coast anticolonialist Joe Appiah remembered that, 'although the press was present throughout, nothing

---

52  Padmore, *Pan-Africanism or Communism?*, pp. 149–50; Adi, 'George Padmore and the 1945 Manchester Pan-African Congress', p. 78.

53  Padmore to Du Bois, 12 April 1945, in *Correspondence of W. E. B. Du Bois*, pp. 63–4.

54  George Padmore, 'Facts behind Jamaica Labour Riots', *New Leader*, 2 March 1946, p. 4.

55  For the broader context, see Epilogue, below.

56  Hakim Adi, *Pan-Africanism and Communism: The Communist International, Africa and the Diaspora, 1919–1939* (Trenton, NJ, 2013), p. 121; Leslie James, *George Padmore and Decolonization from Below: Pan-Africanism, the Cold War, and the End of Empire* (Basingstoke, 2015), p. 64; Holger Weiss, *Framing a Radical African Atlantic: African American Agency, West African Intellectuals and the International Trade Union Committee of Negro Workers* (Leiden, 2014), p. 721.

57  Abrahams, *Coyaba Chronicles*, p. 47.

had been reported in the British papers by the morning of the fourth day'.[58] The *New Leader* declared that 'the Press took so little notice that it amounted virtually to a boycott'.[59]

The ILP itself recognised the congress's significance. The party promoted a demonstration in London on 9 December to advance the congress's demands.[60] A brief 'review of 1945' in the *New Leader* took as its scope the entirety of global politics, and noted that, in October, 'A Pan-African Congress is held in Manchester'. The inclusion of this detail, even if only a sentence (the same space as granted to the World Trade Union Conference in February), illustrates the importance that the ILP attached to the congress.[61] It would be vindicated in granting this significance, as three future African heads of state (Kenyatta, Nkrumah and Hastings Banda) were delegates. The congress forged new pan-African connections, and reconnected old ones that had been disrupted by the Second World War. The ILP, following years of collaboration with the IASB, was a nodal point within this pan-Africanist network.

## The PAF and the British Left During the Postwar Labour Government

In July 1945, Clement Attlee's Labour Party won a landslide victory in the first general election for ten years. This victory was met with ambivalence by the PAF. Labour's paternalistic Africa policy had been expressed in its 1943 statement, *The Colonies*: 'For a considerable time to come these peoples will not be ready for self-government, and European peoples and States must be responsible for the administration of their territories'. This paternalistic logic was further evident in the contention that these territories 'should be administered by colonial powers as a trust for the native inhabitants'.[62]

Nevertheless, the PAF believed that it was worthwhile appealing to a Labour government, even if only to use its own rhetoric to expose its

---

58  Joe Appiah, *The Autobiography of an African Patriot* (New York, 1990), p. 166.

59  'Africans to Protest in London', p. 2.

60  Ibid., p. 2.

61  'Review of 1945', *New Leader*, 29 December 1945, p. 2.

62  Labour Party, *The Colonies: The Labour Party's Post-war Policy for the African and Pacific Colonies* (London, 1943), p. 2.

hypocrisy. After the general election, the PAF sent an open letter to Attlee, declaring: 'To condemn the imperialism of Germany, Japan and Italy while condoning that of Britain would be more than dishonest, it would be a betrayal of the sacrifice and sufferings and the toil and sweat of the common people of this country. All imperialism is evil.' Attlee failed to respond.[63] In September 1945, Padmore explained to Du Bois: 'While the Colonial peoples expect a more sympathetic attitude towards their problems and aspirations from Labour than from the Tories, they have no illusions about either party, for on matters affecting imperial policy there is only a difference of degree rather than of kind.' He elaborated that, if Labour's promises of greater freedoms for colonial peoples went unfulfilled, 'we shall expose them even more ruthlessly than the Tories, for the Tories never promised us anything but blood, tears, toil and sweat.'[64] After the Paris Peace Conference, held the following year, Padmore wrote that 'the Labour Party have sold the future of Britain, lock, stock and barrel to the United States, in the hope that America will underwrite the remnants of the British Empire.'[65]

By the end of 1945, Wallace-Johnson was publicly raging against the Labour government. He expressed scepticism about Labour colonial policy in October 1945, when he argued: 'Labour cannot fulfil its obligations to the Colonial peoples by means of the Tory watchdogs who have been placed in control of Colonial affairs.' He worried that the government saw the replacement of personnel in the colonial authorities as 'of minor importance', and warned: 'If Labour fails to give them attention, those responsible will soon find that they have "cut their noses to spite their faces" in so far as British influence over the darker races is concerned.'[66] Labour's new colonial secretary was George Hall, whom Black radicals had earlier maligned as under-secretary. In November, Wallace-Johnson criticised Hall's 'indecision' about meeting a West African farmers' delegation.[67] By December, he was vociferously denouncing the government for its role in the repression of the Indonesian

---

63  Padmore, *Pan-Africanism or Communism?*, pp. 157–8.

64  Padmore to Du Bois, 18 September 1945, in *Correspondence of W. E. B. Du Bois*, p. 87.

65  George Padmore, 'Review of the Paris Conference', *Pan-Africa*, January 1947, p. 9.

66  I. T. A. Wallace-Johnson, 'Labour's Greatest Job', *New Leader*, 13 October 1945, p. 4.

67  I. T. A. Wallace-Johnson, 'Mr George Hall Should Stop and Think', *New Leader*, 24 November 1945, pp. 4–5.

Revolution. He pleaded with Attlee to 'maintain the dignity of International Socialism', and warned: 'Britain is treading the same path that led the people from World War No. 1 to World War No. 2.'[68]

Arthur Creech Jones was Hall's under-secretary, and then colonial secretary himself from October 1946. He had previously enjoyed a warm relationship with the British pan-Africanist movement. His subsequent role in the Labour government was particularly disappointing not just to the PAF, but also to WASU, which became rapidly disillusioned with the postwar government.[69] The disillusionment with Creech Jones in fact began before the 1945 general election. In April 1944, he had written that Britain 'has an Empire it cannot shed'. Making an argument for the gradual abolition of empire under a paternalistic Labour government, he submitted that it was 'one thing' to rail at colonial exploitation and advocate the breaking of 'monopolistic trading interests', but asked, 'how is it to be done?'[70] Padmore observed that the question asked by Creech Jones ('who has so often championed the Colonial peoples in Parliament and exposed their grievances') was the same as that asked by Lenin, 'and we have seen how he solved it: how he removed the vested interests of Czarist Imperialism by superseding them entirely'.[71]

The PAF's criticisms of Creech Jones were thus not entirely personal attacks, but rather stemmed from a Leninist understanding of imperialism and the state. A 1946 article by Abrahams contrasted Creech Jones's earlier 'thunderous denunciations' of imperialism with his record in office. It added that, as far as colonial peoples were concerned, 'that Mr Jones is really good-intentioned, but weak and over-ruled by the machinery of the Colonial Office is also beside the point. They are not interested in how Mr Creech Jones makes peace with his conscience.'[72] A 1947 article in the PAF's journal *Pan-Africa* commented on Creech Jones's speech at the annual meeting of the Anti-Slavery and Aborigines' Protection Society. The article stated a belief in Creech Jones's sincere desire to

---

68  I. T. A. Wallace-Johnson, 'Mr Churchill Wants a United Europe', *New Leader*, 8 December 1945, p. 4.

69  Adi, *West Africans in Britain*, p. 120.

70  Arthur Creech Jones, 'British Imperialism and the Colonial Empire', *Left News*, April 1944, pp. 2, 818–20.

71  George Padmore, with Dorothy Pizer, *How Russia Transformed Her Colonial Empire: A Challenge to the Imperialist Powers* (London, 1946), pp. 171–2.

72  Peter Abrahams, 'The Colonials Can't Live on Promises!', *New Leader*, 20 April 1946, p. 7.

bring his socialist principles into the Colonial Office, but scoffed at Creech Jones's suggestion that there had been a significant change in the character of imperialism.[73] For Black radicals, Labour imperialism was not the failing of Creech Jones personally, but of social democracy and liberal parliamentarianism as a whole.

The Labour Party thus occupied a strange space in PAF thought. Leninist theory allowed Black radicals to see the Labour Party as representatives of the labour aristocracy, who were invested in imperialism. Even the honest anti-imperialists like Creech Jones were constrained by their parliamentarianism. But the PAF also recognised the Labour Party's hold on the British working class and wider labour movement, as well as its declared commitment to gradualist anticolonialism – or at least colonial reform. A Labour government was therefore attacked in a manner different from that deployed against a Conservative government – but the PAF never placed its hopes for liberation in Labour's electoral success.

Perhaps the most important moment of disillusionment came in 1947, when left-wing Labour MPs R. H. S. Crossman, Michael Foot and Ian Mikardo published the pamphlet *Keep Left*. It was an essentially nationalist pamphlet, couched in the language of maintaining Britain's place as a global power that could forge a path between the United States and the Soviet Union in the incipient Cold War. It argued that African soldiers should be recruited to reduce the burden on British manpower after Indian independence, justifying this position through an emphasis on the educational value of military service for colonial peoples.[74] The authors criticised the exploitation and immorality of the old imperialism, but clearly still viewed empire as an important British asset. They also offered no prospect of African independence, stating that their project of African development 'should be our main colonial responsibility for the next twenty years'.[75]

Padmore savaged the pamphlet, arguing that the authors 'can only think of Africa in terms of exploitation', and predicted that they would 'be found in the Yankee camp of imperialism should there be another world war'.[76] The importance of the publication of *Keep Left* derived

---

73  'Halcyon' and 'What Will the Harvest Be?', *Pan-Africa*, May 1947, pp. 6–9.
74  R. H. S. Crossman, Michael Foot and Ian Mikardo, *Keep Left* (London, 1947).
75  Ibid., p. 44.
76  Padmore, 'Review of the Paris Conference', pp. 15–16.

from the fact that it came from the most significant section of the post-war Labour left. As Stephen Howe has observed, 'During the 1945–50 Government the Labour left did not mount any significant challenge to the colonial policy of George Hall and Arthur Creech Jones.'[77] This lack of dissent stood in marked contrast to the anticolonial politics of the Socialist League during the previous decade. Coupled with the ILP's dramatic decline in the years following the Second World War, Labour's stance determined that Black radicals in Britain increasingly had to look to individual sympathetic socialists, rather than any form of institutional support.

Despite the ILP's postwar decline (accelerated by Maxton's death in 1946 and the exodus of many leading figures to the Labour Party), the PAF still looked to the party as its most valuable ally on the British left. PAF members began to devote more energy to building pan-Africanist networks. They therefore contributed fewer articles to ILP publications than they had previously, but Abrahams, Padmore and Wallace-Johnson continued to write for the *New Leader* and to speak at ILP meetings.[78] The ILP even consulted the PAF on draft pamphlets about colonial issues before publication.[79] After speaking at the 1947 summer school in Bangor, Abrahams wrote to thank McNair 'for the very glorious time I had with you and other comrades'. Abrahams was particularly struck by 'the truly international spirit of the comrades there', as political relation-ships developed into personal friendships.[80] Stock served on the editorial committee of *Pan-Africa*, launched by Makonnen in January 1947. The August 1947 issue regretfully announced her departure for India, remarking: 'We think of her not as a European, but as a person with all the characteristics of true greatness.'[81]

There was also an attempt to revive the interwar British Centre Against Imperialism (BCAI). As Howe has noted, 'There is no record of the BCAI having undertaken any activity beyond holding a single "Annual Confer-ence" in February 1946 and, in conjunction with the Pan-Africanists,

---

77  Stephen Howe, *Anticolonialism in British Politics: The Left and the End of Empire, 1918–1964* (Oxford, 1993), p. 147.

78  ILP, *Annual Report of the NAC, 1946* (London, 1946), pp. 10–11.

79  BLPES, ILP/3/34, Meeting of NAC, 15 and 16 June 1946.

80  Peter Abrahams, 'Letter from a Lecturer', *Between Ourselves: ILP Internal Bulletin*, October 1947, p. 6.

81  *Pan-Africa*, August 1947, p. 3.

attempting to publicise Kikuyu grievances over land rights in Kenya.'[82] Makonnen, as ever, was concerned about Black involvement in the BCAI: 'Now when I saw Africans hiving off to work under this umbrella movement, I felt it was a disaster. The whole point of our creating first the IASB and then the federation was to break with the age-old tradition of blacks depending on white organizations.'[83]

But Padmore was a central figure in the short-lived attempt to revive the organisation, of which Fenner Brockway was the driving force. In promoting the single 'annual conference', the ILP traced the BCAI's lineage to the League Against Imperialism, lamenting: 'Alas, however, the Communist International which started this hopeful movement also killed it off!' The BCAI had been formed in response to this.[84] The conference was held on 23 and 24 February 1946, in Denison Hall in Victoria. Representatives of anticolonial movements from across the British Empire were present. Padmore's speech surveyed the history of imperialism, discussed the militancy of the 1945 Pan-African Congress, and appealed to his British audience: 'You need our help as much as we need yours. Let us join hands together . . . Let us make this anti-imperialist centre a worthy instrument in a worthy cause.'[85] While pan-Africanists would soon refocus on a strategy that placed less emphasis on metropolitan alliances and more on activity in Africa itself, it should be apparent that there was no instant break in 1945.

The end of the war also failed to resolve tensions between the PAF and the CP. The Communist vision of the postwar world was aligned with Soviet foreign policy interests. The party congress of October 1944 declared for 'A world peace settlement, based on the principles agreed at Teheran and at Dumbarton Oaks, and embodied in the British-Soviet Treaty; the close co-operation of Britain, France, the United States, the Soviet Union and China, and the establishment of a world organisation of democratic nations for the maintenance of peace against aggression.'[86]

The party campaigned for a Labour victory in the 1945 election. After Labour's victory, it adopted a strategy of attempting to push the Labour

---

82 Howe, *Anticolonialism in British Politics*, p. 177.

83 Makonnen, *Pan-Africanism from Within*, pp. 178–9.

84 'The Socialist View', *New Leader*, 2 February 1946, p. 2.

85 'World-wide Link-up against Imperialism', *New Leader*, 2 March 1946, p. 3.

86 Communist Party, *Victory, Peace, Security: Report of the 17th National Congress of the Communist Party, 1944* (London, 1944), p. 38.

government to follow more left-wing and pro-Soviet policies. As Howe has written of the November 1944 memorandum, *The Colonies: The Way Forward*, it 'represented only a slightly more radical variant on official Labour policy'.[87] The memorandum promoted self-determination (though without preaching anticolonial revolution) and highlighted the role played by colonial peoples in the antifascist struggle; but there was no place in its narrative for anticolonialists who had not supported the Allied war effort.[88] The members of the CP's Colonial Committee resolved in February 1945 that self-determination must come through 'agreement' rather than revolution, and that self-determination was only useful so long as it strengthened the alliance of the 'Big Three' (the Soviet Union, Britain and the United States).[89]

The colonial resolution adopted at the November 1945 congress signalled a slight change in tone, welcoming 'the growth and strengthening of the national liberation movement in the Colonies during wartime'. But the focus of the resolution was on demanding greater concessions from the Labour government.[90] Imperialism was evidently still peripheral to CP thinking: an August 1945 memorandum of the eight 'main tasks of the Communist Party' featured no mention of anti-colonialism.[91] The fracturing of Soviet alliances and the early stages of the Cold War, however, induced something of a return to Communist anti-imperialist militancy. At its February 1947 congress, the CP proclaimed 'solidarity with, and full support of, the struggle for the self-determination of the subject peoples'.[92]

In London, shortly thereafter, from 26 February to 2 March 1947, the CP hosted the Conference of the Communist Parties of the British Empire. Alongside these empire parties, the LCP, WASU and Nkrumah's new organisation, the West African National Secretariat (WANS), were

---

87  Howe, *Anticolonialism in British Politics*, p. 124.

88  Communist Party, *The Colonies: The Way Forward* (London, 1944).

89  LHASC, CP/IND/DUTT/15/13, A Note on the Points Raised at a Special Discussion of the Colonial Committee, 24 February 1945.

90  Communist Party, *Communist Policy for Britain: Report of the 18th National Congress of the Communist Party, November, 1945* (London, 1945), pp. 71–2.

91  LHASC, CP/CENT/CIRC/71/1, Executive Committee to Members, 20 August 1945.

92  Communist Party, *19th National Congress: Resolutions and Proceedings* (London, 1947), pp. 14–19.

invited to the conference.[93] The PAF, conversely, was not invited.[94] Indeed, the *Daily Worker* also refused an advertisement for Padmore's *HRTHCE*, and the Communist bookshop refused to stock the book.[95] The conference recited Popular Front-era calls for colonial charters of rights for colonies (but independence in South Asia and the Middle East). R. P. Dutt stated that immediate independence could not be demanded for tropical Africa in the way that it could for India and Egypt, due to the lack of 'developed national movements'.[96]

Nkrumah's presence at the conference was telling, as he and WANS became increasingly involved in Communist networks after his move to Britain. Sherwood has argued that 'Nkrumah was definitely interested in communist philosophy and analyses of colonialism and capitalism. If he wanted an international political party's support for his aim to free Africa, or at least West Africa from colonialism, he could not turn anywhere but to communism.'[97] Of course, Nkrumah, like most of his colleagues in the PAF, could have turned to the ILP rather than the CP; but it seems likely that Nkrumah, aware of the greater resources of the CP (and the Soviet Union), saw the situation in the terms described by Sherwood. Nkrumah remembered the *Daily Worker* 'as the only paper I really enjoyed reading' during his time in Britain, and the intelligence services recorded a flurry of contact between Nkrumah and the CP in 1947.[98] During that year, as a result of its relationship with Nkrumah, the CP set up fortnightly study courses for West African students, which were run by Emile Burns.[99] Even a decade later, Nkrumah recalled that the CP 'was fortunate in having among its leaders personalities such as Emile Burns, Palme Dutt and Harry Pollitt'.[100]

---

93  For more on WANS, see Marika Sherwood, *Kwame Nkrumah and the Dawn of the Cold War: The West African National Secretariat* (London, 2019).

94  LHASC, CP/CENT/INT/55/3, Organisations Invited to Empire Parties' Conference, 1947.

95  Carol Polsgrove, *Ending British Rule in Africa: Writers in a Common Cause* (Manchester, 2009), p. 86; 'Guide to Books', *Empire*, January 1947, p. 10.

96  Communist Party, *We Speak for Freedom* (London, 1947), p. 28.

97  Marika Sherwood, *Kwame Nkrumah: The Years Abroad, 1935–1947* (Legon, Ghana, 1996), p. 186.

98  Nkrumah, *Autobiography*, p. 49. For Nkrumah's contact with the Communist Party, see TNA, KV 2/1847 (Nkrumah).

99  TNA, KV 2/1847 (Nkrumah), G. T. D. Patterson to C. Burgess, 6 August 1947.

100  Nkrumah, *Autobiography*, p. 51.

Writing to Du Bois in the months before the 1945 Pan-African Congress, Padmore declared that, since Black people in Britain organised in colonial organisations rather than multiracial political groups, as they did in the United States, debates about Communism and Stalinism were less prevalent in the movement. He added: 'This does not mean that there are no individual Negroes who subscribe to political philosophies, whether they be Socialism, Communism, Anarchism, etc. But these are more in the nature of personal idiosyncrasies than practical politics.'[101] This statement seems, more than anything, to have been an attempt by Padmore two months before the congress to convince Du Bois that the political gulf between him and Moody was not as wide as in fact it was. Furthermore, Abrahams, Makonnen and Padmore protested Nkrumah's relationship with the CP.[102] Arguments about Stalinism and Communism, contrary to Padmore's claim to Du Bois, continued to animate the PAF in the postwar years. In fact, Padmore in 1946 contributed an oft-misunderstood intervention to this debate.

## Padmore and the Soviet Model of the British Commonwealth

In *How Russia Transformed Her Colonial Empire* (*HRTHCE*), written in collaboration with Dorothy Pizer, Padmore appealed to the Soviet end to the Russian Empire as a model for the future of the British Empire:

> If it is possible for the former colonies of the Czarist Empire to come together in fraternal co-operation, there is no reason at all why a Socialist Britain, for example, should fear to extend the Right of Full Self-Determination to the subject peoples of the British Empire. Once these dependent territories are given the right to plan their future, in their own interests, they would link up with the more advanced sections of the new Socialist Commonwealth.[103]

---

101 Padmore to Du Bois, 17 August 1945, in *Correspondence of W. E. B. Du Bois*, pp. 77–8.

102 Makonnen, *Pan-Africanism from Within*, pp. 262–3; Sherwood, *Kwame Nkrumah: The Years Abroad*, p. 161.

103 Padmore, with Pizer, *How Russia Transformed Her Colonial Empire*, p. 63.

This jars with the traditional historiographical view of Padmore's relationship with Stalinism and the Soviet Union. James Hooker made his thesis clear when he subtitled his book *George Padmore's Path from Communism to Pan-Africanism*. For Hooker, there were two Padmores: the young, dogmatic Communist and the older, wiser pan-Africanist.[104] In this narrative, Padmore became in the mid 1930s an avowed pan-Africanist and anti-Communist – thus corroborating, in the words of Vincent Thompson, 'the assertion that "youth dares and age considers".'[105] Rupert Lewis suggests that Padmore became in this period a 'full-blown anti-Stalinist'.[106] As late as 1946, however, Padmore argued that the British Empire should transform itself in the same manner as the Soviet Union. While no longer a member of any Communist organisation, Padmore in 1946 still found in the Soviet Union a path to the future, making the case for a simple rupture in 1934 far from persuasive. Indeed, Padmore's ideological continuities are crucial in understanding his intellectual history.

The Bolshevik Revolution galvanised African diasporic interest in socialism.[107] For many Black radicals the Soviet Union would provide a model for the rest of the world; both the perpetrators and victims of imperialism and racism could transform themselves in the Soviet image. Bill Mullen, in his study of Du Bois, has observed 'Stalin's tragic influence' on the 'diasporic international' of left-wing thinkers with world-revolutionary objectives.[108] Mullen notes that this was a contradictory influence, as the Soviet Union became a revolutionary model while at the same time the Comintern stifled the goal of world revolution in favour of defending 'Socialism in One Country'.[109] This observation aids our understanding of the tensions within Padmore's post-Comintern output, as he heaped praise on Soviet domestic policy while maintaining a distance from Soviet foreign policy in favour of a world-revolutionary goal.

104　James R. Hooker, *Black Revolutionary: George Padmore's Path from Communism to Pan-Africanism* (London, 1967).

105　Vincent B. Thompson, 'George Padmore: Reconciling Two Phases of Contradictions', in Baptiste and Lewis, *George Padmore: Pan-African Revolutionary*, p. 134.

106　Rupert Lewis, 'George Padmore: Towards a Political Assessment', in Baptiste and Lewis, *George Padmore: Pan-African Revolutionary*, p. 151.

107　See Introduction, above.

108　Bill V. Mullen, *Un-American: W. E. B. Du Bois and the Century of World Revolution* (Philadelphia, 2015), p. 9.

109　Ibid., p. 10.

The remainder of this chapter argues that Padmore's commitment to the Soviet model of colonial transformation, best exemplified in *HRTHCE*, is essential in understanding his form of Marxist pan-Africanism. Furthermore, it undertakes an analysis of the function of Padmore's book as a *manifesto* rather than simply a *history*. Here, Laura Winkiel's study of modernism, race and manifestos is instructive. Although *HRTHCE* does not call itself a manifesto, it sits with other documents containing what Winkiel calls 'functional similarities' to manifestos. Salient features of manifestos include 'seek[ing] to break from the past' and 'draw[ing] attention to the present moment in order to generate a radically different future, changing the world and starting the revolution . . . now!'[110] Particularly useful is Winkiel's idea that manifestos reveal a 'crisis of modernity'; there was 'a counter-history, a black revolutionary tradition, that existed in relation to European modernity and its history of slavery', which 'articulated alternative modernisms'.[111] But it should be added that Padmore was located within the networks of European socialism as well as those of Black radicalism. These overlapping movements both possessed a language of alternative modernisms.

*HRTHCE* can be located within the context of the latter half of the Second World War and the immediate postwar period, as part of a trend of internationalist optimism that pervaded the socialist and Black radical milieus in which Padmore operated. As Frederick Cooper has argued, 'the formulation of alternative modernity is empty unless one can demonstrate both the alternative and the modernity'.[112] For Padmore and his comrades, 'modernity' was defined by advanced methods of production, which were linked to forms of democracy and citizenship. Actually existing capitalist modernity created and depended upon forms of 'backwardness' in the colonies, and offered only limited forms of democracy and citizenship to limited groups of people. The 'alternative' was thus a socialist modernity in which the means of production would be commonly owned, in which 'backwardness' would be ended through the dissolution of distinctions between centre and periphery, and in which

---

110  Laura Winkiel, *Modernism, Race and Manifestos* (Cambridge, 2008), p. 12.

111  Ibid., pp. 30, 41.

112  Frederick Cooper, *Colonialism in Question: Theory, Knowledge, History* (Berkeley, 2005), p. 130.

more meaningful forms of democracy and citizenship would be extended to all people.

The political thought of Ridley, Padmore's comrade in the ILP, as well as the decisions of the Fifth Pan-African Congress, offer useful points of comparison for Padmore's own political thought. Ridley was a leading member of the ILP, and particularly prominent in the movement for a United Socialist States of Europe. As well as enjoying a personal and political relationship with Padmore, Ridley was therefore also part of the same global mood of internationalist postwar optimism – as was the Pan-African Congress, which advocated for a Socialist United States of Africa. These blueprints for postwar reconfigurations – influenced, like Padmore's, by an analysis of the relationship between capitalism and colonialism – provide a lens through which Padmore's political thought can be placed in context. Furthermore, studying Padmore and his comrades allows us to zoom in on the permeable boundary between the histories of Western socialist and Black radical thought, rejecting any neat distinction between the two.

After his break from the Comintern in the 1930s, Padmore continued to defend Stalin's domestic policy, most notably its domestic racial and national relations. In *How Britain Rules Africa*, he argued that racism 'does not exist in the Soviet Union where capitalism has been abolished'.[113] Maintaining this analysis in the postwar period, *HRTHCE* took as its starting point Bolshevik ideas of self-determination and federation as propounded in the 1910s. Padmore frequently cited Stalin's *Marxism and the National Question* (1913), and Lenin and Zinoviev's *Socialism and War* (1915). These foundational Communist texts were written partly to explain how the Bolsheviks proposed to end the Russian Empire and put in its place a multinational socialist federation. By recognising national oppression and defending the right to self-determination, they aimed to create the conditions under which formerly oppressed nations would use this right to enter voluntarily into a union with the formerly oppressing nation.[114]

Padmore attempted to demonstrate how Lenin and Stalin successfully applied these ideas in the Soviet Union. Large parts of *HRTHCE* were

---

113  George Padmore, *How Britain Rules Africa* (London, 1936), p. 335.

114  Joseph Stalin, *Marxism and the National and Colonial Question: A Collection of Articles and Speeches* (London, 1942), pp. 18-19; Grigory Zinoviev and Vladimir Lenin, *Socialism and War* (London, 1931 [1915]), pp. 25-6.

devoted to demonstrating how the Soviet Union had successfully industrialised and combated illiteracy in the 'former colonies' and – pertinently in the context of the Second World War, and in contrast to the rapid loss of British territory in Asia – produced a unity of interests between Russian workers and the colonial peoples. Following Lenin's analysis that imperialism, characterised by colonialism and monopoly capital, was a stage of capitalism, Padmore stressed that socialist revolution was a prerequisite for unity between metropole and colonies. 'Only the proletariat can cut the Gordian knot which binds the subject peoples to the yoke of imperialism', he wrote.[115]

To treat *HRTHCE* primarily as a work of historical scholarship, however, is to miss its function as a manifesto for the postwar global order. The subject matter and significance of the book extended far beyond the boundaries of the Soviet Union. Aiming his book at both British socialists and colonial radicals, Padmore hoped to align these forces in reshaping the British Empire through simultaneous revolution. As the Second World War came to an end, the transition of the British Empire into the Commonwealth of Nations was already underway. Padmore believed that a transformation that retained the bourgeois and racialised facets of the British Empire would be inadequate in addressing the problems of the colonial peoples. He mined Soviet history with a clear eye to its utility as a model for post-imperial development, writing: 'It is not enough to describe and admire the achievements of the Soviet Union' without also attempting to infer from these 'the solution of the Colonial Question in Asia, Africa, the Pacific, and the Caribbean.'[116] Throughout the book, he drew parallels between the British and Russian empires. He used his historical analysis of Soviet colonial policy to conclude that the British Empire should follow this model and transform itself, through revolutions in both the metropole and the colonies, into a *socialist* commonwealth.

There has recently developed a historiographical interest in the postwar 'federal moment'. Of particular importance is Cooper's argument that it was not inevitable that empires would be replaced by independent nation-states. Cooper 'tells the story of how it happened that in 1960 the political actors of France and French West Africa ended up with a form

---

115 Padmore, with Pizer, *How Russia Transformed Her Colonial Empire*, p. xiv.
116 Ibid., p. ix.

of political organization that neither had wanted during most of the previous fifteen years'.[117] He contends that, though there were of course programmatic differences about precisely what form such a union should take, 'French West African political leaders sought . . . to transform colonial empire into another sort of assemblage of diverse territories and peoples: a federation of African states with each other and France'.[118] This bears a similarity to Padmore's plans for the federation of the British Empire into the British Commonwealth, though Padmore abandoned the project much earlier than 1960. Moreover, even if we accept Cooper's argument as correct, Padmore's federalism differed from the projects of many of Cooper's subjects in that it was dependent on socialist revolution in Britain, not a political union to be achieved through constitutional reform.

Cooper has been criticised for his lack of attentiveness to the limits placed on federalism by capitalism, racism and the Cold War. As Samuel Moyn observes, metropolitan France did not desire a politically equal union, while former colonial subjects did not desire one that was unequal.[119] Richard Drayton criticises Cooper for his failure properly to acknowledge the barriers to federalism caused by racial capitalism: 'there was a fundamental tension between France's grand strategy, for which colonies were a source of national power and wealth, and the idea of a shared future, in which the former would always win out'.[120] It is difficult to see how these tensions could be resolved through reform, and Padmore, writing in a British context, clearly did not believe this to be possible. Drayton further criticises Cooper for a lack of understanding of the impact of the Bolshevik Revolution on the 1946 moment. The prominence of French Communists instilled hope in actors such as Léopold Senghor and Aimé Césaire that a socialist French Union could be achieved, before these hopes were dashed following the marginalisation of the Communists after 1947.[121] Nevertheless, it is important to remember that Black radicals

---

117  Frederick Cooper, *Citizenship between Empire and Nation: Remaking France and French Africa, 1945–1960* (Princeton, 2014), p. 3. See also Gary Wilder, *Freedom Time: Negritude, Decolonization, and the Future of the World* (Durham, NC, 2015).

118  Cooper, *Citizenship between Empire and Nation*, p. 2.

119  Samuel Moyn, 'Fantasies of Federalism', *Dissent* 62 (2015), p. 148.

120  Richard Drayton, 'Federal Utopias and the Realities of Imperial Power', *Comparative Studies of South Asia, Africa and the Middle East* 37 (2017), p. 404.

121  Ibid.

were engaged in a process of what Adom Getachew has called 'world-making', in which they 'reinvented self-determination' to extend beyond nation-building to a 'project of reordering the world'.[122] Getachew observes that Nkrumah 'envisioned national independence as the first step in constituting a Pan-African federation and transforming the international order'.[123] The replacement of empires by nation-states was certainly not inevitable.

Padmore was aware that a reconfiguration of the British Empire, whether from above or below, was likely. Michael Collins has shown that much of the drive towards the Commonwealth came from the imperial centre. The Commonwealth was seen as 'a way of reconfiguring the politics of collaboration' in order to 'maintain key British spheres of influence'.[124] Figures such as Jan Smuts promoted a vision of commonwealth that would retain the racialised order of empire as the best means to defend the interests of his country.[125] Padmore was entering an active debate with high stakes.

Unfortunately, the most important element of *HRTHCE* – its manifesto for the British Empire – was overlooked by reviewers. Upon publication, the book was criticised by many on the British left because of its defence of the Soviet Union. Walter Padley, who around this time left the ILP to rejoin the Labour Party, argued, with much justification, that Moscow had maintained an imperialistic relationship with Eastern Europe.[126] Conversely, he had nothing to say about Padmore's proposals for the transformation of Britain. Even in a positive review, Ridley similarly failed to engage with the book-as-manifesto. He simply praised Padmore's analysis of the Soviet Union and criticisms of the British Empire without joining the dots between these arguments.[127] Recently, Carol Polsgrove and Leslie James have observed that the Soviet Union functioned in *HRTHCE* as a 'model' and 'blueprint', respectively.[128]

---

122  Adom Getachew, *Worldmaking after Empire: The Rise and Fall of Self-Determination* (Princeton, 2019), p. 2.

123  Ibid., p. 1.

124  Michael Collins, 'Decolonisation and the "Federal Moment"', *Diplomacy & Statecraft* 24 (2013), p. 24.

125  Mazower, *No Enchanted Palace*, p. 20.

126  Walter Padley, 'Padmore, Stalin and POUM', *Socialist Leader*, 11 January 1947, p. 9.

127  F. A. Ridley, 'Searchlight on Imperialism', *Socialist Leader*, 14 December 1946, p. 7.

128  Polsgrove, *Ending British Rule in Africa*, p. 62; James, *George Padmore*, p. 108.

Padmore's use of the Soviet Union as a model provokes the question of whether he was more invested in providing a historically accurate account of the Soviet Union or in offering an idealised model that could be applied to other empires. McNair, in an interview with Hooker, remembered that 'in debates with communists during the war Padmore used to claim that the "Russian Communists were the worst of all Imperialists in their subversion of the Baltic Provinces, their attack on Finland and their record in Poland"'.[129] Hooker himself believed that, once Padmore 'had written a manuscript, he could not bear to have it overtaken by events'. He therefore suggests that the delay in publishing *HRTHCE* accounted for Padmore's defence of the Soviet Union as late as 1946.[130] In fact, Padmore publicly criticised the Soviet invasion of Finland before he began writing *HRTHCE*. During the Winter War of 1939–40, he wrote that the Soviet invasion was a response to the danger of imperialist war being waged against the Soviet Union. This danger was itself 'the logical outcome of Stalin's fundamental error of attempting to build "Socialism in a single country," at the expense of the Revolution abroad'.[131] Padmore did not shy away from criticising Stalin, but made it clear that the Soviet Union should still be defended against capitalist aggression. It is here that we can see the tension in the influence of Stalinism on world-revolutionary politics, as observed by Mullen.

Leslie James is less dismissive than Hooker of Padmore's sincerity. She argues that 'the consistency of his statements on Soviet anti-racism shows that he seems to have genuinely believed his main argument to be true'.[132] James is more convincing than Hooker on this matter. Padmore was a committed anticapitalist who admired the Soviet Union because of its challenge to global capitalist-imperialism. Padmore was consistent in praising Soviet antiracism, and continued to do so until his death in 1959 – well after the publication of *HRTHCE*. His comments on Soviet foreign policy were usually critical but sympathetically contextualised, as his analysis of the Winter War illustrates.

---

129  Hooker, *Black Revolutionary*, p. 72.

130  Ibid., pp. 72–3. Padmore finished the first draft in 1942, but redrafted it as the war progressed.

131  George Padmore, 'Hands Off the Soviet Union', *Left*, February 1940, p. 47.

132  James, *George Padmore*, p. 110.

## F. A. Ridley and the United Socialist States of Europe

Other socialists also offered visions of the postwar peace, as the left attempted to shift the new internationalism into more radical channels. As soon as war began, the ILP asserted that it must be followed by the creation of a United Socialist States of Europe. In Leninist terms, the party saw capitalist-imperialist rivalry as the main cause of the war. Following this logic, the internationalism of the nascent UN would be insufficient to achieve lasting peace. This was another alternative modernism. No one embraced this idea as enthusiastically as F. A. Ridley. Born in 1897, after flirting with Trotskyism and anarchism he joined the ILP in 1938, and was elected to its National Administrative Council in 1943. He linked the need for a USSE to his theory of a crumbling British Empire no longer able to support a labour aristocracy: 'Socialism in Britain must, necessarily, presuppose one of two things; either a socialist Britain is supported by the tribute of the (non-socialist) Empire throughout the transition, or it goes into Socialism as part of a socialist Europe.'[133] What is especially noteworthy is not Ridley's combination of Europeanism and anticolonialism, but his implication that socialism in the colonies, and therefore a socialist commonwealth, were impossibilities.

Ridley's dismissiveness was not lost on other members of the ILP, who occasionally challenged him. In 1943, Brockway wrote a comment on Ridley's plans for a new socialist international. Ridley suggested that any new international should be limited to socialists in countries that had industrialised. Brockway responded: 'I recognise that Europe is likely to be the scene of the next mass movement towards Socialism and that one cannot step from primitive conditions . . . into full Socialism. Nevertheless, any New International must also represent the socialist forces in India and the Colonial countries.'[134] Brockway believed that industrialisation and proletarianisation were powerful currents of revolutionary potential, but rejected Ridley's dismissal of the socialist potential of colonial liberation movements. In the event, the ILP delayed the decision, and the new international did not materialise.

---

133  F. A. Ridley, 'The Socialist Attitude to an United States of Europe', *Left*, October 1939, p. 267.

134  BLPES, ILP/3/31, Comment by Fenner Brockway.

Ridley's agitation for a USSE continued as he co-authored a book with Bob Edwards in 1944. Ridley wrote the first half of the book, declaring: 'World-Socialism – the United States of the World – is our majestic goal.'[135] This was consistent with Padmore's goal in *HRTHCE*. Both texts took as their starting point the Leninist explanation of war and the need for socialist revolution to achieve meaningful peace. Similarly, both Padmore and Ridley accepted a Marxist idea of the stages of history, whereby societies progressed from feudalism to capitalism, and eventually to socialism. They therefore agreed that most of the world outside Europe was, to a greater or lesser extent, 'backward'. Padmore observed that imperialist powers were guilty of preserving this backwardness by using colonies primarily to extract raw materials to be processed in the metropole.[136] For Padmore, 'backwardness' was an economic category, though one with cultural implications. Colonial peoples were not innately inferior, but, in intentionally undiversified agrarian economies with limited educational opportunities, ignorance abounded and national cultures were poorly developed.

The role played by capitalist-imperialism in this underdevelopment meant that, in Padmore's formulation, a socialist commonwealth could overcome these problems. Padmore used the Soviet Union to illustrate the possibility of this. He asserted that the Soviet Union was 'a political federation of multi-national Republics in which all peoples, *irrespective of their degree of civilisation and social development*, enjoy equal political, economic and social status'.[137] For Padmore, then, it was crucial to use *HRTHCE* to document the Soviet Union's efficacy in combating illiteracy, promoting national languages and cultures, and achieving industrialisation in formerly 'backward' territories – all of which demonstrated the possibility of achieving similar results in the British Empire.

Conversely, Ridley argued that it would be 'a great exaggeration to state that all traces of pre-capitalist barbarism have been already abolished, and that the whole world is equally ripe for the social transformation'.[138] Africa and Polynesia, in particular, were deemed 'still

---

135  F. A. Ridley and Bob Edwards, *The United Socialist States of Europe* (London, 1944), p. 8.
136  Padmore, with Pizer, *How Russia Transformed Her Colonial Empire*, p. 25.
137  Ibid., p. x. Emphasis in original.
138  Ridley and Edwards, *United Socialist States of Europe*, p. 8.

more primitive' than 'the nations of the East'.[139] Like Padmore, Ridley believed that 'backwardness' was the result of imperialism, but did not propose a basis for a relationship between a socialist Europe and its former colonies as a path towards socialist partnership. Instead, Ridley argued that the means of production must be sufficiently sophisticated to be socialised: 'One cannot profitably socialise a dust-bin, nor divide a desert!'[140]

While this latter comment was particularly crass, Ridley should not be understood as rejecting African agency. Indeed, throughout 1947, Ridley wrote a series of articles celebrating the Zulu king, Shaka, as the 'African master of total war' for *Pan-Africa*.[141] As we have seen, Ridley regarded the PAF as an organisation of great historical significance. His rejection of socialism in Africa as something that could be achieved in the near future should be ascribed primarily to his particularly deterministic understanding of the stages of historical development (although it is impossible to dismiss the idea that his analysis of African preparedness for socialism was not also informed by racism).

The differences between Ridley's Europeanist socialism and Padmore's pan-Africanist socialism were mainly matters of emphases, priorities and timeframes. Abrahams stressed in 1946 that 'the Socialist Federation of Europe, right and intelligent as it is', would not be possible so long as Europe maintained its empires.[142] Like Padmore, in an April 1946 article he argued for the 'transformation of a subject Empire, seething with bitterness and suspicion, into a group of partner states, free and autonomous'.[143] Ridley would not dispute the incompatibility of colonialism and socialism. Likewise, Ridley, Padmore and Abrahams all argued for world federation – though this was further on the horizon in Ridley's programme. Despite their varying degrees of optimism as to how quickly colonial peoples would overcome their 'backwardness', their Marxism meant that they shared a definition of that term.

But there was a more important programmatic and theoretical distinction. For Padmore, the key to understanding the coming world

---

139  Ibid., p. 53.

140  Ibid., p. 50.

141  See *Pan-Africa*, June, July and August 1947.

142  Peter Abrahams, 'Imperialists Cannot Make Peace', *Socialist Leader*, 7 September 1946, p. 3.

143  Abrahams, 'Colonials Can't Live on Promises!', p. 7.

socialist transformation was the interdependence between metropolitan and colonial revolutions. Conversely, Ridley concluded that 'the *primary* aim of the coming Revolution, and of the International that will lead it to ultimate victory, must be confined to European soil'.[144] This belief explains his clash with Brockway on the proposed socialist international. For Ridley, the European proletariat was more than capable of achieving socialism by itself; it would simply divest itself of colonial possessions once power was achieved.

But Ridley did not speak for the entire ILP. Brockway also wrestled with the nature of the postcolonial state. He positioned himself closer to Padmore than to Ridley, again illustrating the impact of the IASB on the ILP. When theorising about the relationship between a socialist Britain and newly liberated colonies, he suggested: 'In many cases the liberated colonies would wish to remain in close association with a Socialist Britain, but that would be for them to decide'.[145] He continued:

> *A Socialist Britain would go beyond extending political liberty to the colonial peoples.* It would restore the land and the natural resources which have been appropriated by British capitalists . . . Within a generation the 'backward' races would have disappeared. The advance in material welfare and education among the subject peoples of the old Czarist Empire since the Soviet Government was established shows what the possibilities are.[146]

These ideas of consensual federation, a materialist definition of 'backwardness', and even a reference to Soviet colonial transformation illustrate the ways in which Brockway was in this period Padmore's closest White ally, barring Pizer and perhaps Nancy Cunard. Indeed, Brockway's later citation of Padmore's pan-Africanism as one of the major influences in shaping his understanding of imperialism suggests that Padmore was likely responsible for these ideas.[147]

It would be a mistake to characterise the political relationship between Padmore and Ridley as conflictual. As we have seen, Ridley reviewed

---

144 Ridley and Edwards, *United Socialist States of Europe*, p. 56. Emphasis in original.

145  Fenner Brockway, *The Way Out* (London, 1942), p. 17.

146  Ibid., pp. 17–18. Emphasis in original.

147  Howe, *Anticolonialism in British Politics*, p. 171.

*HRTHCE* positively upon its publication – although his focus on the book as a history of the Soviet Union rather than a manifesto of course allowed him to ignore some fundamental political differences. For his part, Padmore in *Pan-Africanism or Communism?* listed Ridley among a select group of British activists who had championed African freedom struggles – high praise indeed when one considers that Padmore had pulled few punches in the book.[148] Nevertheless, they advocated different routes to their shared goal of world socialist federation.

## The Pan-African Congress and the Socialist United States of Africa

It was in this same context of postwar optimism and dreams of imperial transformation that the 1945 Pan-African Congress was held. A memorandum to the UN demanded that Africans be represented in the organisation, but this approach was generally eschewed throughout the congress.[149] Instead, as we have seen, the congress focused on the self-organisation of Africans and people of African descent, particularly through labour organisations. Solidarity was expressed with liberation struggles in India, Indonesia and Vietnam, and Abrahams underlined the significance of the Subject Peoples' Conference by saying that it had contributed to 'the closer establishment of fraternal contacts between the African and Asiatic liberation movements'.[150]

It is necessary to interrogate what 'pan-Africanism' means in this context. While Padmore identified continuously as a pan-Africanist after his break from the Comintern in the mid 1930s, in *HRTHCE* he advocated a socialist federation based on the territories of the British Empire. This encompassed regions of not only Africa, but also Europe and Asia. There was no overt advocacy of 'pan-Africanism', leading Leslie James to observe that this was 'perhaps the book where Padmore "the anti-imperialist" is most clearly evident'.[151] The 1945 congress demanded the complete independence and federation of West Africa, self-government and federation in the British West Indies, and racial

---

148  Padmore, *Pan-Africanism or Communism?*, p. 365.
149  Padmore, *Colonial and . . . Coloured Unity*, pp. 57–9.
150  Ibid., p. 61.
151  James, *George Padmore*, p. 109.

equality in South Africa, with an eye to an eventual 'Socialist United States of Africa'.[152] The role of the European proletariat was barely discussed at the congress. The idea that self-determination might lead to a voluntary federation with a socialist metropole was absent from the resolutions. But although the Soviet Union was mentioned infrequently at the congress, it was spoken about positively by delegates. While not explicitly advocating a Soviet-style commonwealth, F. O. B. Blaize of WASU remarked: 'Britain left to herself without the resources of the Colonies would not live six months. We have seen the remarkable rise of the Soviet Union. This can be done for the Colonies, and we demand that it shall be done.'[153]

In his study of the national-racial idea of 'Greater Britain' that emerged during the nineteenth century, Duncan Bell observes that the 'history of modern political thought is partly the history of the attempt to confront increasing global interdependence and competition'.[154] Relatedly, Marilyn Lake and Henry Reynolds have charted the spread of 'whiteness' as a 'transnational form of racial identification' that began in the nineteenth century, also observing that this led to 'transnational expressions of counter solidarity'.[155] From the PAF's writings and the resolutions of the Pan-African Congress, we can see the ways in which Black radicals attempted to confront the increasing global interdependence and competition cited by Bell – in a process that, as suggested by Lake and Reynolds, began around 1900. If global White supremacy was forged during the nineteenth century, people of colour responded with their own transnational identities and movements in the twentieth.

There were multiple ideas within pan-Africanist and socialist circles about what the postwar order should be. But what all these proposals had in common were materialist strategies of liberation, with the ultimate goal of world federation, or at least peaceful cooperation between continental federations. The solidarity with Asian liberation struggles expressed at the 1945 congress demonstrates that there is no neat distinction between the pan-Africanism of the congress and the more

---

152  Padmore, *Colonial and . . . Coloured Unity*, p. 61.

153  Ibid., p. 82.

154  Duncan Bell, *The Idea of Greater Britain: Empire and the Future of World Order, 1860–1900* (Princeton, 2007), p. 1.

155  Marilyn Lake and Henry Reynolds, *Drawing the Global Colour Line: White Men's Countries and the International Challenge of Racial Inequality* (Cambridge, 2008), pp. 3, 245.

all-encompassing anticolonialism of *HRTHCE*. Similarly, Nico Slate has observed that, for W. E. B. Du Bois, ' "the race" meant not just African Americans but "negroes" and other colored people throughout the world'.[156] Pan-Africanism was a vehicle through which the new world could begin to take shape – a natural first step based on shared geography, history and economic interests.

*HRTHCE* may appear to be a deviation from pan-Africanism, in that it advocated a postcolonial socialist commonwealth rather than African political unity. But it was consistent with Padmore's internationalist, socialist and anti-imperialist philosophies; these were the most important functions of pan-Africanism for Padmore. His methodology was flexible, and, for a few years in the 1940s, influenced by an analysis of a world in turmoil, he espoused the socialist transformation of European empires as the means by which socialism and colonial liberation could be achieved in Africa. His continued focus on the agency and futures of all African peoples displayed an unbroken pan-Africanist spirit. 'Pan-Africanism' should not be understood as simply a project of African political unification, but rather as  one of liberation that could be pursued through a variety of methods.

Padmore wrote the preface to *HRTHCE* in June 1945, a month after the bombs and bullets of the Second World War ceased scarring Europe's cities, bodies and psyches, as four great powers occupied Germany in an uneasy peace, and as the great and the good gathered in San Francisco to discuss what shape the new world would take. Following two world wars within three decades, it was clear that any reconfiguration would need to take place on a global scale. Padmore used this opportunity to set out his vision for the postwar order. He believed that the solution lay not in appealing to diplomats and politicians, but in creating mass labour and colonial liberation movements.

A crucial element of this postwar reconfiguration was the transformation of the British Empire into a socialist commonwealth based on the model provided by the Soviet Union. This can only be understood through the lens of Padmore's Marxist pan-Africanism. His primary concern was the liberation of Africa and its diasporic communities. Marxism shaped his definition of liberation and his ideas about how it

---

156  Nico Slate, *The Prism of Race: W. E. B. Du Bois, Langston Hughes, Paul Robeson, and the Colored World of Cedric Dover* (New York, 2014), p. 35.

could be achieved. Developing Lenin's ideas as contained in the national and colonial theses, Padmore believed in the interdependence of revolutions: that the European proletarian and colonial liberation movements would buoy each other as they attacked the shared enemy of capitalist-imperialism. An alliance between a workers' Britain and a workers' and peasants' Empire could then be formed as the first step towards world socialist federation. Modern audiences might consider this proposal fancifully optimistic, even eccentric; but 200 copies of *HRTHCE* were seized by customs in Nigeria, and British foreign secretary Ernest Bevin considered the book to be Soviet propaganda.[157] The book was clearly considered dangerous, and its manifesto far from impossible to achieve. *HRTHCE* presents us with one route to a bold political horizon viewed by an optimistic internationalist left in the postwar period – a vantage point that has since been obscured by the Cold War and its aftermath.

This moment of postwar expectation was brief. The idea that the world could be reorganised into a single bloc with a lasting peace did not survive the early years of the Cold War. Hakim Adi, writing about the 1945 Pan-African Congress, has observed that Padmore was 'influenced by prevailing political conditions', and felt the 'near euphoria and great expectations of the victory over Fascism in 1945'.[158] This was followed by a failure to achieve socialist revolution in Europe, desperate attempts to maintain hegemony by the colonial powers, and the fragmentation, repression and demoralisation of the left that occurred as a result of the Cold War. Leslie James has argued that, before 1945, Padmore clung to the prospect of metropolitan revolution. When this was not forthcoming, a strategic realignment saw less emphasis placed on the European proletariat.[159]

At the Second World War's end, however, the PAF continued to regard the British left (or at least sections of it) as crucial allies in the overthrow of capitalist-imperialism. Indeed, I propose that the most significant realignment happened gradually in the two or three years that followed the war, rather than in 1945. McNair's speech to the Pan-African

---

157  James, *George Padmore*, pp. 104–5.
158  Adi, 'George Padmore and the 1945 Manchester Pan-African Congress', p. 89.
159  James, *George Padmore*, p. 123.

Congress was a sign of the continued significance of the theory of inter-dependent revolutions, as the ILP continued to offer hope of European socialist support for the anticolonial struggle. In this respect, the ILP's position stood out from the ambivalence or gradualism of much of the British and European left. But that this ambivalence and gradualism should be deemed so tragic is evidence enough that Black radicals recognised the strategic importance of metropolitan support. The election of the postwar Labour government was met with cautious optimism at best, indifference at worst; by the end of 1945 it had confirmed to the PAF the deficiencies of social democracy. The CP, for all PAF members except Nkrumah, remained too wedded to the concerns of Soviet foreign policy to be an ally, though the comradeship of committed Communist anti-imperialists continued to be welcomed.

The postwar visions of the PAF and ILP imagined a reconfigured world based variously on the United Socialist States of Europe, the Socialist United States of Africa, or even the socialist 'British' common-wealth. These seemingly competing ideas were even held by the same individuals almost simultaneously, and all had as their final objective world socialist federation. There were sometimes disagreements. Ridley's proposed USSE did not leave much space for African socialism (or, at least, not imminently); but this did not cause fundamental ruptures. Brockway criticised Ridley's ideas within the ILP, but no PAF members publicly criticised Ridley's work, and Ridley was himself a regular contributor to *Pan-Africa*. The most significant realignment came shortly afterwards, with the clear failure of metropolitan socialist revolution, the onset of the Cold War, and the increasing maturity of African nationalist movements.

# Epilogue

In October 1959, George Padmore's ashes were interred at Christiansborg Castle in Accra. As part of the ceremony, Kwame Nkrumah, by then the prime minister of independent Ghana, paid tribute to him. Even after his death in autumnal Britain, Padmore's ideas continued to resonate in the spring of African independence. He had died in London on 23 September as a result of cirrhosis. The Movement for Colonial Freedom, the successor to the British Centre Against Imperialism, recorded 'with deep regret the death of George Padmore who contributed so much to the Pan-African idea'.[1] Padmore had lived to see Ghanaian independence, but this was only a partial victory. The system of capitalist-imperialism in Africa had been challenged by Nkrumah's independent nation, but Black radicals recognised that their project of African liberation remained incomplete.

The Independent Labour Party, historically the greatest friend of British Black radicals, entered terminal decline shortly after the Second World War. The party lost both of its giants, Fenner Brockway and James Maxton, in quick succession. Maxton died in July 1946. Padmore wrote: 'The Colonial peoples have lost a great friend and stalwart champion', and spoke of his personal friendship with Maxton.[2] Brockway, meanwhile, excited by the possibilities created by the first majority Labour government, attempted to convince the ILP to reaffiliate to Labour. When

---

1 Movement for Colonial Freedom, *Annual Report 1959/60* (London, 1960), p. 11.
2 ILP, *James Maxton, 1885–1946* (London, 1946), p. 24.

he was unsuccessful, he resigned his leadership positions in May 1946 and left the ILP to rejoin Labour in January 1947.[3] This precipitated a wider exodus of ILP members to Labour, as they hoped to shape the governing party's policies from within.

Importantly, this coincided with the rapid development of African liberation movements and the return to Africa of Nkrumah and Jomo Kenyatta, who would both become the first presidents of their independent African nations. Kenyatta left for Kenya in September 1946. Makonnen accompanied Kenyatta to Plymouth, and wordlessly embraced his comrade as he contemplated what struggles lay ahead.[4] The following year, Nkrumah accepted the general secretaryship of the newly formed United Gold Coast Convention. He left for the Gold Coast on 14 November 1947.[5] Peter Abrahams also left London, moving to Paris in June 1948.[6] Of the old core of the IASB, only Makonnen (in Manchester) and Padmore (in London) remained in Britain.

The return to Africa of Kenyatta and Nkrumah was part of a realignment in pan-Africanist strategy away from Europe and towards the African continent itself, encouraged by the growing nationalist and labour movements there. The PAF's Ceylonese comrade, T. B. Subasinghe, recalled to James Hooker that, in 1945, he 'began to detect a change in George's political emphasis'. Padmore became 'more cynical about the role of the working class and the so-called anti-imperialists of imperialist countries' and 'began to advocate the theory that the liberation of the colonial peoples was their own responsibility'.[7] Similarly, C. L. R. James noted a reorientation after 1945, as a result of the lack of revolutions in metropolitan countries. He observed that 'the Bureau' (or perhaps, more accurately, the Pan-African Federation) retained its 'Marxist foundation', but that it contended that the

---

3 BLPES, ILP/3/34, Meeting of Executive Committee, 12 May 1946; Fenner Brockway, *Outside the Right* (London, 1963), p. 36.

4 T. Ras Makonnen, *Pan-Africanism from Within*, p. 169; Jeremy Murray-Brown, *Kenyatta* (London, 1972), p. 223.

5 Kwame Nkrumah, *The Autobiography of Kwame Nkrumah* (Edinburgh, 1957), pp. 61–3.

6 Peter Abrahams, *The Coyaba Chronicles: Reflections on the Black Experience in the Twentieth Century* (Kingston, 2000), p. 79.

7 James R. Hooker, *Black Revolutionary: George Padmore's Path from Communism to Pan-Africanism* (London, 1967), p. 87.

'actual struggle of the Africans now had to depend on themselves alone'.[8]

However, as demonstrated in Chapter 5, while there were shifts in strategy, there was no abrupt break in 1945. With the postwar world still a haze of competing visions and manifestos, pan-Africanists in 1945 continued to hope for a socialist Europe that would unite in partnership with a free Africa. The failure of this vision became apparent only gradually, and was compounded by the imperialism of the Labour left and the onset of the Cold War. The cracks were beginning to show by the time of the Congress of the Peoples of Europe, Asia and Africa, held in Paris in June 1948. Anne-Isabelle Richard highlights the 'limits of solidarity' between the congress's European socialist delegates (including representatives of the ILP) and the colonial delegates.[9] While most of the European delegates hoped to steer a course between the United States and the Soviet Union, colonial delegates looked upon Europe as the main perpetrator of colonial oppression. They believed anticolonial alliances with the Soviet Union, and even the United States, to be more attractive than a continued relationship with a European labour movement that held the paternalistic views espoused by the likes of Ridley in his enthusiasm for a United Socialist States of Europe.[10] The prospects of a British socialist commonwealth seemed increasingly remote. Nevertheless, Abrahams, representing the PAF, declared: 'we are not prepared to form an organisation which is only nationalist, be it African or Asiatic'. He instead called for 'an international socialist organisation' – while reminding his audience that 'Africa is the second largest continent and it forms part of the world quite as much as does Europe'.[11]

Cooperation persisted between PAF members and the British left. Brockway continued to correspond with Black radicals and speak on their platforms. In 1950, he was greeted by Kenyatta when he visited

8 Rare Book and Manuscript Library, Columbia University, New York, C. L. R. James papers, box 5 folder 21, C. L. R. James, 'Notes on the Life of George Padmore', p. 41.

9 Anne-Isabelle Richard, 'The Limits of Solidarity: Europeanism, Anti-Colonialism and Socialism at the Congress of the Peoples of Europe, Asia and Africa in Puteaux, 1948', *European Review of History* 21 (2014).

10 Ibid., p. 522. Brockway recalled that he was one of the delegates to warn his European comrades of the necessity of centring colonial liberation in the conference's decisions. Brockway, *Outside the Right*, p. 42.

11 *Report of the First International Conference of the Peoples of Europe – Asia – Africa against Imperialism* (London, 1948), pp. 31–2.

Kenya, where he met with leading Kenyan anticolonialists.[12] That same year, Ridley reviewed Padmore's *Africa: Britain's Third Empire*. He agreed with Padmore's criticisms of Labour Party colonial policy and declared that Padmore's formulation, 'British Imperialists have no permanent friends nor permanent enemies, they have only permanent interests', deserved 'to become classical'.[13] Near the end of the decade, in December 1958, Bob Edwards (having returned to the Labour Party and become an MP) attended the All-African Peoples' Conference in Accra. He reported positively on the conference, while despairing that the wider Labour Party and labour movement had ignored the conference.[14]

Pan-Africanists also continued to receive support from British Communists. The Soviet-sympathising barrister and former Labour MP, D. N. Pritt, defended Jomo Kenyatta and the rest of the Kapenguria Six during their trial of 1952–53, after they were accused of being Mau Mau conspirators.[15] Willie Gallacher, an outspoken Communist anti-imperialist since the 1920s, helped to collect funds for the defence (which was ultimately unsuccessful).[16] Nkrumah also stayed in touch with the British Communist Party after his return to the Gold Coast. Though Padmore subsequently played a role in turning Nkrumah away from the international Communist movement, Nkrumah increasingly looked to the Soviet Union after Padmore's death in 1959. In 1963, Nkrumah's personal secretary even wrote to the offices of *Labour Monthly*. She thanked R. P. Dutt for sending a recent edition containing a review of Nkrumah's *Africa Must Unite*, and revealed: 'Arrangements are being made through the High Commissioner for Ghana in London, for the President to receive regular copies of *Labour Monthly*.'[17]

It was Nkrumah's Ghana that epitomised the hopes of the pan-Africanist movement. With independence in 1957, several pan-Africanists moved there – including Amy Ashwood Garvey, W. E. B. Du Bois, Makonnen and Padmore. Makonnen and Padmore in particular became

---

12  Brockway, *Outside the Right*, Chapter 5. Brockway also visited the Gold Coast in 1956 at Nkrumah's invitation. Brockway, *Outside the Right*, p. 119.

13  F. A. Ridley, 'Africa Calling!', *Socialist Leader*, 18 March 1950, p. 6.

14  Bob Edwards, 'All-African Conference Was Biggest Ever', *Colonial Freedom News*, February 1959, pp. 1, 4.

15  See TNA, KV 2/1788 (Kenyatta).

16  LHASC, CP/IND/GALL/2/2, Willie Gallacher to Leslie Hale, 14 October 1953.

17  LHASC, CP/IND/DUTT/6/5, Erica Powell to *Labour Monthly*, 22 July 1963.

deeply involved in Ghanaian politics.[18] Despite this funnelling of activity into the Ghanaian nation-state, Padmore until the end remained convinced of the need for colonial liberation movements that went beyond merely achieving national sovereignty. He was further concerned that African nations should not fall under Soviet influence. A March 1956 letter to Richard Wright declared:

> I am equally pleased to know that you endorse my point of view at which I have arrived after years of reflection and without abandoning Marxism, which to me is merely one of the many effective instruments in waging the fight for freedom. But what I am equally concerned about is: What will take the place of capitalist-imperialism when the whites are driven out of Africa? If the boys fail to provide a dynamic ideology of a distinctive African character even co-operating (*sic*) elements of Communistic ideology and practice, the Kremlin will rush into the vacuum left by colonialism.[19]

For Padmore, Marxism was not a dogma, but rather a vehicle, like pan-Africanism, through which a socialist Africa could be achieved. The above letter is just one piece of evidence that Padmore believed formal independence to be a prelude to socialism in Africa. In another 1956 letter to Wright, Padmore justified his 'concentration' on Nkrumah by asserting Nkrumah's Marxist analysis. He stated that leaders like Nnamdi Azikiwe were 'only the Kerenskys'.[20] As Matteo Grilli has observed, for Nkrumah and Padmore 'the independence of Ghana was not considered as an end in itself, but it was ultimately connected with the attainment of African liberation and unity'.[21]

The deepening of the Cold War in the 1950s strengthened the hand of anticolonialists and made non-alignment a more attractive prospect. The new mood reached its apogee with the 1955 Bandung Conference

---

18  For Padmore's Ghanaian activity, see Leslie James, *George Padmore and Decolonization from Below: Pan-Africanism, the Cold War, and the End of Empire* (Basingstoke, 2015), Chapter 8.

19  Wright papers, box 103 folder 1522, Padmore to Richard Wright, 5 March 1956.

20  Wright papers, box 103 folder 1522, Padmore to Richard Wright, 12 April 1956. Alexander Kerensky was a Russian revolutionary. He achieved power after the February 1917 revolution, before being overthrown by the Bolshevik October Revolution.

21  Matteo Grilli, *Nkrumaism and African Nationalism: Ghana's Pan-African Foreign Policy in the Age of Decolonization* (Cham, Switzerland, 2018), pp. 14–15.

of newly and soon-to-be independent African and Asian states, the spirit of which permeated Padmore's *Pan-Africanism or Communism?* (like so many of his books, written with much input and assistance from Pizer).[22] Padmore's historical analysis of the Russian Revolution had not changed in this time. He wrote that, during the Russian Civil War, the 'reactionaries failed largely because Lenin's bold anti-colonial strategy paid such rich dividends'.[23] However, while he maintained that the Soviet Union had eliminated racism within its borders, Communists in Britain and the United States had retained their 'racial prejudices'. In doing so, they 'destroyed much of the Negro's instinctive sympathy for Russia'.[24]

Instead of seeking alliances with a socialist Europe, Padmore advocated an independent and united Africa that would remain neutral in the Cold War. This was partly due to his growing distaste for official Communism, accelerated by the 1955 Bandung Conference and Nikita Khrushchev's 1956 denunciation of Stalin. Padmore wrote to Wright: 'I want [*Pan-Africanism or Communism?*] in the hands of black Frenchmen. They need our ideology to help them break away from Thorez's influence. I can see them striving but Senghor and these boys can't help as they too are confused'.[25] It is therefore unsurprising that Padmore expressed interest in Aimé Césaire's 'Letter to Maurice Thorez'.[26] Both Césaire's open letter and *Pan-Africanism or Communism?* encapsulated the spirit of Bandung and a break from Moscow.

But Padmore was also aware of Western fears of national liberation movements falling under Soviet influence. He therefore played a strategic game in the book, arguing that pan-Africanist leaders like Nkrumah would not threaten Western powers if they were left free to build their own brand of socialism. The history of pan-Africanism presented in the book was therefore refracted through a Cold War prism. Padmore constructed a narrative that exaggerated the historical divergences between pan-Africanism and organised Communism. With a new strategy to achieve African independence, and little prospect of significant aid

---

22 George Padmore, *Pan-Africanism or Communism? The Coming Struggle for Africa* (London, 1956), p. 10.

23 Ibid., p. 292.

24 Ibid., p. 314.

25 Wright papers, box 103 folder 1522, Padmore to Richard Wright, 29 January 1957. Maurice Thorez was the French Communist leader.

26 Wright papers, box 103 folder 1521, Pizer to Ellen Wright, 9 April 1957.

from European socialists, the calls for interdependent revolutions were almost completely abandoned. Nevertheless, Padmore remembered the ILP as 'the only British political party which has consistently opposed Colonialism'.[27] He concluded the book with a list of British people who had been 'friends' of the Africans 'at a time when it was not considered so fashionable'. Unsurprisingly, these included several ILP members and Nancy Cunard – but also figures like Leonard Barnes, H. N. Brailsford, Reginald Bridgeman, Arthur Creech Jones and Stafford Cripps, who at various times had been objects of contempt for Black radicals.[28]

With Ghanaian independence in 1957, pan-Africanist strategies for decolonisation appeared to be paying dividends. Yet there was some disaffection within the movement. Abrahams was particularly sceptical. He wrote *A Wreath for Udomo* as a cautionary tale for Nkrumah. He believed that Nkrumah 'took his political enemies dangerously lightly'.[29] Padmore was concerned with maintaining the socialist and anti-imperialist character of the movement. At the independence celebrations, attended by many prominent foreign dignitaries, Padmore angrily remarked: 'When Nkrumah was fighting for independence, they were putting all the black people into gaols, now with independence the black people are outside and the white people inside dancing.'[30] Those closest to Padmore were aware of his priorities. Shortly after his death, Pizer wrote to Cunard that 'he lived to have a certain satisfaction in seeing Ghana gain its independence, but he could also see that for many of the erstwhile leaders, the revolution had ended'.[31] Likewise, James remembered that, later in life, Padmore 'spoke ironically of nationalist politicians who were satisfied with "a flag and a national anthem" . . . African independence did not mean for him a mere repetition of the European experience.'[32]

Padmore did not live to see Nkrumah's overthrow at the hands of a right-wing coup in 1966. James lamented: 'The fall of Dr Kwame Nkrumah is one of the greatest catastrophes that has befallen the minds of

---

27  Padmore, *Pan-Africanism or Communism?*, pp. 324–5.

28  Ibid., p. 365.

29  Abrahams, *Coyaba Chronicles*, p. 125.

30  C. L. R. James, 'George Padmore: Black Marxist Revolutionary – A Memoir' (1976), in C. L. R. James, *At the Rendezvous of Victory* (London, 1984), p. 260.

31  Harry Ransom Center, The University of Texas at Austin, Nancy Cunard collection, Pizer to Cunard, 24 October 1959.

32  James, 'Notes on the Life of George Padmore', p. 52.

Africans in Africa, of people of African descent, and all those who are interested in the development and progress of independent Africa'. He believed that Nkrumah had been overwhelmed by the 'economic and political problems' that all newly independent nations face, and had become dependent on a 'huge bureaucracy'.[33] Makonnen bluntly stated the central problem of this bureaucracy: 'You can't build socialism without socialists.'[34] Elsewhere, James wrote of Nkrumah: 'Like Cromwell and Lenin, he initiated the destruction of a regime in decay – a tremendous achievement; but like them, he failed to create the new society.'[35]

Over half a century after the beginning of decolonisation in Africa, it is clear that the process remains incomplete. Formal colonialism may be a largely discredited project, but imperialism continues. Since the beginning of the process of decolonisation after 1945, numerous Third World socialist and anti-imperialist movements (by which I mean movements aiming to alter fundamentally the economic relationship between ruler and ruled, rather than simply to achieve constitutional independence) have been sabotaged by Western intelligence agencies and local elites where possible, and by military might where necessary. Global capitalism, aided by institutions like the International Monetary Fund and World Bank, continues to plunder former colonial nations. What if there had been revolution in Europe at the end of the Second World War, and Black radicals had not subsequently resolved to win freedom by themselves? Would the project of African liberation, battered by powerful enemies, remain so incomplete? And would the modest gains of the European left in the aftermath of the Second World War, reversed over the last four decades and based on conciliation with capitalism rather than its overthrow, have seemed so appealing had larger sections of the European labour movement grasped the nettle of capitalist-imperialism? Perhaps, when such questions are contemplated, the incompleteness of colonial liberation illustrates the validity of the Black radical theory of interdependent revolutions.

However, we also need to be aware of the achievements of this confluence between Black and White socialists. Much as the abolition of

---

33  C. L. R. James, *At the Rendezvous of Victory* (London, 1984), pp. 172–85.
34  Makonnen, *Pan-Africanism from Within*, p. 238.
35  C. L. R. James, *Nkrumah and the Ghana Revolution* (London, 1977), p. 6.

slavery in the nineteenth century was shaped *both* from above by the changing demands of capitalism *and* from below by slave rebellions in the Caribbean and the abolitionist movement in Britain, the imbrication of Black radicalism and British socialism points to the ways in which decolonisation – while shaped from above by forces such as the emergence of new superpowers and the relative weakness of colonial regimes – was also shaped from below by the confluence of anti-imperialists from the colonies and the metropole.[36] Radicalised socialist and anti-imperialist groups emerged from the First World War inspired by the Bolshevik Revolution and frustrated by the folly of European nationalism, or by the lack of democratic rights granted to colonial peoples despite their war service. Figures such as Padmore and Brockway, though they have been considered relatively peripheral to British political culture, pulled the conversation about imperialism into more radical channels. This meant that, by the time of, say, Mau Mau or Suez, the violence and assumptions of European colonialism were increasingly deemed indefensible. When the IASB was formed in 1937, mainstream political opinion scoffed at the idea that Black Africa would be ready for independence in only two decades. The end of European empires (and the accompanying defeat of ideas of inherent and legalised inequalities defined by race) was the global left's most significant victory of the twentieth century.

The degree of solidarity between metropolitan and colonial socialists ebbed and flowed according to world-historic forces. It reached a low point during the 1950s, when confronted by the early Cold War. However, the place of the IASB in the British socialist movement proved an important antecedent to the embrace by many Western leftists of Third Worldism in the 1960s. Revolutionary governments in China, Cuba and Vietnam, and Black radicals in the West, like the Black Panther Party, were seen as the vanguard of world socialism. Victories against Western (and particularly US) imperialism, while failing to achieve world socialism, demonstrated that the forces of capitalist-imperialism could be contained at a national level. Perhaps relatedly, this moment also coincided with the rediscovery of James's work by many socialists after years of relative obscurity.[37] In Britain, the after-lives of the confluence between pan-Africanism and metropolitan

---

36  Eric Williams, *Capitalism and Slavery* (Chapel Hill, NC, 1945 [1944]).
37  *The Black Jacobins* was reprinted in 1963.

socialism were most clearly seen in Brockway's Movement for Colonial Freedom.[38]

This book has demonstrated that, during the 1930s and 1940s, Black radicals took seriously the need to work within the British socialist movement. While their ideas never became dominant in that movement, they had significant influence. These ideas had their seeds in the international Communist movement – first in Lenin's theses on the national and colonial questions, and secondly in the Comintern's embrace of a Marxist pan-Africanism, embodied in the International Trade Union Committee of Negro Workers during the late 1920s and 1930s. It was the ITUCNW that was the crucible of Padmore's most durable ideas about colonial liberation, the relationship between race and class, and the nature of and prospects for the European proletariat. There was a clear lineage from these ideas to those of the International African Service Bureau and Pan-African Federation. In this sense, a line can be traced from Moscow to Accra, via Hamburg, London and Manchester.

Despite these Communist genealogies, the 1935 turn to the Popular Front irreparably damaged relations between Black radicals and Communists in Britain. The CPGB pandered to the exigencies of Soviet foreign policy, thereby compromising its commitment not only to the European class struggle, but also to anticolonialism. But these antagonisms between Black radicals and the CPGB were not as severe as James (as a Trotskyist) and Padmore (writing during the Cold War) later portrayed them to be. Activists like Abrahams, Kenyatta and Nkrumah often had a foot, or at least a toe, in the Communist machinery. Personal relationships with some Communists (especially women and people of colour) remained warm.

From the late 1930s onwards, after a fractious debate about Ethiopia, the ILP was the group on the British left most receptive to Black radical ideas and forms of activism. It mostly, if not entirely, embraced theories about the interdependence of the colonial and metropolitan revolutions. It granted Black radicals platforms in its publications and at its meetings. It is difficult to imagine the ILP's Ethiopia debate occurring in the same way in 1939 as it had it 1936. The shortcomings of the traditional historiography of the ILP, which considers the post-1932 history of the party

---

38  For the Movement for Colonial Freedom, see Stephen Howe, *Anticolonialism in British Politics: The Left and the End of Empire, 1918–1964* (Oxford, 1993), Chapters 6–7.

as one of unmitigated decline, are exposed by this understanding. It was John McNair's revolutionary address to the 1945 Pan-African Congress, rather than the paternalistic gradualism of the Labour Party, that would echo in Nkrumah's independent Ghana.

These examples of Black radical imbrication with metropolitan socialism point to the ways in which the history of European socialism needs to be reconceived. The IASB positioned itself both as a nodal point in the transnational networks of pan-Africanism and as part of the constellation of the British and European left. Its members understood themselves as part of a global movement against capitalism and imperialism, composed not only of Black and White socialists in the metropole, but also, for example, of Caribbean trade unionists and Indian nationalists. There was no British socialist movement insulated from pan-Africanism and other currents of anticolonial radicalism. At a time of calls to 'decolonise' university curricula, a study of Black radicalism and locating it within British socialism shows that this 'decolonisation' (or, to use more radical language, 'liberation') requires us not only to look beyond 'the West'. It also demands that we challenge established ideas of who and what has constituted 'the West'. As Priyamvada Gopal has argued, studying the transnational and multiracial character of British opposition to empire allows Britons to 'interrogate . . . national mythologies' and 'lay claim to a different, more challenging history, and yet one that is more suited to a heterogeneous society which can draw on multiple historical and cultural resources'.[39]

Surveying the history of working-class politics in Britain, it is clear that, while these politics have often been plagued by racism, and by indifference or hostility towards emancipatory struggles, there have also been moments in which sections of the working class and the socialist movement have opposed racism and imperialism. Indeed, it was often 'racialized outsiders', such as the Black radicals who constituted the IAFE, the IASB and the PAF, who created such internationalist currents in Britain.[40] Activists who have followed in these radicals' footsteps continue to promote antiracist and internationalist ideas within the British socialist movement – but the importance of these ideas remains

---

39  Priyamvada Gopal, *Insurgent Empire: Anticolonial Resistance and British Dissent* (London, 2019), p. 448.

40  Satnam Virdee, *Racism, Class and the Racialized Outsider* (Basingstoke, 2014).

contested within the movement, to say nothing of society at large. In the face of a racialised criminal justice system, the demonisation of migrants and refugees, and the continuation of US-led and British-supported imperialism, studying the Black radicals of the past helps us to confront these challenges directly rather than fall into 'nativist socialism'.[41] Returning to the activism of Black radicals such as Padmore, and their allies like Brockway, allows us to imagine a truly internationalist socialism.

---

41 John Narayan, 'British Black Power: The Anti-Imperialism of Political Blackness and the Problem of Nativist Socialism', *Sociological Review* 67 (2019).

# Index